THE COMPLETE GUIDE TO

LANDSCAPE DESIGN, RENOVATION, AND MAINTENANCE

A Practical Handbook for the Home Landscape Gardener

CASS TURNBULL

BETTERWAY BOOKS
Cincinnati, Ohio

Cover photograph by Scott Neuert
Illustrations by Glen Grantham
Typography by Park Lane Associates

96 95 94 93 92   5 4 3

Library of Congress Cataloging-in-Publication Data

Turnbull, Cass
    The complete guide to landscape design, renovation & maintenance :
a practical handbook for the home landscape gardener / Cass
Turnbull.
      p. cm.
    Includes index.
    ISBN 1-55870-208-3 (paperback) : $14.95
    1. Landscape gardening--Handbooks, manuals, etc. 2. Landscape
architecture--Handbook, manuals, etc. I. Title.
SB472.T87 1991
                         712'.6--dc20   91-17996
                                          CIP

Dedicated to Werner Erhard

Acknowledgments

Simply listing the names of the many people who helped with this book seems too small of an acknowledgment. The rough draft was easy, but the rewrites, the search for the publisher, and the hunt for technical and literary inaccuracies were laborious. Thank you all for moral support as well as technical assistance. I hope you are pleased with the final result. What we didn't get this time, we'll get next time.

I thank John Turnbull, steadfast and supportive. Thank you Glen Grantham, illustrator, I'll miss our weekly meetings. Thank you Ron Brightman, Pat Roome, Lisa Hummel, Dorothy Bestor, Lisa Douglas, George Scott, super secretary Mary Barton, Bob Braid for a peaceful place to write, Deb Pederson and Bruce Cowen, the Washington Toxics Coalition, Mike Erb from the Wilber-Ellis Company, Extension Agents Stott Howard and Sharon Collman, Mariah Krone, David VanZandt, Margaret Moynan, and Eileen Niven, last line of defense against bad grammar and spelling.

I especially want to thank the arborists who made this book and the entire PlantAmnesty campaign possible. They have donated countless hours of tree work to help pay for the word processing of the book and have been teaching me the ways of the trees, so that I may better serve them.

Thank you Rob Williams, Doug Clark, 100% sterling silver Chip Kennaugh, Mark Harman, Scott Neuert, Paul Wiltberger, Jon Cook, John Hushagen, and others both near and far.

Thank you also to the people who have taught me most about the wonderful art of pruning. I apologize that at the time I was being given those pearls of plant wisdom I often thought to myself, "big deal" or, alternately, "too radical, this can't be right." Such is the nature of learning. It often takes more than a while to sink in, or should I say to germinate? Thanks to Andrea Furlong, Carol Baker, Lisa Douglas, and Betty Rollefson.

Contents

INTRODUCTION

PART I: PRUNING

Gardening is a Virus 15

The Science of Pruning 18

Tools of the Trade 23

Looking for Dead Wood 25

Timing 27

Pruning Cane-Growers 30

Pruning Mounds 35

Pruning Tree-Likes 37

Pruning Hedges 43

Shear Madness 47

Fruit Trees 50

How to Prune a Tree Limb 57

PART II: RENOVATING THE OVERGROWN YARD

Begin to Bring Order out of Chaos 67

Sorting Out 70

Adding the Lower Story 78

Speaking and Understanding Gardenese 83

Getting Rid of Unwanted Plants 88

Radical Renovation 90

My Tree's Too Big 94

PART III: DESIGNING AND INSTALLING A NEW LANDSCAPE

What Makes a Yard Look Good or Bad 101

Map and Hardscape 107

How to Choose and Arrange Your Plants 113

More Unheeded Advice 120

Installation How-Tos and Tricks 122

PART IV: MAINTAINING YOUR YARD

Taking Care of Your Yard 133

Weeds: Hand-to-Hand Combat 136

Herbicides 142

Fertilizers and Organics 149

Watering 154

Pests and Diseases 160

A Woman: A Plan: An Organization: PlantAmnesty! 167

APPENDICES

1. Cane-Growers, 173
2. Mounds, 173
3. Tree-Likes, 174
4. Best Plants for Formal Shearing, 174
5. Suckering Tree-Likes, 175
6. Tree-Likes Tough Enough to Shear, 175
7. Plants that Take Thinning or Arborizing, 176
8. Short Plants, 176
9. Easiest Plants to Keep at Mature Height of 5 Feet or Less, 177
10. Background Plants for Mass Planting, 177
11. Deciduous Plants for Group Plantings and Seasonal Interest, 178
12. Fun in the Sun Plants, 178
13. Fall Show Plants, 179
14. Plants with Interesting Berries and Things, 179
15. Plants for Winter Interest, 180
16. Plants for Skinny Places, 180
17. Author's Choice Plants, 181
18. More Choice Plants, 181
19. Tough Guys, 182
20. Small Trees/Big Shrubs, 183
21. Strange but Wonderful Plants, 183
22. Planting List for Design-Map and Hardscape, 184
23. Books, Periodicals, Catalogs, 184
24. State Cooperative Extension Services, 185

INDEX 189

Introduction

This book was not written for gardeners, although I'm sure it contains many hints and tips useful to professional and amateur gardeners. This book was written for people with a problem. The problem is what to do with their shrubs, their trees, or their yards.

As a professional gardener I get many phone calls from troubled homeowners. I often hear, "It's all just gotten too big," or "It's out of control!" They can't make any sense out of the pruning books they buy, and the illustrations don't look anything like what's in their backyards. So I've written this book to help people renovate overgrown and overplanted yards, not just to show how to prune individual plants.

Frequently I work on yards that have been previously worked on, or should I say worked over, by homeowners or the people they've hired to cut it all back. Unfortunately, this method of yard control backfires. The trees and shrubs regrow rapidly and wildly. This book includes information on rehabilitative pruning; that is, how to get trees and shrubs back into good shape if they have been previously badly pruned.

Most people have mastered the fundamentals of daily life by age thirty. They know how to buy a car, how to maintain a car, and where to go to have it fixed. They know how to choose their groceries, fix simple meals, and they have located their favorite restaurants. But gardening fundamentals are not as readily or commonly understood. To help alleviate the problem, I have included general descriptions of how to manage the average landscape successfully. For example, Part 4: Maintaining Your Yard explains what people need to know about weeding, watering, fertilizing, and pest control. It is not the complete and final word on these topics, but it should give the home gardener the basics upon which to build. And I have, I hope, included enough information to help you make intelligent choices when hiring work to be done.

Poor design is at the root of most yard owner unhappiness. Pruning and fertilizing are often used, unsuccessfully, in an attempt to compensate for poor design and bad plant choices. Also, many people have empty or dull or disagreeable yards and wish to make improvements themselves. They lack the money to hire a full-service landscape company, and they need more information in order to choose a designer/gardener to assist with a do-it-yourself project. With some basic knowledge, a little courage, and a lot of physical work, they could transform their yards into true gardens. Remodeling the outdoor spaces can be as easy and rewarding as any home remodeling project. Perhaps "easy" isn't the word. Let's say "achievable."

This book is for people with overplanted, overgrown, malpruned, poorly planned, or deadly dull landscapes. If you are one of these people, this book is for you. The book is divided into four sections: Pruning; Renovating the Overgrown Yard; Designing and Installing a New Landscape; and Maintaining Your Yard.

You may discover an added bonus. After you eliminate the clutter and confusion of an overgrown yard or redesign and install a new one, your yard may become a source of pride and solace, as it protects you from the harsh urban world. Its greenness and aliveness may serve to refresh and amuse you, and you may come to feel toward your shrubs as you feel toward your pets—that they are alive and that they do things that give you pleasure.

Beyond controlling Nature comes relating to it and understanding it. It is truly the same Nature that exists in the forests and jungles, and it can and does exist in your own backyard.

The public is, I am convinced, unaware of the source of joy that exists in the 1,000 square feet or so of land around their homes. Joy being a commodity in short supply these days, that land may be worth a second look. Your yard is action packed, in a slow motion sort of way. It is full of sex, violence, and mystery. You just can't see it—yet.

Each section of this book includes mistakes to avoid. I think a lot can be learned from this approach. People persistently try to make plants do what they will not, thinking that shrubs and trees are infinitely malleable. Plants will not, cannot, be made to do whatever we want. There are rules to the game of gardening. Once you know the rules, you will find that plants are very forgiving. If you merely stay away from the big mistakes in your yard, you are more than halfway home. After reading this book, you must be bold and begin to make decisions on your own. There are no absolute right answers (a situation that drives neophytes crazy); there is only a series of choices. Prune this or that branch? Move this shrub? Get rid of that plant? Prune the lower limbs of a tree or shorten the shrub beneath it?

The principles of gardening are the same everywhere, only the names (species) of the plants change. So don't be stymied by unfamiliar shrub or other plant names. If I make reference to a tree or shrub that you don't recognize, rest assured that you have their counterparts in your area, and they will respond in similar ways. Your local County Extension Agent or nursery person should be able to help sort out the particulars of your specific plant material. I have included lessons on speaking and understanding "gardenese" to help you communicate.

I've tried to keep the book brief enough to get you through it before setting you loose with loppers and chain saw. After reading it you will have, I hope, enough fundamental knowledge to keep you out of trouble until practice and observation teach you the rest. For those who just want to know *what* to do, not why or how, I have added a summary for each chapter subject.

HOW TO BEGIN: THINGS TO KEEP IN MIND

When my former partner and I would arrive at the scene of a tangled, overgrown yard we had contracted to restore, we would be totally overwhelmed and would invariably exclaim, "What a wretched mess!" Then, like the cavalry, we would head in to do battle. I've been doing this sort of work for years, and when I see some places I am still at a loss as to where to begin, and I certainly can't visualize the end product in its final state of orderliness. I want to turn and run. My head is swimming and I'm confused. At this point I begin to pick out areas and jobs that I know must be done. This narrows my focus and gives me a starting point. Like so much in life, it's the getting started that's tough.

THE WORST FIRST RULE

You must make yourself begin. When you narrow your sights to a section, a shrub, or a tree, you then begin with what is obviously wrong or *the worst*. Forget the big picture for a while. Weeding and deadwooding are great warmup exercises until whatever else needs to be done occurs to you.

I made up the "Worst First" rule, and I use it a lot. With gardening in general and pruning in particular, it's never all done. It's *not* like fixing a car or a house. Many times you must wait for nature to fix her or your mistakes. This built-in delay also drives homeowners crazy. If what needs to happen is a healthier plant, or if a plant needs to grow and fill in, it cannot be fixed with a pair of loppers. Still, if you follow the "Worst First" rule and then step back, you will, more often than not, see dramatic improvement.

At other times you will be at a loss as to what to do and you may think of the old saying, "Wander, ponder, and prune." This refers to the time good gardeners spend walking around the yard staring at plants and their situations, trying to see what needs to be done next. When pruning and renovating the overgrown yard, you should make tentative decisions while viewing from *outside* the shrubs. You do the work from *inside* them. As you prune your way through the shrubbery, remember to step back out to the lawn every so often to check your progress.

Another adage used by pruners is: "The sign of a good job is one that you can't tell has been done." This is because a well-pruned, well-maintained yard looks as if it's naturally well ordered, not chopped. I know of a landscape supervisor who once told his crew, "You can do whatever you want to the plants as long as I can't tell you've been there." This included dramatic size reduction in some cases. Good pruning is invisible, which is one reason it's not done much; in other words, it's hard to copy.

I define good pruning as pruning that generally enhances the plant's health and promotes its natural form (and indirectly makes the plant more beautiful). Bad pruning (malpruning) is defined as pruning that runs counter to the plant's natural habit or shape and is a drag on its health, as evidenced by increased dead wood, abnormal suckering, and decreased vigor. Such pruning eventually makes plants look unnatural and sickly. At the edges of the science and the art of pruning are those forms that are the exceptions to the rules—these are the tight shearing of topiary (plant sculpture), pleaching (weaving) of trees, pollarding (lollipop trees), bonsai, cloud pruning, espalier, and the like. I recommend that all novices stay away from these specialties, unless they've inherited or want to design a yard specifically for these purposes. These are generally high-maintenance garden practices and look rather pretentious or silly in the middle of an average yard.

SUMMARY

❏ You can't fix a yard all at once. Just go for the worst, follow the rules, and it will look better. Come back next year and do more.

❏ A good pruning and renovating job is invisible.

PART I
PRUNING

Gardening is a Virus

Gardeners are sick, needy people. They can't drive past new nurseries without stopping to browse. They sometimes speak in a dead language (Latin); they crave ever more plants and choicer plants. It's a disease I call "phytophilia" (Plant Lover's Disease—in Latin, of course). Early symptoms include the removal of grass areas to include more plants; phytophiles often hop the fence when they run out of land and take over parking strips and neighboring bare patches. Sometimes in a schizophrenic fit they disown last year's favorites, yanking them out while pronouncing them all weeds, then start a new collection of plants. They can drop two bills on spring bulbs alone. Theirs can be an expensive habit to feed. I know of an otherwise respectable librarian caught by local police "fern-napping" by the side of the road. She has been known to engage in midnight pruning in her neighbor's yard as well.

Advanced stages of phytophilia include a morbid fascination with blood and bone meals, manures and molds, feces and decomposing things, and other substances. Phytophiles congregate with others of their kind to swap dirt recipes, speak in tongues, and do "ID" (plant identification). Gardeners would just as soon never come in from the yard. My husband has often had to point out to me that the sun has gone down and it's too dark to work. During the final stages of this disease, spouses find plastic bags and yogurt containers in the refrigerator containing peat moss and seeds being stratified, or strange and hairy-looking bulbs, corms, and tubers. These late stages of phytophilia can be dangerous for family members when the phytophile is driving the car. He is apt to drive off the road while doing high speed or midnight plant identification.

Thank heaven for the winter, because otherwise we phytophiles might work ourselves to death. It gives us time to rest, but beware! You'll find the ad-vanced gardener in the throes of withdrawal, browsing through the seed catalogs and poking around the yard in late winter, turning over leaves, looking for the first shoots of spring, and examining buds for imperceptible signs of swelling.

CONSIDER THE BENEFITS

Gardening is a sickness, but you won't mind catching the bug. In fact, you're going to like gardening just the way I do because it's so easy! I used to be envious of people who had really beautifully decorated houses and hip clothes and who did creative things. Then I discovered that when you buy a plant and put it in your yard, and it does something neat, *you* get all the credit. I was amazed. I redesigned my yard before I knew anything about plants and you can, too. And my friends and neighbors are truly impressed. If you've never found your creative niche, try gardening. The plants do all the work, and just look at your competition. Only about one out of fifty yards looks even vaguely interesting. You can be the best in your neighborhood—easily. I tell people, "I'm an artist, I work in dirt."

Another thing I like about gardening is that you're encouraged to copy; it's part of the whole game. Good gardeners keep notebooks to jot down good plant combinations to try out in their own yards. And you also get full credit for serendipitous creations—that is, when you throw in a bunch of things that you like, and four of them bloom at the same time and complement or contrast with each other so well that you get credit as a creative genius. This happens a lot in gardens—really, it happens a lot.

Furthermore, your mistakes are easy to fix. Usually, the plant dies, and you can replace it with a good performer. You can move an unhappy plant to a place it likes, where it looks better. Or you can give an unwanted one away to someone who thinks it's choice, even though you think it's now too vigorous or just plain common. The gardening world is not completely full of snobs; it's also full of generous, gentle-hearted people. They will help you trouble-shoot and will be eager to share seeds as well as starts of treasures from their yards.

GETTING PHYSICAL

Gardening is also a great sport for less vigorous humans, and it will keep you well into your old age. Unlike snow skiing, the gardening form of exercise takes no courage, will not break bones, and is easy to do into your eighties and nineties, when you probably shouldn't be driving into snow-covered mountains anyway. It will keep you young and healthy. You always see those old ladies with their broad-brimmed garden hats and the old gents in their overalls out there. They aren't shut-ins. They are the experts! Outstanding in their field, where you should be—out, standing in your field.

People pay attention to old gardeners. This is because gardening is way behind everything else that's being scientifically tested. Horticulturists are just now starting to test some old, wrong assumptions and practices. A great deal of gardening is a guessing game. That's because, when you are dealing with plants, you constantly find that several factors can combine to produce any one effect. This makes it very confusing; yet once you get the hang of it, it's fun, and your opinion and experience are valid. It's easy to become smart fast in gardening. With only a modicum of reading and investigating, you will become the neighborhood expert. And, by careful observation, you can become a sought-out real expert in your old age.

YOU'LL LEARN FAST

Don't be intimidated by all that Latin and all the names. Once you get interested, you will be surprised at how much you learn in a year. I remember being on a garden tour when I knew my shrubs but not my flowers, and I asked someone, "Whatzzat?" He said, "Cosmos." I was astounded. "How do you know all those different flowers?" He said, "You just get to know them." A year later, I knew all those

flowers—at least, all the common ones. It takes a lifetime to know *all* the flowers' names. It's like a good novel that never ends. You'll love it.

You'll love gardening because through it you will return to the surprise and wonderment of your childhood. You will regain that feeling of being connected to nature. You will get the healing, enriching perspective of the world in which a tiny, infinitely complex bud moves you. And, when you plant a tree that will probably live longer than you will, you sense the entire web of living things of which you are only a part. You will glory in the life-and-death drama that's played out in your yard. You will feel like an Olympian god as you watch the ants farming aphids for honeydew, or cheer as the ladybugs decimate the aphids that attacked the maple. The boring round of human routine is replaced with the ever-fascinating change of seasons. You will smell the frost in the air as a winter sun warms your cheek. You will experience the incredible high expectancy just before spring when the first early burst of bulbs and blossoms confirms that winter is defeated and all the best is yet to come.

You will love those lazy, hazy days of summer that are like an old friend you forgot, who returns again, bringing wafts of sweet-scented phlox or heliotrope. And it is confirmed that, yes, life *is* good. And at least once a year in the fall, you look up just as a breeze sends a flurry of golden leaves in a shower down to the ground. Even in the winter as the snow gilds the fine branch patterns and textured plants that you so carefully chose, you know that hiding just beneath the soil (you forget just where) are the bulbs you planted, which will surprise and delight you and your family come February, March, and April.

AND FOR THE LONG TERM ...

About your fifth year into gardening, some of the great philosophical truths will begin to occur to you. You will see that good and bad (weed vs. not weed) really depends on how you look at the plant and at the situation; you will marvel at the incredible tenaciousness of living things; you will fully understand that giving things what they *need* according to their individual habits and types, rather than controlling them and trying to make them do what you *want*, is the real key to success and beauty. You can begin to train your eyes and yourself to see what's needed and wanted in any situation—not just what *you* want. (And, if people ever treated each other or other cultures this way, what a difference there would be.)

I'll tell you a secret. You will get what *you* need in the process. Without ever intending to, you will learn the lessons of gardening. All the things I didn't want to do, you'll do. You'll find out that all things worth having and doing take work and maintenance, but when you love the process, it's no problem. You'll learn (I still hate this one) that it's important to make sure that living things are kept healthy; and (I hated this one the most) you'll learn patience. But it won't hurt, I promise. The good things in life begin with setting up an emotional bond between you and your kids, you and your nice house, you and your pet, you and your beautiful, wonderful garden. It all takes time.

SUMMARY

❑ Several factors combine to create a good-looking or bad-looking plant.

❑ Gardening can be more fun than work.

❑ *You* can be an expert.

❑ Gardening is creative, and good gardeners share plants and ideas, borrowing from each other's wealth.

The Science Of Pruning

There are only two kinds of cuts in pruning. One is the *heading cut*, which means cutting off the tips of branches either bluntly (called *stubbing*), i.e., not to another side branch; or selectively, back to a smaller side branch or to a bud.

Severe heading of trees is called *topping*. Don't do it. An alternative called *dropcrotching* is used by responsible tree pruners when they are forced to try to reduce the actual height (not just the mass) of a tree. It consists of heading a branch or leader back to another smaller (not too small) branch. Other kinds of heading are *tipping back* and very light heading, which is accomplished by just nipping off the tips of new shoots with your fingertips, which is called *pinching*. *Shearing* consists of many non-selective heading cuts. Heading is good to do to your formal hedge or to your young chrysanthemum to make it bushy. In fact, all heading cuts stimulate bushiness at the tips of branches. I call this the *Hydra* effect. Wherever you make a non-selective heading cut you will stimulate many hidden buds to *pop* or *break*, meaning they will grow out near the tip of your cut branch. The non-selective heading cut gets people into trouble. They go out and whack back the tips of all their shrubs and trees in an effort to control size, without realizing that they will stimulate a lot of thick rapid regrowth.

THINNING

The other type of cut, and the one we use most in selective pruning, is the *thinning cut*. You cut branches or twigs back to other branches or twigs or cut out whole canes clear to the ground. Technically speaking, thinning removes a twig or branch back to where it began as a bud. But selective heading, that is, taking a big branch back to a smaller side branch, will thin a shrub out, too. The rule of thumb is to cut to a side branch no smaller than one-half the diameter of the wood you are cutting. Doing this will not stimulate bushy regrowth when used appropriately. This applies to shrubs. Trees, with the possible exception of fruit trees, don't take well to heading, including selective heading.

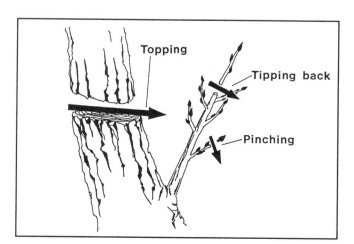

Examples of heading cuts are topping, tipping back, and pinching.

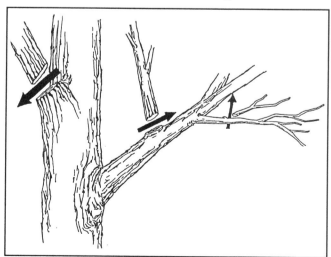

Thinning cuts take branches off where they began as buds.

Selective heading removes a branch where it joins a side branch of sufficient size. This reduces height while retaining some of the natural shape of the shrub.

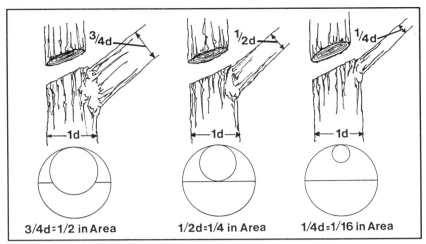

3/4d = 1/2 in Area   1/2d = 1/4 in Area   1/4d = 1/16 in Area

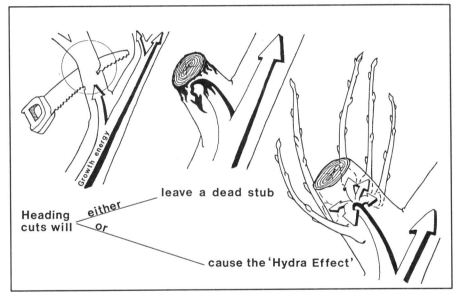

Non-selective heading will cause die-back of the branch or it will stimulate rapid, bushy regrowth.

You can't simply cut back a tree branch to one-half its length and expect it to live. There will not be enough leaf area to gather food to support the mass of the remaining stem. It will either re-sprout vigorously or die. Besides, it looks bad. So it is better to remove the branch totally, taking it off back where it joins a larger stem, if you can, rather than head it severely. Heading is harder on a plant in proportion to the size of the cut and the greater age and bulk of the plant—for example, an old, big tree. Plants also vary as to how much cutting they can take according to their species. Laurel can take it, but a sugar maple may die.

Most people want to prune to reduce the size of their plants and, in fact, many can be reduced dramatically in size, always thinning as you do so. But let me add that most of what I do as a professional is to prune out *internal* branches so that you can see into or through the plant. I also thin to break up the exterior solid ball appearance of both old and young plants. This gives your shrub more character and definition. In addition, I prune to create definition between shrubs, so that instead of a mass of giant greenery jammed against the house, you can see three shrubs of different types, with room between them and the house. You will be able in some cases to see the dirt beneath them.

It is not immediately apparent how following the rules by cutting dead, crossing, and crowded branches will result in a nicer, smaller-looking shrub.

So beginning gardeners will just have to follow the recipe with faith until they see the connection. In the beginning, don't agonize over which one is the right branch, just take your best shot and see how it goes. Stand back and observe the effect on the overall appearance.

When you make your cut, do so just above a side branch or bud, slanting the way the bud is facing. Don't cut too close, but don't cut too far away.

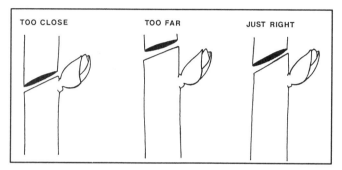

Cut to the node!

PLANT TERMINOLOGY

This brings me to a little plant terminology. A shorthand way of saying "a bud or side branch" is to say *node*. This is your first lesson in how to speak *gardenese*. Knowing to cut to the node separates the pros from the amateurs in gardening. A node can also be a place a leaf or branch used to be, where a dormant bud remains. Such a node will look like a bulge in the stem with a line or leaf scar where the leaf once was. If you cut to the node, a dormant bud will begin to grow out and form a new branch. And

if you say "soil" instead of "dirt," and "shrubs" instead of "bushes" you are well on your way to speaking gardenese.

Plants are categorized by their branching pattern into *alternate*, *opposite*, and *whorled*. The vast majority of plants are alternate in branching. Opposite plants are harder to prune, because it's hard to squeeze the tips of your hand pruners into the "V" to cut so as not to leave a stub to die back. *Stubs* are the dead section of branch that occurred when the last person didn't cut to the node and the branch died back. If buds or twigs are opposite each other, just cut off straight and as close as you can.

There's another reason it is harder to direct the growth of opposite plants: often the branch you chose because it was headed in the right direction (out from the center) is accompanied by one going the opposite (wrong) way. Do the best you can. One solution is to cut off the inside branch as well.

A little more terminology, now. *Suckers!* Technical types like to point out that suckers are the straight-up shoot growth that comes from the base or roots of the plants, and *watersprouts* are the skinny, ugly, straight-up growth that occurs on branches. Common usage has it, however, that all young, straight-up new shoots are called suckers. I like the way it sounds, too. I like the verb *suckers-back* to describe what happens when the hapless homeowner hammers his hawthorn in a misguided attempt to keep it small. Next to dead wood (including stubs) we want to reduce or eliminate watersprouts or suckers on plants. Straight-up growth is generally less pretty than curving growth. For more information on suckers you will need to read the sections on "Fruit Trees"

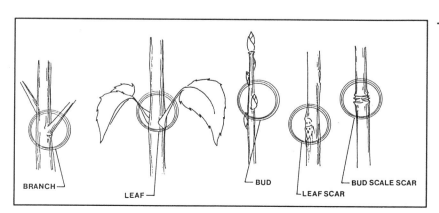

Types of nodes.

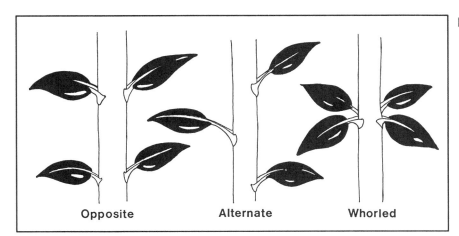

Branching patterns.

Opposite   Alternate   Whorled

How to make a stub.

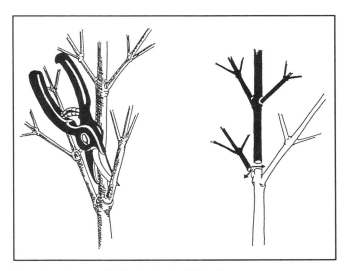

Pruning "opposite" plants is difficult.

and "Rehabilitating Shrubs."

I often tell people that pruning is a skill like any other. You must pay attention and then practice. Learning to do a decent job of pruning takes more time and effort than learning to vacuum, but less than learning to play basketball. The sport of pruning takes about as much time and attention as learning to play a decent game of ping pong. In this chapter we have gone over some rules of the game. Now you must go out and practice, practice, practice.

SUMMARY

❑ Pruning—especially heading—stimulates growth.

❑ Use thinning cuts. Avoid cutting ends or tips of branches to make things smaller. This action of-

ten backfires.

Heading cuts:

❑ Non-selective heading is good to stimulate bushiness. Examples: sheared hedges, chrysanthemums.

❑ Selective heading is the cutting back to a side branch or bud. The remaining branch should be at least half the size of the one being removed. This reduces the plant size and is less likely to stimulate sucker resprouting or create dead stubs.

Thinning cuts:

❑ Thinning cuts remove branches to the point where they began as buds or remove total canes to the ground. They are better for the health and good looks of plants, especially trees, than heading cuts.

❏ Thinning reduces bulk and sometimes height of shrubs (when canes are removed).

❏ Shrubs and trees vary in the degree of thinning they can withstand. A pine tree will take a lot of thinning; a cherry tree resents even moderate thinning.

Tools of the Trade

Personnel at the Parks Department where I worked used to drive the warehouse people crazy by ordering the same tool by several different names. We were going to assign every tool a permanent Latin name, but the idea was voted down. I had one worker whose vocabulary was minimalist to the point that he called a pitchfork a "pick." Anyway, we had many such wonderfully named tools as square-point shovels, "madaxes" (mattocks), "baby rakes," and rock forks.

I will cover here only the tools I think you'll need as a homeowner and save the more technical stuff for my second book.

If I were shipwrecked on a desert island, I would most want to have my Felco® #2 hand pruners, their quick-draw holster, which attaches to my belt, and my spring/fan rake. Next, I would want a blue plastic tarp, a plastic bucket, loppers, a folding pruning saw, and a hand cultivator (the claw, or scratch tool). I need wood-handled loppers with rubber lopper bumpers to cushion the impact the cutting has on my hands. Next, I would want a dandelion weeder, a garden fork, a garden hoe, a scuffle hoe (for weeds in cracks and tiny, baby weeds in beds), a half-moon edger, a round-point and a medium-sized square-point shovel, a wide tine pitchfork, a mattock, a three-point 8-foot orchard ladder for uneven ground, a large wheelbarrow, and then a pair of hedge shears. My round-point shovel would have a straight shank, which is good for digging, not a curved shank, good for scooping.

After that I want a stiff (sawed or cut-off) house broom, a not-too-stiff/not-too-fine street broom, a bow/hard rake, a small chain saw, a blower, power hedge shears, a $3/4$-ton pickup truck, and a "swamper." A swamper is the person who sits next to the driver and gets out to open the gate. They are also known as "gofers" and "grunts." I don't want a mower or power weed cutter, since there is no grass on my island.

All my tools will be painted bright fluorescent red instead of tasteful garden brown, so that I won't lose them in the piles of weeds and leaves. I also want a lifetime supply of leather gloves made for smaller hands, medium size, please.

Don't buy cheap tools. Good ones are worth the money. For pruning tools, Felco® and professional-grade Corona® and manufacturers used most often by people who use such tools every day.

SUMMARY

Necessary tools in order of importance:

❑ Felco® #2 pruners with holster

❑ Spring/fan rake

❑ Tarp

❑ Bucket

❑ Loppers

❑ Folding hand saw

❑ Hand cultivator

Hand pruners and holster with a fan rake.

Shown left to right, top to bottom: tarp, bucket, folding saw, loppers, hand cultivator, dandelion weeder.

Left to right on wheelbarrow: scuffle hoe, half-moon edger, garden hoe; left to right: square point shovel, round point shovel with straight shank, spading fork, pitchfork, hedge shears, three-point ladder, mattock.

Left to right: power hedge shears, chain saw, blower, garden rake, stiff house broom, street broom.

Looking for Dead Wood

One of the great secrets of successful pruning, and the only rule for all of the time is: *prune out the dead wood* (it's also a favorite adage of politicians). Dead wood makes an amazing subconscious impact on the viewer: the landscape seems messy and dirty. I would estimate that more than 50 percent of my work involves pruning dead wood. You cannot hurt a plant by cutting dead wood; there is no correct season for such pruning; dead wood cannot possibly grow new leaves and adds no beauty.

Summer is a good time to prune out dead wood on deciduous trees and shrubs, especially small-leaved, fine-branched plants. In the winter it is much more time-consuming to sort out which branch is dead on shrubs like deciduous azaleas, viburnums, and lilacs. In the summer, you need only note which branches have no green leaves.

SIGNS OF DEAD WOOD

New gardeners will have to train their eyes to see dead wood. I can't stop seeing it. I see it on your house plants, I see dead wood even when I'm going 55 miles an hour on the freeway. You can tell if a branch is dead even in the winter, because the wood is a different color from the plant's live wood, and it is brittle. Gardeners are always gently bending branches to see if they are brittle and dead and shaking them to see if there are live leaves on the ends. Sometimes merely tapping the branches with your pruners will snap them off; cotoneasters, for example, are easy to clean up this way. Another tipoff is that dead branches have dead buds. Any time of year your healthy plants will have live-looking, plump buds on the tips of their branches. Dead buds are smaller, browner and, well, dead looking. Dead or dying branches will sometimes have orange coral fungi on them, sunken spots or wounds, or persistent dead leaves.

HOW TO CUT BACK DEAD WOOD

At first you will need to cut the branch back a little bit (branches die from the tip back), until you find out where it is alive again. Look at the inside of the part of the branch you just cut off by looking at its cut end. If it's brown inside, it's dead. If it's light tan surrounded by green or all green, it's alive. As you get more experience, you will just know. Equally important is pruning off any dead stubs you may find. These stubs also have a profound effect on the overall appearance of the plant. Finally, you can always nick the bark with your pruners to see if the wood is alive or dead: if the area just under the bark (called cambium) is green, the branch is still alive; if black or brown, it is dead.

It is not possible to prune dead wood at a distance. You are going to have to put on your grubbiest clothes, get on your hands and knees, and crawl into the shrub! Now sit there and stare at the branches. Spot the dead wood? Sometimes it helps to start from the bottom and work up, following one branch at a time. Don't just take the largest ones, get all the tiny twigs, too. Be patient, move slowly. If you are in a hurry, you will not see what is needed, and you will probably put your eye out, not to mention cutting off some nice live wood. Keep in mind that this large-scale cleanup needs to be done only once—the task will be only a minor job in coming years.

By the end your underwear will be full of twigs and you should be feeling about as awful as your shrubs have been. But when you have finished, after, I estimate, from half an hour to two and a half hours per old shrub, then walk or crawl outside and see what you have unveiled. I promise a miraculous improvement on any shrub, if you just believe me and prune out the dead wood *before* you do anything else. Most people ignore this part, yet this is real pruning.

USING THE FAN RAKE

The second great professional secret is the wonders worked by that little-known tool, the fan rake. Raking out the leaves from under trees and plants invariably makes things look enormously better. If your plant has had blackened or scorched-looking leaves, don't use them in the compost, since they may have a bacterial or fungus disease that is overwintering on the ground and getting ready to reproduce next year. Using the fan rake may also destroy some slug egg homes, too—slug condos, we used to call them at the Parks Department. In some situations, however, good gardeners will rake leaves *into* the beds, the theory being that they act as a nice blanket of mulch to prevent weeds from germinating, and also that the leaves will decompose and make good compost for your soil. I guess ideally you should rake out healthy leaves and then cut them up in a machine called a shredder. Shredded leaves look nicer and will decompose faster. Then reapply them to your yard. You decide which you prefer. In any case, rake or push out the mess you just made pruning out the dead wood.

YOUR PLANTS WILL THANK YOU

Just a word or two on dead wood and plant health. When I was a novice gardener I wondered what the big deal was about improving air circulation for the health of shrubs, which the professionals kept saying was the point of pruning. I thought the point of pruning was to make shrubs smaller. I know better now. Your plants will love you for taking out the dead leaves and dead wood. (They'd do it themselves, but they can't move.) I have brought many plants back from death's door by pruning out the dead wood. I don't know how plants know, but they love it. Not only do they look infinitely better, but they grow better and are able to ward off disease better as well. Healthy plants simply look better. In fact, "healthy" is to plants as "fresh" is to fish.

So, be a hero or heroine: prune out the dead wood.

SUMMARY

❑ Take out the dead wood. Do it first; do it always.

❑ Prune from inside the plant and from the bottom up.

❑ Use your fan rake to remove debris.

❑ Note the signs of dead wood:

1. No leaves or dead leaves on dead branches.

2. Dead-looking buds.

3. Wood is a different color.

4. Branch or twig is brittle.

5. Cambium layer just under bark is not green.

Timing

New gardeners are often overwhelmed by the deluge of conflicting advice they get as to the right time to prune. Some experts say to prune "when the shears are sharp," while others, warning about the way trees bleed in the spring, urge "dormant pruning."

I'd like to introduce the general rules of good timing and mention some specifics, too. A little-known or little appreciated fact is that *pruning* (especially heading cuts) stimulates *growth*.

SPRING

In the early springtime your plants are most vigorous, and pruning will stimulate new growth the fastest; it's also the best time for a plant to recover from severe pruning since it is followed by the longest period of benign weather. Try to wait until the danger of frost is gone, because if your pruning stimulates lots of new soft growth, this growth might freeze off. It will not freeze the old "hardened off" wood, though. Spring is a good time to renovate your giant aucuba ball, when you will be cutting into all that black-looking inside growth, and this will give it maximum time to "green up" again. When you radically reduce the size of a hedge, you expose ugly, dead-looking branches. If you must do this, know that early spring is when the new growth will come back fastest. Spring is a good time to prune anything that you are worried about killing with heavy pruning. Rhododendrons are touchy, and sometimes when you prune back to an old node (branch or bud), the whole branch simply dies. Early spring is when they are most vigorous, and you can spot swelling hidden buds along the stems and cut back to these. If you do this, you will have a better chance of stimulating growth.

Spring is the time for bud work. You can rub off new buds growing from places where you've thinned off branches before. This may stop them from becoming suckers (or watersprouts). In my area, where the climate is mild, early spring (Washington's Birthday) is when we heavily prune back hybrid tea-type roses. It is easy to spot the swelling buds to cut back to. Later in the spring is the time to prune the elongating buds called "candles" from the tips of pines. The Japanese either twist or cut them off, or even cut them in half. This prevents pines from getting bigger and gives them the "puff of clouds" look. It's almost impossible to make pines smaller again without ruining their natural form. It is far better to thin or layer your pines as they grow than to wait until you think they are suddenly too big and then try to make them smaller.

Contrary to common practice, spring is not a good time to prune fruit trees or flowering ornamentals (flowering and fruiting cherries, plums, crabapples). This is because these plants are prone to suckering back. Suckers, you recall, are the weak, wild, skinny, upright branches that often result from wounding or pruning. The more heavily you prune, the more suckers you get. So always go lightly in pruning these trees, say one-eighth of the total green area in any one year. Avoid heading cuts on the ornamentals (which means those trees that are not fruit trees).

Other plants that sucker easily are magnolia, dogwood, witch hazel, fig, parrotia, and hazelnut (filbert). You should generally prune these in the summer to reduce sucker regrowth. There is another group of trees (maple, dogwood, pine, birch) called "bleeders" that lose sap at a frightening rate if you prune in the spring. I am told that this loss of sap does not actually endanger the plant's health, but it looks messy. Prune these trees in the summer or winter.

Avoid pruning all trees during the weeks in spring that they are forming leaves, and during the time the leaves are falling in the autumn. These are times of low energy for your trees and the added stress of pruning is not good for them.

SUMMER

Summer pruning is less stimulating to plant growth. It is, however, somewhat more stressful to the plant, so be sure your plants are well watered and healthy and don't pick on rhododendrons or other touchy shrubs. Summertime is great for spotting dead wood, as you know. Because of the non-stimulating effect of summer pruning, it is a good time to tidy up that laurel hedge or those abelias, because they won't grow back right away. Summer pruning in the Pacific Northwest means June and July. In hotter climates, ease off even earlier. Summer is a good time to snap out new sucker growth or cut it off. Battling suckers is much of what I do as a pruner. Avoid heavy pruning (except for suckers) during droughts. Drought is stressful on plants; so is heavy pruning. Also, it will take a long time for your plant to regrow. You may burn some previously shaded leaves or the bark inside your plant or tree.

FALL

Fall pruning is risky only with certain plants. Some plants are considered tender, which means their tips freeze back easily, and sometimes whole branches do so. (In my climate zone, roses, choisya, laurestinus, raphiolepis, and laurel are tender.) I have noticed that many of these are the plants that take full sun. It makes sense that these plants, perhaps from warmer climes, are not used to colder weather. Also, in the fall, when the days are somewhat warm and wet, plants are occasionally tricked into thinking spring is back, so you may not wish to chance stimulating more soft tender growth. Some people feel that fall pruning is rather stressful on plants, but a little thinning and touching up are always in order in any season. You can, of course, always take out the dead wood.

WINTER

Winter is a favorite time for professional gardeners to prune, especially trees. That's because we are usually too busy weeding and doing absolutely essential pruning in the spring and summer. In winter we have the time to get out our ladders, dive in among the branches, and really sort the garden out. Winter pruning also stimulates growth (which will happen next spring), but not as much as spring pruning does. When all the leaves are gone, it's easier to see the branch pattern on some of the big deciduous shrubs, such as forsythias and European cranberries (*Viburnum opulus*).

BLOOM TIME

Another consideration for deciding when to prune is flower production. You will read that some plants bloom on year-old wood, or two-year-old wood, or on buds set up this season, or that are maximum on three-year-old wood. This is all very confusing. A good rule of thumb is to prune right after blooming so that the plant has time to set up buds for the next year. But it's just a consideration for gardeners who are really into their flowers. You know it does not hurt the shrub to prune it at the wrong time. You don't shock buds into not forming, you just cut off some. In fact, some gardeners prune before blooming so that they can bring in the barren-looking twigs of, say, forsythia, quince, or sweet-smelling witch hazel, put them into vases of water, and force them to bloom early in their warm homes. Such are the rewards for clever gardeners.

If you are selectively pruning and thinning your shrub or tree, this should not make a big difference to the casual observer come bloom time. It makes a big difference only if you shear or otherwise head back all the branches of your shrub after it has made its flower buds; then you will be cutting off all the buds. But you shouldn't be shearing your flowering shrubs, anyway. I pay closer attention to bloom time when pruning plants that have one big show and then quit, as opposed to ones that push out flowers on and off throughout the season.

Now you have the facts before you, and you may decide for yourself when to prune. There are many oddities to know about plants that you can look up in a pruning encyclopedia for your region (or check the Appendix for titles). You will, however, have to know the names of your shrubs first. I suggest you make a little map and get the lady with the great-looking yard down the block to come help you identify your favorite plants; she will be flattered. Or you may want to hire a professional gardener; he or she can get you off to a good start, too. In any case, don't be intimidated by the notion of right-time pruning. If you are out renovating your yard, it's then that you "prune when the shears are sharp."

SUMMARY

❏ People make too big a deal out of proper timing. General thinning is okay almost any time of year. Following are general results of pruning at different seasons of the year.

Spring:

❏ Pruning in spring produces rapid regrowth. This is a good time for any bud work. Watch out for "bleeders"(maple, dogwood, walnut, grape, birch).

Summer:

❏ Summer has a somewhat dwarfing effect, but is harder on the health of the plant; it's a good time to battle suckers and to spot dead wood on deciduous plants.

Fall:

❏ Pruning in fall may be stressful on plants and may stimulate tender growth that will freeze when winter comes. General light thinning is always in order.

Winter:

❏ Winter is a good time to prune deciduous plants and is the traditional time for pruning fruit trees. Winter is a good time for undertaking heavy work and will stimulate growth next spring.

Pruning Cane-growers

When I decided to give my first lecture on pruning, I had to decide what to say. The principles of pruning are the same for every plant, but I knew that I approached a forsythia with a different mental attitude from that in which I approached, say, a star magnolia. I concentrated on different kinds and sizes of branches. With the forsythia I spent most of my time sawing out large canes to the base; I didn't worry about its ability to recover. The magnolia required dainty, thoughtful pruning and was more a matter of art. I realized that there were many plants that I pruned pretty much like forsythias, and that I could tell how to approach most plants by simply observing their "habit" or natural shape.

This is how I came to divide plants into three broad categories. This classification is convenient, not scientific, but it will help you to decide how to prune your plants by learning to read their habits. I have labeled these groups *Cane-growers*, *Mounds*, and *Tree-likes*. You can start looking at plants on your block and deciding which type they are. Many plants have an in-between habit; just train yourself to observe a plant's character.

DEFINING A CANE-GROWER

Cane-growers include a large category of plants referred to in garden literature as "deciduous flowering shrubs." They are often vase-shaped or fountain-shaped, with many trunks or canes coming up from the base. The bases of deciduous flowering shrubs are usually a clump. A forsythia is your basic cane-grower, as is a rose. Cane-growers renew themselves by sending up new canes; hence they can afford to lose their old canes to injury or pruning.

Some cane-growers spread by way of underground stems or roots rather than by staying in one clump. Examples of *running cane-growers* are bamboo and

kerria. There are also intermediate cane/tree-likes and cane/mounds. More on them later.

STARTING TO PRUNE

Deciduous flowering shrubs are chosen and planted mainly for their flowers, although some have a habit and foliage that's interesting, too. Forsythias can look great when in bloom and then pretty uninspiring the rest of the year. Many of these plants have an optimum age of each cane for flower production, say, canes three or five years old. By cutting back the oldest canes to the ground level and encouraging some of the new canes, you are planning for good flowers in coming years. This cutting back is not necessary; the shrub will bloom anyway, but it is desirable for those who really care about having the maximum quantity of flowers. Taking out one-eighth to one-fifth of the old canes each year will also keep your plant from getting too big, as nothing in there will be more than five to eight years old. While you are pruning out two or three or five of the biggest, oldest canes, take out some of the newest ones, too. Pick only the nicest arching or healthy ones to remain. Cut out some puny, too straight, or too crowded ones, also. On the other hand, if you would like your forsythia to be 10 to 15 feet tall, just let it be. Shrubs don't *need* to be pruned.

LOOK FOR DEAD WOOD

On many of these old cane-growers you will find a lot of dead wood. The shrub can afford to let canes die back, because it's easy for it just to send up a new cane as a replacement. Old deciduous flowering shrubs often have big stumps of dead wood at the base. Weigela and forsythia will show many stumps where old canes were cut back to 3 inches or 6 inches. They will be dead and punky or dry as

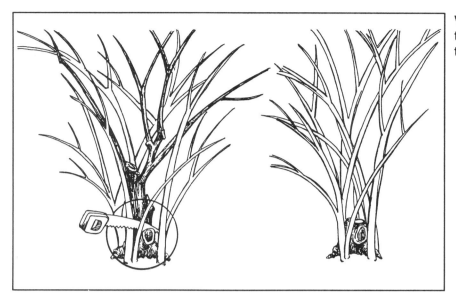

When pruning cane-growers, spend the most time thinning out canes at the base.

powder. I'll never forget the look on a client's face when I went over to her forsythia and pushed on a giant old hunk of dead wood that just snapped out in my hands at the base. It had looked as if I would have to take a saw to get it out. It was in the winter, and she must have wondered how I knew it was dead.

CUTTING LIVE CANES

Speaking of sawing, after you prune or push out the dead wood, you will have to saw out some of the big old *live* canes, too, especially the ones crowding and rubbing in the middle. These are the hardest ones to get at because all the others are in your way. You will have to scoot around the plant to find the best position to get at the target cane. Sometimes it is not possible to saw it or cut it off right at ground level; just do the best you can. Sometimes you have to sacrifice a couple of outer canes that are in the way. But don't risk destroying your shrub to get at the inside canes. When pruning an inside cane, the space is often so tight that you can only saw with the very tip of your saw. Keep at it! When you finally make it through that big old cane and haul it out, you will be amazed and deeply gratified because you have dramatically reduced the bulk and clutter of your plant. You can pull out your cut cane by tugging on it down and out from the base; check to see if it's catching on anything big. Sometimes you can push it up and out. Sometimes, if it's really wrapped

around other things (and these canes are the ones you're after), you may have to cut it into smaller pieces where it's hung up. It only takes the removal of a few big canes to alleviate big problems.

A TRAINED EYE

But, before you cut, you need to train your eye. Stare at your shrub. Deciduous flowering shrubs are easier to stare at in the winter when all those leaves aren't hiding the branches. Pick a couple of canes and follow them; see where they go and what they run into. Visualize how the plant would look without this or that cane. Look for canes that are too crowded, or that twist around, or that badly rub other canes. Look for canes that start on one side of the clump and head the wrong way through the center and out the other side. Look for ugly branches, by which I mean branches that are too straight (if it's supposed to be an arching shrub). This is a tough one on forsythia and weigela, because it's the older canes that develop this nice arching habit. The new canes tend to be straighter, with flower buds spaced farther apart. You may encourage some of these young canes to fork and start curving by cutting (heading) at a bud at the height you want. Look closely at these buds. The way the buds face is the way your new branches will go. Visualize! Are your new branches going to go where you want (and not into the center)? Do not be afraid to head back a large cane to a place you intend it to bush out and fill in.

Now that you have been staring at your shrubs for a while, you realize that there are tons of wrong branches and canes. You can't get them all, so pick two or three of the worst ones and *cut*! Voila!

Cane-growers are good for the novice to work on because they are, generally speaking, really tough stuff. It's hard to hurt them or ruin their shape. In fact, you can renovate them by cutting them totally to the ground and starting them over. Really, it's okay! Don't try it with your rhododendrons, though. (See the section on "Renovation.")

PLANT SIZE

Something you should know about cane-growers and plants in general is this: they *have a size they like to be*, and it's not usually a convenient 3 feet by 4 feet. Lots of the deciduous flowering shrubs like to be 5 to 10 feet tall. I remember when my mentor, Andrea, pointed to some mock oranges (*Philadelphus*) and said that these plants like to be about 8 feet tall. I thought, good grief, don't plants grow to whatever height I cut them? How will I take care of something 8 feet tall? But really, it's easy, as I found out. It's hard only when you work *against* what a plant wants to do. When you try to keep a plant smaller than its mature height, it loses its nice, natural shape. And you wind up cutting off most of its flowers. The harder you prune, the harder it grows, and you soon find that you have to be out there whacking away at it all the time. So, although your cane-growers can take it, don't work against them. Fortunately, horticulturists are breeding smaller varieties of many of our pretty, giant cane-growers like forsythia and spirea, for smaller yards. If your cane grower is really, really too big, read the renovation section.

After taking out the dead wood and some old canes in your shrub, move up to the top and sort out some (rarely all) of the crossing and ugly branches (use thinning cuts and selective heading). If your plant's tips hang down to the ground, cut them back a bit. If one branch sticks way out, cut it back to a side branch that is the right height. Be aware that there is another workable way to prune cane-growers. The

British develop a low (4- to 12-inch) framework called a "stool" and cut the canes back to it.

HOW TO PRUNE A ROSE

When people speak of garden roses, they are generally referring to hybrid teas. These are pruned heavily and greatly shortened to force them to produce bigger flowers and to keep them to a manageable height.

You prune a rose as you do any other cane grower, only more so. After pruning too big, too small, too crowded branches, by cutting out at the base, you shorten all the canes drastically. You cut to a side branch or promising bud facing, generally, out from the center. Gardeners like pruning roses because it's so dangerous with all those thorns. (You know, some people climb mountains.) In the early spring you find gardeners standing on their heads looking for tiny, swelling pink buds on the sides of canes.

When cutting out rose canes to the base, most people prefer to take out canes that are thinner than a pencil, as well as a few of the fattest ones. People disagree on how far down to head the remaining canes. But do make the skinnier canes shorter and the fatter ones taller. I like to keep a cane that is as fat as a cigar and about as long. Rose fanciers in the midwestern states will cut them as low as three buds from the ground! One rose expert I know teaches new rose pruners the chant, "You can't kill a rose by pruning it. You can't kill a rose by pruning it," to give them courage.

Prune roses as you would other cane-growers, then reduce height dramatically. Gardener shown is trying to locate out-facing buds to cut above.

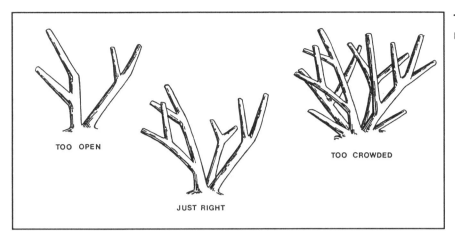

TOO OPEN

JUST RIGHT

TOO CROWDED

Thin out roses and other shrubs, but not too much.

When you begin to shorten your canes, you will find that the place that seems like the right height usually has a bud facing the wrong way (i.e., facing toward the center), and vice versa. As with most pruning and renovating, it's a matter of just doing the best you can. Pruning instructions are always guidelines, rarely hard and fast rules.

You should also be aware that many roses are grafted. The above-ground portion of the shrub is spliced onto a tougher root stock. Sometimes the roots send up shoots of their own, especially after a freeze. You need to cut off these unwanted canes or your rose will revert to the rootstock rose.

A good thing to remember about pruning a rose or any other cane-grower or plant of any sort is not to take everything out of the middle or everything down low; leave something there. We want to thin it out, not gut it.

Besides hybrid teas, there are other kinds of roses: shrub roses, old roses, climbers, ramblers, miniatures, and floribundas, to name a few. You prune all these less severely. For people interested in a more in-depth description of rose pruning, I suggest Brickell's *Pruning* (New York: Simon & Schuster, 1979). Usually a little light thinning and sorting out will suffice, however, for the average homeowner's non-hybrid tea rosebush.

PRUNING "RUNNING" CANE-GROWERS

There are many other miscellaneous cane-growers that are not deciduous flowering shrubs. These are plants like bamboo and Oregon grape that spread with runners. Heavenly bamboo (*Nandina domestica*) stays in a clump, but is not deciduous (it usually keeps its leaves all winter). Kerria is deciduous and flowering but it runs. You can tell the type by observation. All cane-growers look better if thinned by cutting some canes to the ground, unless you are using them as a hedge. There is a general rule about plants to the effect that you can encourage either tall, thinned out plants or low bushy ones. When you cut them down drastically to reduce height, they tend to get busy and send up new canes and new side shoots to make up for it. A combination of thinning and shortening is usually best, depending on what you are trying to do.

Plants that run, which is to say ones with a mat of roots spreading across the top layer of dirt, can be easily reduced in size (width) by grubbing out the roots. For bamboo, this works only on new growth. The old growth is about as tough as rebar. To reduce your mahonia (Oregon grape) or kerria, loosen the dirt with a shovel and pull canes up and back toward the center of the plant. Use an old pair of loppers (so you won't mind if they get dull cutting down in the dirt) to cut the roots where they're too matted or well rooted. Prune with vigor! You won't hurt what's left.

PRUNING "IN-BETWEEN" PLANTS

Many other plants that I have categorized as "mounds" or "tree-likes" have a sort of in-between habit. They, too, will benefit from your cutting some canes down to the ground. A lilac, which is mostly tree-like, sends up suckers or canes from the base.

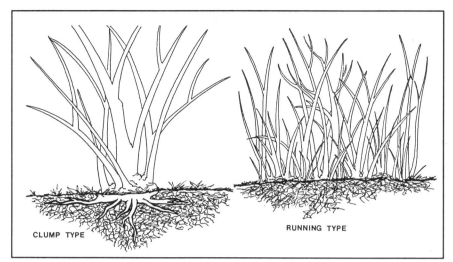

CLUMP TYPE

RUNNING TYPE

Some cane-growers are vase-shaped and grow from a clump. Others increase in width by "running" with their roots. Reduce width of the latter by digging and cutting back roots to desired shrub size.

Usually you cut these out, but you may want to choose one to develop into a nice new trunk. Or you may wish to renovate your lilac slowly by taking a big cane down to a side branch or out at the base. In fact, many people treat lilacs as cane-growers—sacrificing branch patterns for lower blooms, pruning them almost like a forsythia.

SUMMARY

- ❑ Cane-growers are tough.
- ❑ Thin out canes to the base.
- ❑ If it's not broken, don't fix it. Shrubs and trees don't *need* to be pruned.
- ❑ Each species has a size it likes to be—its "mature" height. You cannot usually keep a plant smaller than its "mature" height without doing great harm to its looks, its health, or your

own pocketbook.

Cane-grower pruning punch list:

1. Stare at your shrub.

2. Take out all dead wood—always do this first.

3. Take out some (one-eighth to one-fifth) of the oldest canes to the base and some of the puniest new ones every year, if you like.

4. Pick out the worst-looking canes that rub or cross each other, look sick, go the wrong way, or are ugly.

5. In general, prune to open up the center.

6. Tidy up the rest of the plant, always cutting to a side branch or bud (node).

7. Prune with vigor!

Pruning "Mounds"

You will recall that cane-growers are generally very tough; you can cut them totally to the ground and they will renew themselves by sending up new canes.

The shrubs I refer to as *mounds* are not quite as tough as that. But they can generally take some pretty serious selective pruning to reduce height and bulk without drastic results. I would say you can safely take out one-third of the total plant area without inflicting stress on the plant. Mounds are the easiest of the three types to keep to a given height.

A mound's natural growth habit is generally just that. They tend to be wider than they are tall. Many send up canes like cane-growers (i.e., spirea); others are more twiggy and tree-like (*Viburnum tinus*, *Ceanothus sp.*), but they all have a more or less mounded look. Some people tend to shear them for this reason, but please don't. Most of them are planted for their flower show, which will be reduced or eliminated if you shear them. They generally have small leaves and short spaces between leaves on the branches (short internodes) and their branches are fine or soft, a habit that tempts people to shear them. They make nice informal hedges and mass plantings.

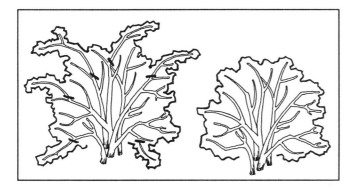

When pruning mounds, hide cuts down inside the plant. Your shrub will be shorter and tidier but natural looking.

FINDING THE BRANCHES TO PRUNE

Upkeep on these plants is quite simple. After they are through blooming, you wade into the shrubs with hand pruners in one hand. You train your eye to pick out the very longest, most unruly strand or branch, grab it with your free hand, and follow it with clippers down inside the shrub, 2 inches to 1 foot below the general surface of the planting; then snip it out. If possible (some say it's a must), cut to a node. Now don't seek the next *closest* unruly branch, but the next *most* unruly, too-long branch in the vicinity. This is the grab and snip method! You wander around taking *only* the worst or longest branches. After cruising the whole area once, step out and look. Miraculously, everything will be tidier and shorter, but it will also look natural and unpruned. By the time the branches from the nodes to which you cut grow back up, they will be about the right height. By cutting to nodes you will not cause cut branches to die back, leaving unsightly dead stubs, or cause them to sprout back in a snarl.

Stand back and judge your work; ask yourself if you're done. Does the shrub need to be shorter? Are there some uglies you missed? Is there dead wood, or are there weeds spoiling the looks of things? A good pruner is always standing back and seeing whether it's time to stop or to ask what else needs doing. Sometimes you may want to tip back (cut off the tip) a branch to a certain length. That's all right, too, but the more *whole* branches you leave, the better your flower display will be next year, and the more natural it will look.

More serious pruning of these shrubs should be done also. You can do some every year as you tidy up. Or you can "sort them out" all at once. By "sorting out" I mean that you should remove some of the oldest branches to the base, especially ones clogging up the center, or twisting around other branches, or rubbing them. And as always, *remove any dead wood*, which will, trust me, improve the looks of things dramatically.

ABELIA

Abelias are shrubs that tend to send up rockets for new growth. The more you prune, the more moonshots you get, so go lightly. Light pruning in the late summer helps reduce this wild-looking regrowth and, as I have said before, the older branches develop a more graceful arching habit. Often you find abelia with a sort of thick lower story and a cap of new, straighter, thinner top growth. The temptation is to cut it all back down to the mounded part, but this just perpetuates the problem and may keep the shrub too small. Instead, try to create a balance by opening up the shrub. Remove whole canes to the base, especially very long, leaning ones. Thin out the lower story, especially if it's crowded at the base or skirt. Then selectively grab and snip the worst of the top growth. Also tip back a few to promising side branches, and you've got a more uniform shrub. This is good general advice for pruning trees and shrubs. Instead of trying to remove growth that doesn't "match" the rest of the tree or shrub, make it altogether more uniform. Thin out some of the too bushy parts and head back (thus thickening) some of the too sparse or leggy parts. It is a longer-lasting and better-looking solution.

CHOISYA

A word about choisya or Mexican orange (not mock orange). Choisya is a soft wooded shrub that breaks and freezes easily. A cold snap may cause branches to die back, even much later—perhaps next summer. But it is a tough plant, nonetheless, in that it readily sends up new growth from the underground root system and will easily "break bud" from branches cut back to any length. These buds will form new, green, leafy side branches in no time. So don't worry if you have to cut choisya way back at some times and in some places. Don't cut in the warm weather of fall, because you will stimulate new, soft growth that will freeze easily, but wait to prune it in the spring or summer.

ESCALLONIA

Escallonia will similarly break bud down the branch. If you cut escallonia back hard, it will look bare and ugly a little longer than choisya. However, the plant will assuredly return. Its new growth is also prone to freezing, so prune escallonia in the spring or summer as well.

If you choose to reduce the size of your mound-type plant dramatically, be sure to do it to a few feet lower than you want it to be eventually, so that it has some room to grow back bushy. Or, if you prefer, put these plants on the five-year plan and reduce them a little more each year.

Mounds are easy—just grab and snip.

SUMMARY

❏ Mounds are the easiest type to make shorter and keep small.

❏ Use the grab and snip method, hiding cuts down inside the shrub.

❏ Sometimes it is better to make a plant more uniform (thin bottom to match top, or vice versa) than it is to cut off all the "funny" top growth.

Pruning Tree-likes

In this section, we'll talk about tree-like growers. Rhododendrons are tree-like. In fact, some say they are trees (*rhodo* means red, *dendron* means tree). Other examples are pieris and camellia. Many deciduous plants, like azalea and snowball bush (*Viburnum opulus*), witch hazel and lilac, are tree-like. They generally have stiffish branch patterns, medium to large leaves, and large internodes. They grow from one main trunk or group of trunks and branch many times. I call them tree-likes because their habits are much like trees.

TREAT THEM GENTLY

Whereas cane-growers can be renewed by cutting them totally to the ground if need be, and mounds take some serious thinning and lowering, you cannot deal with tree-likes with a heavy hand. Heavy pruning and shearing place a serious stress on some of these plants and can start them on a downward spiral ending years later in death.

Some tree-like shrubs are prone to suckering. Suckers (also "watersprouts") ruin the good looks of these plants and should be removed unless you want to train one into a branch in two to five years. (See the section on "Renovation.")

Do not prune tree-likes heavily and don't "head" or cut off all the ends of the branches. Many of these deciduous plants' star attributes are their winter branching patterns, which thoughtless pruning destroys. The Japanese maple is king of these. In the winter, raindrops hang onto the branches outside my window like a string of pearls. When laced with snow, the tree is exquisite. Magnolias, with their fuzzy buds, double-file viburnums with their very angular (double-ranked when in flower) branches, and the arching cotoneasters are prime examples of growth habits that should under no circumstances be altered by heading cuts. These cuts constitute a crime against nature that is not easily undone. Avoid even selective heading. Invariably these plants look better when branches are thinned out, cutting a smaller branch off where it joins the larger parent stem.

TREE-LIKES LIKE TO BE BIG

Most of these shrubs are best left to grow big. Pruning on these plants is the most difficult of the three types. Rules for pruning them can and should be applied to other types as well. Restoring plants of this sort that have been badly pruned is indeed an art, and I will speak to that in the renovating section. The point of pruning tree-likes is rarely, if ever, to reduce their size. When you prune them you are trying to thin them out so that they are open looking, less oppressive, more distinct. Thinning and pruning the finely branched shrubs will enhance their good looks, and you will be able to "read" the branch pattern. You may need to remove the interfering branches—ones that head out into the sidewalk, touch the house, lie on the roof, or crowd too far into neighboring plants. You are then channeling the growth into branches that can grow without interference. Only occasionally do you head back a too-long or too-leggy perimeter branch to force it to bush out down inside the tree-like shrub.

It is with tree-likes that the invisible and somewhat magical art of pruning is most apparent. Shrubs and trees are no smaller, but somehow they are transformed into less oppressive, cleaner, nicer, more beautiful plants.

GETTING STARTED

Again, put on your old clothes and crawl inside the shrub with your hand pruners, loppers, and hand

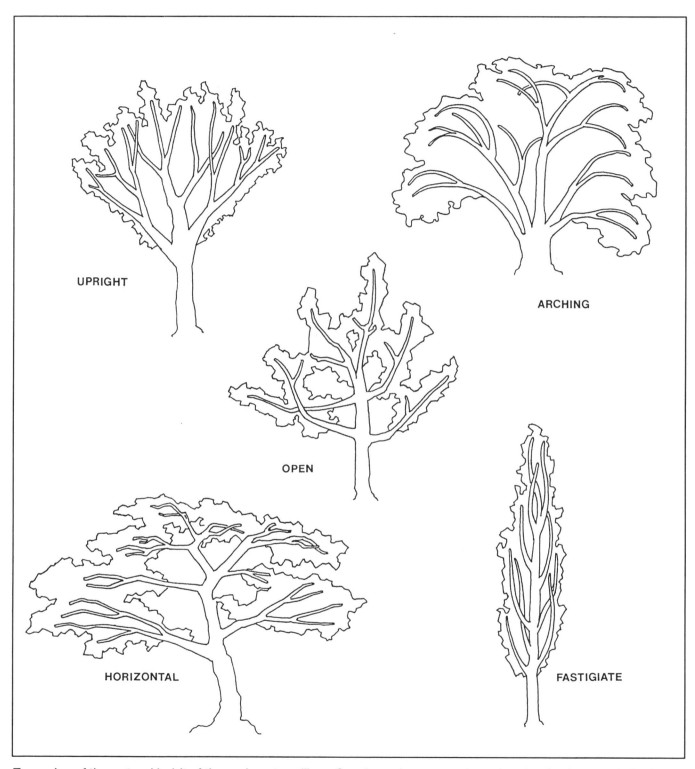

Examples of the natural habit of the various tree-likes. Good pruning never alters the plant's characteristic shape.

saw. Sit down and start staring at your shrub's branch pattern. It takes anywhere from one-half to three hours to prune an old tree-like shrub, so take your time. First spot the dead wood and any stubs where a branch not cut at the node (side branch or bud) has died back. Take it all out, even the tiny dead twigs, cutting close to the main branch. In many cases, dead wooding is all you need to do with tree-likes. This bears repeating. *In many cases, dead wooding is all you will have to do.*

As for the rest of sorting out your shrub, start at the base and work up and out, saving until the very last any size reduction of the shrub by heading back branches.

In all cases except dead wood, you will want to cut out the worst offending branches; rarely can you eliminate everything that is going the wrong way. Do not remove more than, say, one-eighth to one-fourth of the total plant in any one year. So if you decide to take out one big branch, don't take out all the little wrong branches, too. Save that for future years. Generally, you are helping the plant to attain its natural growth habit by removing branches that rub or interfere with others. Remember, most cuts made in this situation are true *thinning* cuts, taking small branches back to bigger branches.

In general, prune to open up the middle, so as to enhance the natural habit. If your shrub is horizontally branched, cut out some of the branches that head straight up or down. If it's arching and floppy, prune to enhance this shape. Frequently crawl back out to see how things are going. It's easy to do too much. Once you start seeing "wrong" branches, you want to take them all out and finish the job. Some old, mangled shrubs will have nothing left if you do it all. As with a haircut, it's easy to take it off, hard to put it back. So stand outside frequently and see whether it's time to stop, or if the shrub is unevenly thinned, or if you've missed something.

THE OVERVIEW

Back to nuts and bolts: (1) Take out dead wood. (2) Take out suckers at the base and any other straight up growth. (3) Starting at the base, look for any large branches that may be making the shrub too crowded or that may be seriously twisting or rubbing around another big branch. Taking out one big errant branch may solve a host of problems. But be cautious, it may make things very bare. So study your two entwined branches to decide which one stays, or whether you must perhaps leave them. You may wish to look from different sides and from the outside. Don't wait to do this until the very last, because you may need all those other small branches for cover when you take out a big one. *So, early on, take out any big, crossing branches.* (4) Take back any branches that are hanging down on the ground. (5) Take out the worst of the smaller, rubbing, crossing branches, choosing the healthiest or best placed one of each pair to remain. (6) Prune or shorten the worst of the branches that start from outside of the shrub and go the wrong way back through the center and out the other side.

Now, we are getting into some of the more artistic stuff. (7) Branches naturally arrange themselves in layers, alternating around the trunk. Each branch holds a network of smaller branches, generally on the same plane in a more or less fan-like pattern. Sometimes a branch will send out a stray that heads too far up into the next plane, or crosses two or more planes, or goes too far down. Pruning off these will add definition to your shrub, thin it out, and make it look more open. This is especially good for pines and camellia. This is just something that makes the plant look a little better.

(8) You are nearing the end of the job now. Sometimes several branches are doing the work of one. That is to say, you have two or three branches that exactly parallel each other. It will look better in many cases to remove one of two parallel branches, or the center one of three. Parallel branches are disturbing to one's aesthetic sense when they are close to each other. Dogwood trees, especially, have doubled branches that may look better removed. (9) At the very end, you may wish to head back, that is to say, cut off, the tops of some of the taller branches to shorten them to a side branch of your tree-like shrub. This should be done last. Frequently people find that by thinning, sorting out, and cleaning up the insides of their big old shrubs, they no longer appear so oppressive and big. Rarely is your tree-like too big. It's really just too confused and cluttered.

Take out dead wood. Do this first and always.

Take out the worst of the crossing/rubbing branches.

Take out suckers.

Take off branches actually touching the ground.

Take off the worst of the wrong-way branches. Look for ones that head back toward the center of the plant.

Take off the worst of the branches that head too far up or too far down.

Take off parallel branches to give more definition to the plant.

In Japanese gardens, the gardeners carefully train their rhododendrons, magnolias, and laceleaf maples so that there is a sort of see-through outer shell and you can look inside to see the "bones" of the plant; the dappled light thus created is an added aesthetic attraction. Use the helpful lists in the Appendix to find out which plants take heavy thinning and which do not.

SUMMARY

❏ Don't prune tree-likes very much.

❏ Most plants will eventually grow to about twice their "mature height." They finally stop at their "ultimate height." Some plants are easy to control heightwise and some aren't.

❏ Tree-likes are the most complicated to prune and the hardest to control in size. Give them the room they need to reach their "ultimate" size. Take out dead wood and little else.

❏ Avoid heading cuts.

❏ Thin offending branches (ones that hit the house, go too far, or are most in the way) back to a larger parent stem or trunk.

❏ Sucker regrowth is an exact reflection of too much or the wrong kind of pruning.

Punch list for tree-likes:

❏ Take out:

   1. Dead wood

   2. Suckers from trunk, roots, or branches

   3. Crossing/rubbing branches (the worst ones)

   4. Branches hanging on the ground

   5. Wrong-way branches

   6. Too-far-up/too-far-down branches

   7. Parallel branches

❏ Head back to shorten (if necessary) on shrubs, not trees.

❏ Tree-likes vary in the degree to which they may be thinned before they sucker back or suffer dieback. Removal ranges from approximately one-eighth to one-third total leaf area.

Pruning Hedges

Hedges can be grown in two styles, the formal and the informal. Formal means that you shear them, informal means that they look more natural and you *selectively* prune them to control size and maintain their good looks.

A big difference between formal and informal hedges is the amount of time it takes to maintain them. Formal hedges have to be sheared all over to keep them looking tidy. Shearing may be fast, but it must be done frequently. To control size you cannot miss a year. Informal hedges can be selectively pruned, and therefore generally need only touchups of unruly branches. They are easier to reduce in size and look better when reduced this way. Both styles of hedges have the purpose of providing a natural screen or wall. A formal hedge (in addition to performing a function) is a good contrast with other plants. Contrast is one of the major elements of an esthetically pleasing yard. So that, whereas an en-

tirely sheared yard may look dumb and dull to some people, a perfectly straight sheared hedge behind your perennial flower bed constitutes valuable contrast in your yard and is very tasteful.

AVOID LEGGY HEDGES

Avoid creating a hedge with legs. It is considered uncouth to have such a hedge. You want a hedge that is dressed to the ground, as in totally formal. Hedges get leggy when sun cannot reach down low, so that lower leaves are shaded out. The way to prevent this is to shear your hedge in a slightly pyramidal fashion so that the top does not shade the bottom. By fall, the top will have grown back more vigorously than the bottom and it will look more nearly square. In the colder part of the United States, the pyramidal form helps prevent damage to the top from heavy snowfall as well.

To prevent leggy hedges, shear top slightly narrower than the bottom.

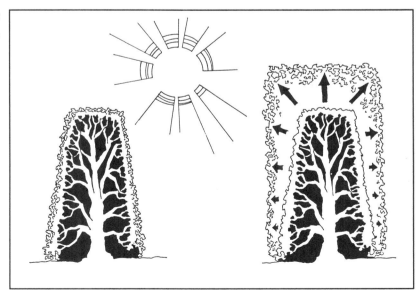

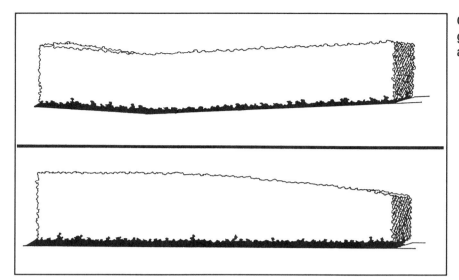

Common mistakes are following the ground level and lowering the hedge as your arms get tired.

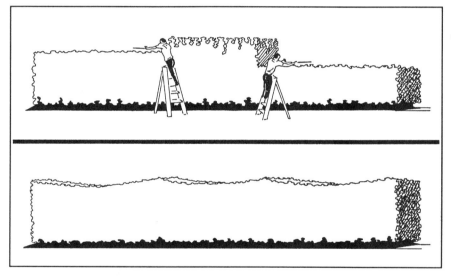

Other errors: two people doing the job; trying to follow a string tied to the chain link fence.

CREATING A NICE HEDGE

The major criteria for nice hedges are levelness and straightness. This is a lot harder to achieve than one might suppose. As people who have sided a house or laid bathroom tile know, the work may look even close up, but when you stand back, OOPS!

Mistakes to avoid are (1) following the ground level, (2) lowering the hedge top as your arms get tired, (3) following last year's mistakes—cutting just above the old cut, (4) having two people do it, and (5) following a string tied between two posts or tied along the adjacent chain link fence.

Some people try using a carpenter's level on a board,

or they rig up a one-dimensional hedge template and move it along. Some pick a part of their body to cut to. Once Norman the Foreman at the Parks Department where I worked told the crew to cut at knee level, which, of course, varied according to whose knees you were talking about.

For very tall and very long hedges, rent scaffolding to help you cut the hedge perfectly level. The best method I've found for general hedge cutting is the haircut method: take a little off at a time and frequently, stand back and walk around, looking at your hedge from different angles. Get it right the first time using loppers—then follow your old cuts the next year using shears or hand pruners.

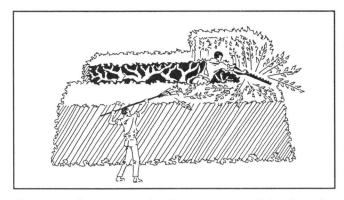

For very tall, very wide hedges, create a "false front," then shear the top from inside.

HEDGE WIDTH

A hedge needn't, shouldn't, be wider than one person on a ladder can reach across. If your hedge has gotten very broad, consider serious reduction. When you drastically reduce the height, or more likely the width, of your hedge, you will want to do it in the early spring so that it will most quickly and vigorously hide those ugly bare branches. Be sure your hedge is the type that will green back up if pruned hard; many needled evergreens won't. If you are a lazy gardener and want to shear only once a year, try a tidy cut in June or July, when it is least likely to promote new shaggy growth. If you have a truly giant laurel or boxwood hedge with only one side facing the public, you may want to turn it into a false front by taking out the unseen inside, or make it into a horseshoe by chain-sawing out the inside. This will make it possible for you to set up your ladder inside or behind and shear the top.

Have you ever wondered about those giant sheared things on English estates? How do they do that? That giant holly gumdrop? That two-story yew that looks like an elf hat? Well, first off, these plants have been sheared from the time they were little, every year, so that they are incredibly bushy and dense right through to the very inside, and the gardener actually stands or ties the ladder onto the shrub itself. The plants chosen are slow growing and only need to be done once a year, usually. Generally the leaves are small.

HEDGE SIZE

Which brings us to the point of your laurel or pho-

tinia hedge. You (or someone else) planted laurel or photinia because you wanted a wall *fast*. Since these bushes really want to be trees, they oblige you by growing fast. But they don't stop when they get to the size you want, they keep growing—fast. They are prone to developing legs and their big leaves don't look as nice sheared as do fine-leaved plants. That's what you get for being so impatient.

You will probably want to shear laurel and photinia more than once a year to keep them looking nice, and after you shear them, go back over everything with your hand pruners and selectively prune out the ugly stubs and exposed branches. If either of these has been let go so that you've had to place a twelve-year-old kid on a plywood board on top of the hedge to shear the 8-foot expanse on top, you may rest easier knowing that these incredibly tough plants can be pruned back hard, which is gardenese for cut *way*, *way* back, to a couple of feet off the ground if you like.

Do not, however, try this radical reduction with your needled evergreen. It won't work. Most of the conifers and needled evergreens, except yews, develop a dead zone of bare wood on the inside of a sheared plant. This zone gets bigger every year. If you shear deeply into it, it will not green up again. So, generally speaking, every year your needled evergreen hedge must get incrementally larger.

The qualities of a plant that make it good shear material are that it has small leaves, spaced closely together, it is slow growing, and it is tough enough to take it.

DECIDUOUS HEDGES

Some people plant deciduous shrubs for hedges—privet, hornbeam, and the like. They often need more severe early training than conifers in order to build a dense, bushy framework, especially around the base. It is even possible to use blooming things like forsythia, escallonia, quince, and camellia. I wouldn't, but I'm prejudiced. Pyracantha is often used as hedge material and is also valued for its decorative berries. Your timing may vary in order to retain as much "show" on these berried and flowering plants as you can. Do not top your conifer hedge until it reaches the height you wish it to be. Shear

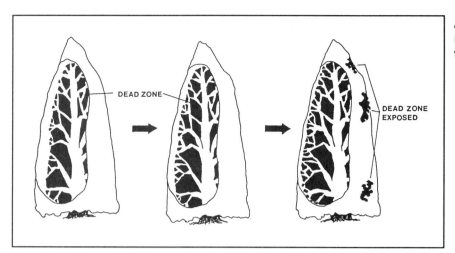

Avoid cutting into the dead zone on needled evergreens. If cut deeply, they will not "green back up."

deciduous material all over repeatedly as it grows to its desired height.

POWER TRIMMING

If you have inherited a home with a veritable fortress of hedging around the perimeter and you want to keep it (I'd take it out and plant a perimeter of tasteful groupings of shrubs), you may choose to invest in a pair of electric or gas-powered hedge trimmers. The two most hated pieces of power equipment in the Parks Department were chain saws and power hedge shears. That's because they rarely made it through a group project alive. I always loaded up as many as I could lay my hands on, so that when one died, I could switch to a new one. It reminded me of a pony express rider changing to a fresh horse. I also brought two extra chains for the chain saw and some WD-40® for the blades of the power hedge shears, to use when they got sticky and wouldn't move.

It's a wise idea to sharpen both of these pieces of equipment before, during, and after a big job. This is because the amount of physical effort required increases exponentially with the dullness of the blade. Also you can get into serious accidents with both these power tools, the chances of these accidents also increasing as you get tired from forcing dull blades through your shrubbery. People are very reluctant to stop to rest once they start this equipment, especially when it's taken thirty-five pulls to get it started, thus ensuring operator exhaustion from the beginning. Tired people with dull chain saws cut their foreheads open (tip kickback); tired

hedgers tend to saw into their thighs. These tools are, on the other hand, useful time- and labor-saving devices, if you use the best and the sharpest and take the time to rest and resharpen. I use my local saw sharpener a lot, and I keep extra chains on hand. I sharpen things after I'm done, so that my chain saw or trimmer is ready when I go to use it six months later. Electric saws and shears tend to start more easily than gas-powered ones and are much lighter weight, so you don't get as tired. Also, you don't get gassed to death by the exhaust fumes. Be careful with your cord in the rain, however, and don't cut it and electrocute yourself.

People just don't realize the danger, drama, and high excitement that waits for them in their own backyards. Now that you know all about hedges, you are ready for the assault. Let's be careful out there!

SUMMARY

☐ Good plants for shearing have small leaves spaced close together. They are slow growing and tough. They will not become diseased or die back as a result of repeated shearing.

☐ Formal sheared hedges should be level and thin enough for one person to reach across.

☐ Make the top of a hedge narrower than the bottom.

☐ Needled evergreens (hemlock, pyramidalis, etc.) cannot be radically reduced in width. They will not readily break bud and green back up, as will most broadleaf plants.

Shear Madness

The overuse and misuse of sheared shrubbery are among the most common forms of landscape mismanagement. Sometimes shearing shrubs is considered a matter of taste and sometimes it is not. Selective pruners refer to over-sheared shrubs as "green meatballs," "hockey pucks," and "gumdrops"; they spoof sheared landscapes as "tombstone" or "lollipop" yards and generally lament the presence of ubiquitous "poodleballing." I call it "shear madness."

To the novice eye, a sheared yard looks tidy and interesting. To seasoned selective pruners, a sheared yard seems pretentious and betrays an ignorance of good pruning techniques. Whereas tree topping is a crime against nature, poodleballing is regarded as the hallmark of bad taste in gardening.

Shearing is, in itself, not bad. Whether or not shearing is appropriate depends upon the style of the garden and the species of the shrub. Both criteria must be met for sheared material to "work."

FORMAL LANDSCAPES

The style of the yard must be formal as in a topiary, rose, knot, or Japanese style garden. A sheared plant can be used as a single formal element of contrast. For example, a straight, sheared hedge may serve as a backdrop for a border of perennials; or a walkway might be bordered by sheared globes as commonly seen on estate grounds. In England one is apt to find countryside cottages featuring large boxwood shrubs sheared into the shapes of hens. What fun! In a Japanese garden setting, massed plantings are sheared to imitate a vista of low rolling hills. The lower story of sheared material is contrasted with a pond and open, sparsely branched trees.

SPECIES FOR SHEARING

Whether or not shearing is appropriate also depends upon the species of the shrub. All good pruning enhances the natural growth pattern or habit of the plant material itself. Shearing is no exception. As mentioned before, the criteria for good shear material are small leaves spaced close together and a plant tough enough to take the shears repeatedly. Ideally, the plant chosen for shearing should be capable of greening back up if it has to be reduced in size. This makes broadleaf evergreens somewhat more desirable than needled evergreens. Sheared evergreen (broadleaf or needled) shrubs and trees are preferred over deciduous material because they look nice all year round. The ideal plants for shearing are boxwood, holly, yew, privet, pyracantha, and box honeysuckle, followed by some santolinas and some finely needled evergreens such as juniper, thuja, and hemlock. Other plants such as forsythia and *Philadelphus* are tough enough to withstand tight shearing but the leaves are too large and, therefore, are not as attractive when sheared. Barberry and spirea have small leaves but are not tough enough to take tight shearing. They will develop dead spots, "bird's nesting" and generally look "ratty." Species planted for their flowers will lose their spring display.

Some shrubs, such as escallonia, abelia, and osmanthus, are the object of debate among gardeners because they do have small leaves spaced close together, and they are tough enough to take shearing. Some gardeners don't like to see them sheared because the fine flower display is compromised by heavy shearing done at the wrong time of year. Evergreen azaleas are the perfect example of this. Many selective pruners feel that azaleas should be allowed to be themselves, but many Japanese gardeners, and others who like the tight look, do shear them. If done at the right time, the azalea can have wonderful flowers as well.

DON'T MISUSE SHEARING

Aside from considerations of taste, there are other good reasons to avoid the use and misuse of shearing as a pruning technique:

1. It locks you into a high-maintenance routine.
2. It is difficult in the long run to control the size of your shrub.
3. It is a drain on the health of the plant.
4. It subverts the purpose of many shrubs, sometimes by eliminating their flowers or, more unfortunately, sometimes destroying their branch patterns and texture.

DON'T SHEAR TO CONTROL SIZE

Because shearing is non-selective heading, you will stimulate bushy regrowth. You create a twiggy outer shell on sheared plants. This layer of twigs shades out the interior, which then becomes leafless and full of dead leaves and dead wood. Meanwhile the outer shell becomes thicker and larger every year because, as it is sheared repeatedly, it must be cut a little farther out to retain its greenery. This dense, twiggy outer shell makes size reduction difficult because cutting back too far exposes that ugly dead zone inside the shrub. It is also physically difficult to cut through the thick, twiggy mass. Although most plants will eventually green back up when they are pruned back into the dead zone, as you now know, the needled evergreens, such as junipers, won't. Therefore, shearing is not a good way to control the size of a shrub. Selective pruning utilizing the thinning cut ensures that there will be a green twig or branch to cut back to and can therefore be employed to reduce a shrub's size while retaining its natural look.

ONLY TOUGH PLANTS TAKE SHEARING

Shearing is also a drain on the health of plants. Selective pruners spend most of their time opening up the plant to let in more light and air and to reduce the buildup of dead wood and disease. Shearing plants creates the antithesis of a healthy environment, making shrubs more prone to insect attack,

dead wood, and dieback. It adds a general stress on plants because the rapid, profuse growth promoted by repeated heading depletes their energy, and their resulting weakness and tender growth make them more susceptible to injury from freeze or drought. This is why care must be taken to pick plants that are tough enough to take repeated shearing. Even then, the shearing must commence when the plants are young to avoid the sudden stress of shearing after they have reached maturity. Even on plants that are appropriate to shear, the good gardener will take time to reach inside and clean out the buildup of dead wood and dead twigs.

SHEARING IS HIGH-MAINTENANCE

Another problem with shearing is that it is a high-maintenance chore. The growth that results from the heading cuts grows rapidly straight up and looks rather wild. The tidy look that the first shearing created is soon destroyed. Although shearing the plant may take little time, it gets undone very quickly and locks the practitioner into frequent re-shearing.

When plants are selectively pruned, the new growth matches that which already exists in the plant and it looks more natural. The growth from a selectively pruned plant continues at about the same rate. Therefore, a selectively pruned plant stays in control longer. Shearing is a labor-intensive form of pruning. I have even heard it compared to drug abuse: the first time through is very gratifying and very quick, but the unwary wielder of hedge shears will soon be locked into a high-maintenance habit. It will take more and more shearing to keep a plant looking its same tidy way, until one day the hapless homeowner can't see out the window or open the door blocked by a giant ball or box. And eventually, the plant's health will begin to show signs of deterioration.

OTHER DRAWBACKS

Aside from maintenance and health considerations, the gardener must also consider the purpose of plants when deciding how to prune them. Shearing often defeats the purpose of shrubbery, usually by cutting off the flowers. But other characteristics are subverted as well. True genius in landscaping is obtained by balancing theme and contrast. One of the elements of contrast is texture (for example, the fine leaves of a boxwood, the fluffy look of spirea, the bold, deep leaf of a viburnum). Shearing will eliminate contrast of texture. Everything begins to look the same.

Finally, shearing does great violence to plants that have been chosen for their secondary characteristic of fine branch patterns. Such a plant is the star magnolia, which is valued for its flowers, but is also valued for its beautiful branch patterns and fuzzy buds. Other trees and shrubs highly valued for their fine branch patterns are the double file viburnum, Harry Lauder's walking stick, Japanese maple, and Eastern dogwood. Shearing ruins them.

So if you have a sheared hedge and do rent a pair of power shears, restrain yourself from taking on the rest of the yard. Don't get carried away with shear madness.

SUMMARY

Good to shear:

Yew
Japanese holly
Boxwood
Box honeysuckle
Privet
Pyracantha

Optional to shear

English laurel
Quince
Some junipers
Osmanthus

Hemlocks
Evergreen euonymus
Arbor vitae
Oregon grape
Holly
Photinia
Abelia
Escallonia
Bamboo
Cotoneaster

Do not shear:

Deciduous flowering shrubs (forsythia, deutzia, kolkwitzia, philadelphus, weigela)
Lilacs
Roses
Viburnums
Rose of Sharon
Rhododendrons
Pieris/Andromeda
Most barberries
Kalmia
Spirea
Deciduous euonymous
Aucuba
Camellia

Criminal to shear:

Laceleaf maple
Magnolia
Deciduous azalea
Witch hazel
Harry Lauder's walking stick
Dogwood
Contorted or weeping things
Double file viburnum

Fruit Trees

Ask five knowledgeable gardeners how to prune fruit trees and you may well get five very different answers. This is because fruit trees have grown for centuries as food sources rather than ornamental trees. Therefore, everybody and his brother have developed a system to maximize fruit production and to make it simple to pick all the fruit, *fast*, and to make it easy to spray and to do more intensive pruning to produce more and more fruit.

IF YOU ONLY WANT FRUIT PRODUCTION

If you want to maximize your fruit production, most County Extension Services have inexpensive bulletins. They will explain early training of young trees, pruning for production, and what to do with that ugly old apple tree to bring it back into good shape. You will learn the single leader method, the open center method, and the modified central leader method. You will learn about Type IV tip bearers with "blind wood." You will learn how to spread open young limbs (some people use clothespins) or to shore up old limbs with 2 x 4s to keep them from breaking. All the information in these bulletins will help you produce lots of fruit, but if it seems like too much work and you don't want to learn that much, try the Turnbull method of pruning fruit trees. It is less work and you don't have to concentrate as hard. It makes your tree look good and will produce enough fruit to feed all your friends and family before the fruit rots.

PRUNING ERRORS

But first, let's go over what *not* to do. The two most common errors in pruning fruit trees are: (1) topping and (2) creating umbrella trees with ugly, sucker-laden crowns.

Topping is unequivocally bad for any tree, including fruit trees. The suckers that shoot back up from a topped fruit tree will not only be ugly, they are too busy trying to get enough leaves back in order to feed the tree to make much fruit.

However, many orchardists will radically reduce the height of apple and pear trees using the *dropcrotch* method of lowering trees. Dropcrotching means you selectively head back to a side branch of a decent size, say one-half the diameter of the parent stem. This is hard on the health of old trees and opens them up to rot. Younger (fifteen years or less) trees withstand this height reduction better. Dropcrotching reduces the amount of sucker regrowth, as compared to topping, but does not eliminate it. Do not use it as a way to keep your ornamental tree small. (More on that later.) Don't prune too much (no more than one-fourth total leaf surface) in any one year. And don't try to fix it all in one year. If you have a tree that needs a lot of work, do it over several years.

The second error is the creation of "umbrella" trees. This happens when the pruner cuts to an outside branch year after year—something you might be tempted to do if you already know something about pruning. This is called *bench-cutting*.

APICAL DOMINANCE

We now need to understand apical dominance. This is the only hard, technical part. Here is some basic tree and plant biology, which, when you get it, will make everything else clear to you, and you can also impress your friends with some fancy words.

First, we will talk about the last bud on the end of a branch (the *terminal bud*). This bud releases a chemical that, moving via gravity, keeps the buds on down the line rather subdued. Think of it as the

Two common errors in fruit tree pruning.

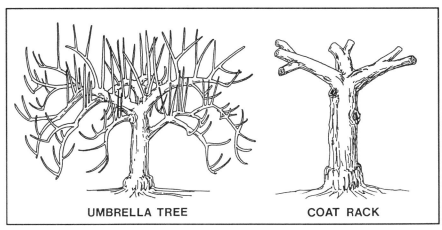

UMBRELLA TREE　　　　COAT RACK

boss bud. When you cut off the end boss bud, or even pull it over, the chemical flow is disturbed and the other buds begin to grow.

Umbrella trees have terminal (boss) buds that are too low. Gravity prevents the chemical from reaching buds down the line, so a crown of suckers develops at the top. To help keep your old apple tree from excessive crown suckering, thin back low branches (they look like hooks) to a branch facing more up and out.

Pick out a major (scaffold) branch and follow it with your eyes. Does it dip down quite far, crossing other, lower scaffold branches and cluttering things up? Then you may selectively head back (prune) to one of its side branches that faces more upward and outward (40° to 60° is ideal). The scaffold branch now ends in a boss bud with greater *apical dominance*. This will reduce the number of returning crown suckers farther back as well as improve the looks of your tree.

Keep in mind apical dominance if you attempt to reduce the height of your apple or pear tree. It is a good idea to cut back a tall vertical branch to a shorter branch that also faces upward. Basically you are not trying to eliminate all vertical branches. You are simply replacing them with shorter, younger, and fewer vertical branches. This retains some apical dominance and allows the tree to grow a little every year. It's like a volleyball game—you rotate out a few of the tallest old suckers every year.

You may have a forest of suckers that are the result of previous bad pruning. If you remove all of the suckers, they all come back. Leave some to apically dominate the rest, shorten some to create a second story up, and thin out the rest.

Note that the natural state of many old fruit trees is an umbrella, which is all right if the umbrella is low down on the tree where you can get the fruit, and if you don't care how it looks. But often the umbrella occurs high up on the tree, shading out the fruit below, and spoiling the overall good looks of the tree.

PRUNING FRUIT TREES

So, how do you prune a fruit tree? The easiest way is just to prune it like other trees: for health and good looks. First, and always, take out the dead wood. Be thorough. Then take out some of the worst crossing or rubbing branches, the worst branches going the wrong way. These are the ones that start on one side of the tree, head the wrong way through the center, and come out on the other side. Also, thin back some of the branches, especially toward the top (even a few big branches) to increase light penetration and to lower your tree. This helps ripen the fruit lower down. It increases air circulation, too, which is important in order to discourage the numerous bacterial and fungal diseases that spoil the fruit. Look for narrow, weak big-branch crotches. Heavy, fruit-laden branches need to be strong. Narrow crotches are the ones that break.

Now, you could stop here and you would have a pretty good-looking apple or pear tree without too much trouble. It will have fruit. But if you want to do more, read on.

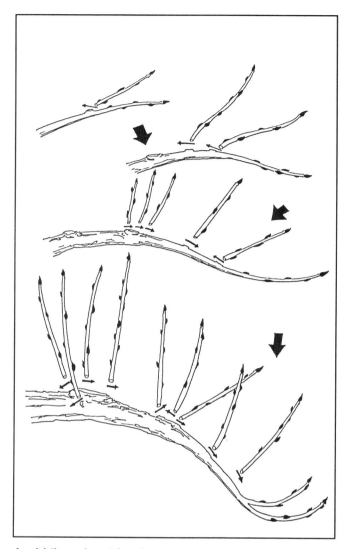

Avoid "bench cutting."

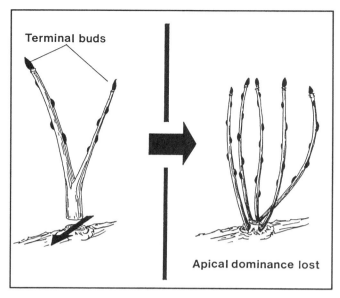

Bench cutting removes terminal buds. Apical dominance is lost and the result is unwanted sucker regrowth.

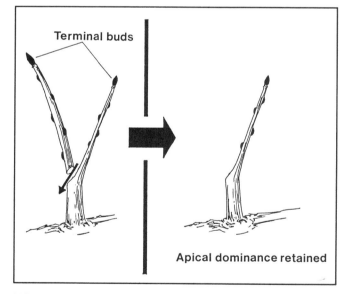

When lowering a large branch, try to retain apical dominance by cutting to a vertical side branch or bud.

PRUNING FOR FRUIT PRODUCTION

Certain kinds of branches make more fruit buds or spurs than others. These are the ones that are situated in a not-too-horizontal position. You can pull or push new branches into such a position, or you can just start cutting out the ones that aren't in the right place and leave the ones that are. Nature makes fruit by sending up a young, straight-up soft branch. It flowers on the tip, and the flower turns into a fruit. The weight of the fruit pulls this supple branch over. As a branch gets older, it stiffens in a more horizontal position. As the branch tips over, the apical dominance of the terminal bud weakens, and buds farther down the branch are released to

How Nature makes fruit.

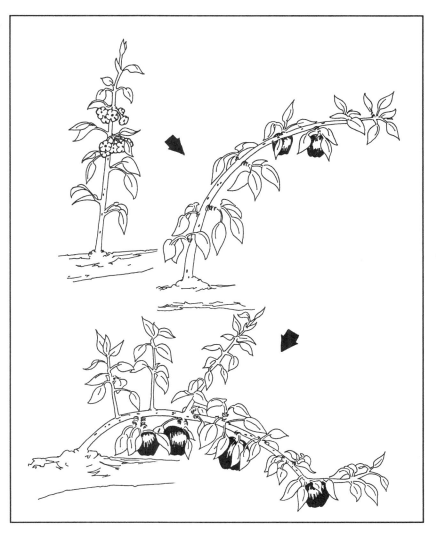

form nice little side branches (*laterals*) and on them, teeny, tiny ¼-inch branches called *spurs*. These tiny spurs have fat flower buds (fruiting buds) rather than skinny leaf buds. We want the laterals and spurs.

In the winter, it is the fat-budded spurs that you see on trees that make you think what you're looking at might be a fruit tree. You can encourage some, but not all, of your side branches (laterals) to make spurs by heading (also called tipping back) to two or three buds. This works on pears and apples, but it doesn't work on cherries.

Now, if your main branch gets pulled too far over—past 90°—apical dominance is diminished, too many buds are released, and those miserable suckers start charging back up.

In some senses pruning fruit trees breaks all the rules for ornamental tree pruning. You try to keep your tree small, something that should never be done to other trees. Pruners often reduce fruit trees dramatically, which would be extremely bad pruning on a maple or oak. We also head a lot. We head side branches (laterals) to force them to make spurs. We shorten major scaffold branches with heading, especially young ones, so that they won't swing in the wind and lose fruit. Heading causes these branches to get fatter or stouter. We need stout branches to hold up heavy fruit. On apples and pears, especially, we do a lot of heading. Peaches, nectarines, and Japanese prunes really like it when we whack and whale. However, don't do it to your cherries or European plums.

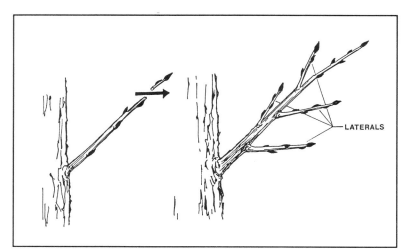

Head branches to force laterals.

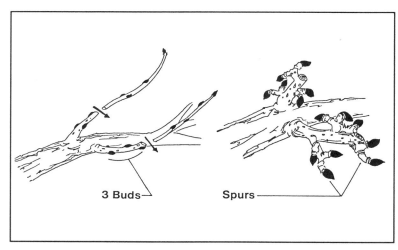

Head laterals to force fruit spurs.

Let's recap what we've gone over thus far. Prune your fruit tree like any other tree:

1. First, and always, take out all of the dead wood.
2. Take out the worst crossing, rubbing branches.
3. Take out the worst wrong-way branches.
4. Take out some, not all, of the suckers.
5. Remove weak crotches if they are or will become part of the main framework (scaffold) branches.
6. Thin (don't strip) all those branches rather than heading them, and do more thinning on the top to encourage light penetration and air circulation.

When dealing with suckers on your fruit tree, remember to: cut some out altogether; leave some alone (don't cut off the tips), since they will flower and fruit and be pulled over and produce more spurs later; head back some suckers to thicken them up into second story branches. Try to head back to another upright side branch and not to a horizontal branch that would sucker back madly.

If you want to encourage more fruiting on your apples and pears, you can prune for more horizontal branches. You can head back laterals to force more spurs to form. See, you're an expert already!

MORE ABOUT FRUIT TREES

Here is more information about fruit trees.

❏ Pruning of young trees (under six years) is done to develop strong, low framework branches and not much else. In fact, it may take a while longer for your tree to fruit. Go easy in the early years. There are some newer varieties that fruit earlier.

❏ Old trees can be invigorated by heavy pruning to produce new wood and spur systems, although you may experience a temporary drop in production when you cut off older and lower limbs or "hooks."

❏ Summer pruning of fruit trees is all right if the tree is vigorous and healthy and well watered. Summer pruning can be useful for spotting dead wood (no leaves). It can be useful in reducing the spread of fungus-bacterial diseases that like damp weather, and it will help reduce suckering. It generally slows the growth rate and will help restrict the size of your tree. It is harder on the plant, however, so go easy, and never prune during a drought.

❏ Proper horizontally-placed branches are only one factor in fruit production. Many fruit trees need a cross-pollinator tree in the neighborhood. The Cooperative Extension Service in your area has lists of what type of tree pollinates what for you and which fruit trees do well. Cross-pollinators are something to consider when you are planning your orchard.

❏ New dwarf varieties called "spur type" apples don't need to be pruned to make them set up spurs. They do it themselves. In fact, be careful that you don't prune them off.

❏ Bee activity is needed for pollination. If it has been a very wet spring, you may not get enough bee activity. Bees, like some Parks Department workers I know, won't work in the rain. On the other hand, if you don't see any bees and it has been sunny, it may be that someone in your neighborhood has inadvertently killed them with pesticides. Misapplication of some commonly used pesticides can wipe out entire hives. If your neighbor doesn't read the label and applies something like Sevin® on plants in bloom during the middle of the day, a bee might bumble into a flower and then carry the poison back to the hive and kill the entire hive. This is a tragedy for the orchardist as well as the bees.

❏ Fruit trees need sun in order to flower and fruit. If your tree never sets fruit, stand next to it and look up. If you see big trees or condominiums, this may be your problem. You're in too much shade. Try removing your fruit tree and planting

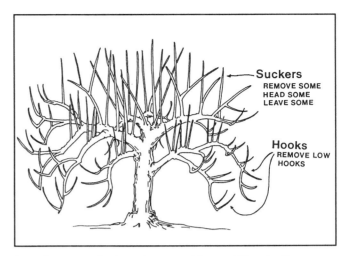

Locate unwanted suckers and lowest "hooks."

With regard to suckers: leave some, cut some out altogether, and shorten some. Remove "hooks" to reduce suckering and to make the tree look better.

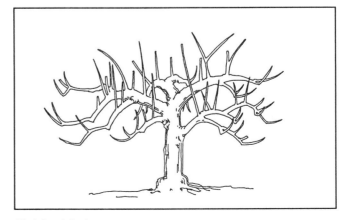

Finished fruit tree.

a vine maple, Japanese maple, or other under-story tree. These look nice and do well in these conditions.

❏ Fruit trees, especially Gravenstein apples, sometimes get into an every-other-year routine, which can be modified by pruning. If you wish, you can ignore it. Your tree may be too young. You'll have to wait, be patient! Your tree may be too old. You'll have to prune it or remove it and replace it with something you like better.

❏ You can improve the size and quality of your fruit by thinning branches so more light gets to the interior of the tree. Also, you can thin spurs and baby fruit, so that more energy gets put into the remaining branches or buds for bigger, tastier fruit. Don't go overboard though, you might get "bitter pit," "cork," or other fruit tree maladies. Now that you know the basics and how to be patient and moderate, you can develop your own best method of pruning.

❏ There is a difference in the severity of pruning of European and Japanese plums. Japanese plums should be pruned heavily, like peaches; the strong upper wood should be cut back to weaker branches. Whack! Whack! Whack! Japanese plums and European plums will not cross-pollinate each other.

❏ These days you don't have to suffer with big fruit trees; nurseries now have new dwarfing rootstocks. So if you want fruit and less work, chop down that old tree and plant a new dwarf one. Dwarfing rootstocks come in small, smaller, and very small. Check it out with your Extension Service. A really smart-sized fruit tree is about 4 feet tall. Unless, of course, you love that old tree—then keep it.

❏ Do not try to make your cherry tree small again by topping it. It won't work. They have yet to develop a really good dwarfing rootstock for cherry trees. That's why that big bucket truck with the 70-foot extension is called a "cherry picker."

❏ People often want to lower cherry trees because they cannot stand the waste of the fruit on the top where they cannot reach. Removing the top would not actually increase cherry production

down low. Other people welcome the day when the tree gets tall enough that the birds leave the lower cherries alone.

If after reading this chapter it all seems very confusing and self-contradictory, well, it is. Even people who specialize in fruit tree pruning are often unsure and easily swayed to other methods and ways. Take heart—teachers send students out to practice on apples and pears because these trees are so forgiving. In eastern Washington, machines mow them to force fruit production. Stay away from topping—especially your cherry tree—and you'll do okay.

SUMMARY

❏ Traditionally, fruit trees, like roses, are for people who like to prune and spray a lot. Try buying very, very disease-resistant dwarf trees to reduce these maintenance chores.

❏ You can, if you like, prune fruit trees as you would ornamentals, for health and good looks, and leave it at that.

❏ Horizontal branches bear more fruit than vertical branches.

❏ All fruit trees are not created equal.

Group A:

Peach	Head a lot
Apricot	Prune hardest
Nectarine	
Japanese plum	

Group B:

Apples	Keep young trees short
Pears	Head laterals to encourage fruit spurs
	Prune medium

Group C:

Cherries	Hard to keep trees short with pruning
European	
plums	No topping
	No heading laterals
	Least pruning
	Train early by bending branches

How to Prune a Tree Limb

Thank goodness for Dr. Shigo! He is the world-renowned tree expert who has scientifically proven what many gardeners suspected all along. He has shown that what a lot of other experts have been doing is *wrong*. Dr. Alex Shigo has degrees in biology and a Ph.D. in plant pathology from West Virginia University. Between 1959 and 1985 he was employed by the U.S. Forest Service as Chief Scientist and Project Leader of a pioneering project on discoloration and decay in forest trees. He has dissected more than 15,000 trees with a chain saw. He has studied trees in many countries. His research has yielded 270 publications, and he has received many honors and awards. Shigo is Who's Who in the world of arboriculture. He is famous for his amazing energy, inquisitiveness, and for his fearlessness in challenging old truths. His respect for trees and the people who actually work with trees is inspirational. He has shown why topping (also called heading, stubbing, or dehorning) is very bad.

DR. SHIGO DEBUNKS MYTHS AND DISPELS MISCONCEPTIONS

Shigo has proved that the common practice of flush-cutting limbs off trees is bad, and that tree wound paints and seals don't do any good whatsoever (except perhaps on rose canes, or with some special sprays that may aid the reduction of suckers on some trees). He and his cohorts have done this by scientifically testing these products and practices and their effects on trees. He cuts and drills and wounds and saws trees by the scores and later dissects them to see what's really happening. He refers to himself as an "inside man" because he likes to look inside the trees. (I call myself an "inside woman" because I like nothing better than to crawl inside a tangled mass of overgrown shrubbery and prune it back to good order.)

Dr. Shigo's findings are very bad news for many professional pruners who learned to do it wrong at their daddy's knee. Experts have been passing on misinformation for decades, sometimes centuries.

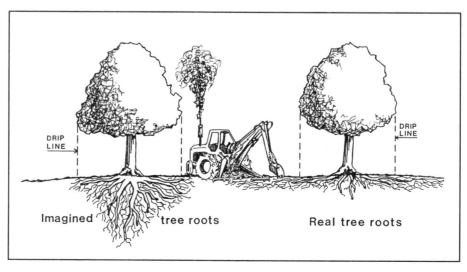

Tree roots extend well beyond the drip line and are found mostly in the top 18 inches of soil.

Trees do not heal; they set up barriers to rot and then they try to outgrow it.

Don't cut too far out, don't cut too close, cut just to the branch collar.

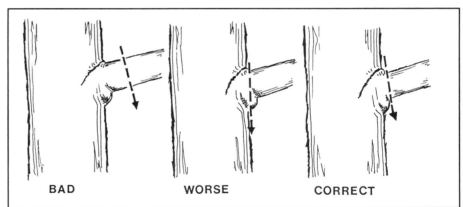

BAD   WORSE   CORRECT

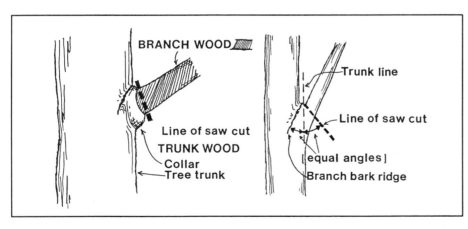

The angle of the branch collar varies. If you can't find the collar bulge, you will have to use geometry to figure out where to cut. Start by locating the branch-bark ridge, and make equal angles with regards to the trunk.

Dr. Shigo has also pointed out the damage done by the commonly reprinted picture of a tree's root system that looks like a giant underground carrot, or inverse tree. It's misrepresentative of the group of plants we call trees, which tend to have a flatter, broader root system. This misconception about tree roots becomes more germane when the bulldozer starts pushing dirt near them, when trenches are dug, cutting off one-third of the roots, or when herbicides put on the lawn or driveway wind up killing the tree.

Dr. Shigo also can tell you exactly why digging and carving out that old rotten hollow in your tree back into nice live wood is precisely *not* the thing to do, and in fact, does great and brand new harm to your tree. What some "professionals" do to trees borders on the criminal.

Although Dr. Shigo is highly respected and famous and his evidence is practically indisputable, people often refuse to change. Those who do change tend to do so very, very slowly. Even new books on pruning, written by authors who know of Shigo's work, often repeat misinformation, although with a little less certainty. I intend to give you the straight skinny here, somewhat simplified, but I trust not oversimplified.

SOME TREE BIOLOGY

The world can be roughly divided into objects, plants, and animals. Animals often avoid injury and death by moving away from the wound source. Pain caused by, say, fire, is the signal to move away. Trees cannot move rapidly away from the source of the injury. They wall it off internally and then outgrow it. If a limb gets injured, it will get rotted out by microbes, and ultimately it dies. The reason the injury doesn't usually kill the tree is that the tree sets up an interior barrier or wall around the rot, which stops it. That's why that pocket in your tree where a tree limb rotted out doesn't get bigger, it just makes a cute home for a squirrel. When some of that rotten branch gets trapped inside the growing tree, it is totally stopped and surrounded by a wall. It's the knothole that drops out of a piece of lumber. It's easiest for a tree to wall off a dead or dying limb. It's somewhat harder to wall off the gash you left when you backed into the trunk with your car after the last Christmas party. It's hardest for it

to wall off all the rot that comes charging down the trunk when you top it. It's sort of the difference between bruising your knee, cutting off your hand, and cutting off your head.

Whether your particular tree dies back totally or partially when wounded depends a lot on how well it walls off wounds generally. This varies according to its genetic makeup or species, and even among members of the same species there is genetic variation. There are several types (species) of trees that do not compartmentalize well; in the trade they're called "rotters." They include bigleaf maple, alder, willow, poplar, tulip poplar, elm, and madrona.

Rotters often make up for their lack of toughness and short life span by reproducing like crazy. You want to help these plants by prompt removal of injured limbs and by avoiding wounding or cutting (pruning) healthy green wood. Cut out the dead wood and little else. Leaving dead wood rotting on a tree acts, as Dr. Shigo says, as a "big stick of sugar" drawing in the rotting bugs. Besides, it's UGLY.

Dr. Shigo tells us that branch wood is different from trunk wood (see illustration). When you go to remove a limb for whatever reason, you should be careful to cut off only the branch wood and to avoid cutting or wounding the trunk wood, which would doubly injure the tree. You will know where to make your cut on many trees because you will see a bulge or collar of trunk wood at the base of the branch.

The right place to cut is almost like a dotted line. It's also the most logical, the easiest place to cut; lazy gardeners have always cut there, as do the ones to whom natural things look right. The chain saw enabled a lot of damage to occur with little effort. For literally decades arborists have been doing things wrong. They have recommended "flush-cutting," which wounds well into the collar, which is trunk wood, not branch wood, thus causing a second and worse type of injury. How did this happen?

GREAT MISTAKES IN TREE HISTORY

Dr. Shigo and his associates can trace the way the mistake has been passed on from generation to generation back to an old arborists' convention. Probably Dr. Shigo even knows the arborists' names!

They were sitting around talking shop talk, and they all had noticed that the branch collar or callus "rolls over" the cut area and covers it up faster when it's sliced into than when you cut to just outside it. They declared that this was the wound healing and just assumed that the wound healed faster with a flush cut. Actually, trees are not healing with the "callus roll" as it is called. The real work is going on inside where things are being walled off. Cutting the collar opens the trunk to rot and is responsible for many serious problems that show up years later.

If you can't see where the collar is on a tree, you may wish to refer to a somewhat geometrical method of determining the dotted line in the accompanying illustration.

MORE OVERSIMPLIFIED TREE BIOLOGY

Let's divide a tree into four sections. The outside section is the protective bark. Just under the bark is where all the action takes place; this part of the tree is made up of the *cambium*, the *phloem*, and the *xylem*. The cambium is where all the growth happens. It pushes out the cells that turn into everything else, including the phloem and the xylem. These cells conduct nutrients and sugars up and down the plant. Phloem and xylem are the major plumbing area. Just inside this high activity area is the sapwood, which is just the major regular old wood part of the tree. It's actually old xylem. It conducts nutrients up the plant, too, but less energetically. Very old, old xylem at the central core of the tree is called heartwood and is often darker in color. Scientific types argue about whether this part is alive or dead.

When you nick the bark to see if a branch is alive or dead, you're checking out the green cambium. When you saw down a big tree and paint the edges with a deadly chemical to keep it killed, you are painting the cambium. Cambium is important stuff.

It is essential that people understand that the most living, most vulnerable part of a tree is like a sheath just under the bark. When you strip the bark and cambium all the way around the base of your tree, in the fashion of a ring, you have *girdled* the tree. It cannot wall off the wound or send nutrients up to the part above the ring. It will die down to the stripped section, or perhaps it will die altogether. If it's a good compartmentalizer, it will wall off just below and send up new shoots from the roots or trunk just below. Don't girdle your young tree by scraping a lawn mower around the base, or by weed-whacking that soft young bark and cambium off of it. You will get lots of suckers at the base where you wounded it, and you'll risk its total death when

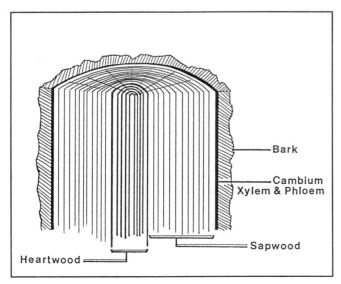

Inside a tree. Remember, the most living, most vulnerable part of a tree is the cambium, just under the bark.

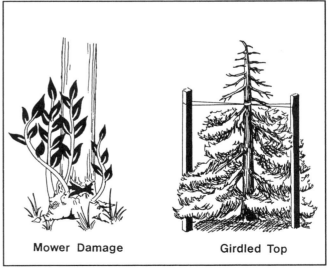

Mower Damage   Girdled Top

Don't wound or girdle trees with string trimmers, lawn mowers, or tree stake ties. Doing so can and will shorten the lives of even old trees.

The two most common errors in limb removal. Forgetting to make an undercut will cause the limb to rip down the trunk. A narrow branch angle will cause the pruner to saw off the bottom of the collar inadvertently.

someday you finally strip it all the way around. You can girdle the top of your tree by leaving something tied around it; an old tree stake tie is the favored thing. Once we managed to top five little Douglas firs at Discovery Park where I worked by forgetting to untie harmless-looking burlap tree stake ties. In two years we had topped all five by simply ignoring them.

TREES DIE FROM A SERIES OF WOUNDS AND STRESSES

People mistakenly assume that since your tree didn't die right after you drove nails or your car into it, it's all right. Wrong! Trees usually die from a *series* of blows over a long time and when one dies, it is from the proverbial straw that broke the camel's back. You may have a giant column of dead rotten wood walled off inside your tree from some old wound and when the drought hits, well, WHAMMO! you've got a dead tree. Or, as Dr. Shigo explains, wounds and injuries, including flush cuts, will often "cock the gun" and a freeze or bright sun will "pull the trigger," so that frost cracks or sun scald will appear a year or years later. The sun or the frost gets the blame. Your trees can wall off a lot of abuse, but that doesn't mean you should abuse them.

HOW TO PRUNE A BIG LIMB

The major objectives in taking off a big limb are: (1) to remove all the limb so that a big stub is not left to look ugly, sucker back, and/or die and rot, and (2) not to injure the branch collar, which is trunk wood. If it's a big branch, this may not be as simple as it sounds. Most people start at the dotted line and cut

down. This will cause two bad things to happen: the weight of your big limb will cause it to break and rip down the trunk wood when you get about three-quarters through; or, if your branch crotch angle is too narrow, and you saw down from the top, you will saw off the bottom of the collar. This is also bad.

To avoid these hazards, use the three-cut system. Somewhat farther out on the branch than you plan to make the final cut, you make a bottom cut and then a top cut that doesn't quite match up; this will act as a hinge so that your limb will gently fold down to the ground instead of dropping on your leg. Or you can just saw it off some distance out. This relieves the weight of the branch and makes an accurate pruning cut easier and safer. When you have a narrow trunk branch crotch, you will have to use the somewhat

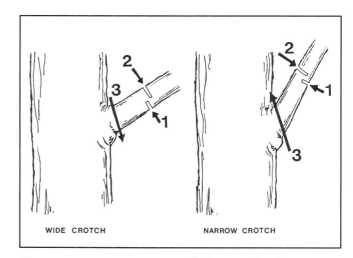

The proper way to remove a limb uses the three-cut system. On narrow, angled branch crotches you may have to saw entirely from the bottom upward.

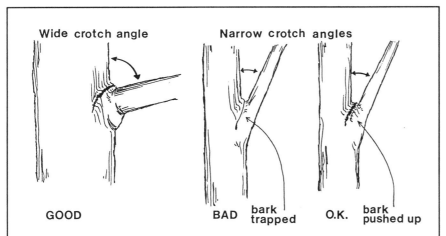

A narrow branch crotch will sometimes have "included" bark. Bark disappears inside the trunk, where it is trapped, causing limbs to break out even on large, old trees.

awkward method of sawing up from the bottom to avoid cutting into the collar. If you ignore this and cut from the top down, you cannot appropriately angle your saw and will wind up sawing through the collar. Even when the angle is wide enough to cut from the top down, always, always make a brief undercut to keep the branch from ripping the bark down the trunk.

LOOK FOR NARROW BRANCH CROTCHES

Speaking of narrow branch crotches, you should be looking for these on your tree. Narrow crotches are the ones that break in storms, causing a big limb to fall on your car. Bark gets trapped between limbs (called *included bark*) in narrow crotches and prevents them from holding together: as the limb gets bigger and heavier, it is more likely to fall apart. Check out the branch bark ridge between the trunk and the limb—does the bark disappear into the tree? Bad news! If the bark is being pushed up, you're okay. Irresponsible pruning by growers early in a sapling's life can cause narrow crotches that fifteen years later turn into dangerous limbs. So look for narrow crotches or crowded branches and remove them if to do so will not ruin your tree. Some species, such as plums, just grow that way. As with all pruning, you use logic and good sense. You just do the best you can in the less than perfect plant world.

CORRECT DOUBLE LEADERS

Another situation to correct in a tree is a *double leader*, which often is a narrow branch crotch as well. You don't want double leaders on your tree. Double leaders are often caused by topping. If it's a young tree (under fifteen years), you can cut out one of these leaders. If it's an old tree and it would ruin its good looks to take out one leader, you could hire a qualified arborist to cable the leaders together, if they pose a threat to life or property. When arborists cable, they put bolts through the branch and the trunk and cable them together. This causes less injury than tying something around a branch, which would girdle it. Sometimes, as in the case of my young katsura, I'm letting two leaders duke it out for awhile to see if one will naturally win. Gardeners have such an odd sense of time. They're always watching their plants, whose lives are action-packed in a slow-motion sort of way.

SUMMARY

❏ Trees don't need much pruning. Taking off a few lower limbs, even big ones, is okay, as long as the limbs are only a small portion of the whole tree, no more than one-eighth of the total. Don't top trees. Here's your list of do's and don'ts for proper tree care:

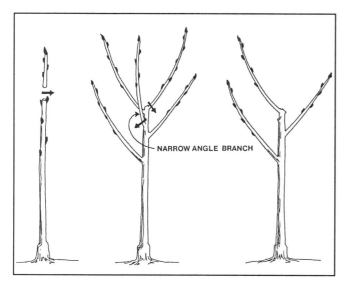

Early pruning of a tree to force branching will sometimes cause crowded branches and narrow crotches to develop. Corrective pruning is shown.

Prune to prevent your tree from growing up with a double leader.

Don'ts:

❏ Don't leave stubs.

❏ Don't paint cut or wounded places on limbs or trunks.

❏ Don't flush cut.

❏ Don't girdle.

❏ Don't top—unless it's a hedge.

❏ Don't leave things tied around your tree.

❏ Don't wound carelessly.

❏ Don't drill holes to drain water from cavities.

Do's:

❏ Do take out dead wood.

❏ Do prune off, to the collar, any limbs you don't want, especially lower limbs.

❏ Do remove narrow crotches and double leaders, or have qualified arborists cable them if they are a potential hazard.

❏ Do remove tree stake ties as soon as trees are established—within a year or two at most.

❏ Do hire a qualified arborist (one who does not advertise topping) to prune large trees or to give you a hazard tree evaluation.

PART II
RENOVATING
THE OVERGROWN YARD

Begin to Bring Order out of Chaos

So you've read the first section on pruning and you know it's not going to be enough. You have bought a yard where everything is enormous; you sense that some plant-happy person planted it thirty years ago and stopped taking care of it ten years ago. Or perhaps you never knew what to do yourself, so rather than ruin everything by pruning ignorantly, you let it all get way out of hand. Something has to be done.

Maybe you bought a yard full of giant sheared poodleballs, globe aucubas, camellias; or something seems wrong with the fruit trees, maples, and dogwoods (they were topped or stripped and now are suckering back like crazy!); or you made some mistakes yourself. You know better now and you're ready to do right by your yard.

This is your section of the book. If you haven't read Part 1: Pruning, do so now, so you don't get into trouble again, then come back to this.

Before you are allowed to begin major renovating you must read two case studies, to get your attitude adjusted. Then you can begin your chain saw work.

CASE STUDY #1: A LADY WHO KNOWS HOW TO TREAT A TREE

I got a call from a lady a few years ago who wanted help in her yard. I knew I wanted to work for her just from the way she talked about her Empress tree. She called it her "grand lady." She proudly referred to the month in spring when its giant purple (foxglove-like) blooms made such a spectacular show that she could hear the squeal of brakes as passing motorists stopped to take a longer look.

This lady, Ms. K., has caught the gardening bug, and she has a bad case. She gladly pays the price of owning a huge (65 foot) and uncommon tree. It's a big price. For one, the rest of her yard and house

are rather small and shrub bed space is at a premium. It's difficult to grow things under a tree that takes up half her front yard. She must add lots of fertilizer and seek out tough plants that can survive the shade and root competition. She must water extra diligently in the summer since the thick canopy of leaves prevents rain from reaching the plants below. She's done a great job.

The Empress tree is a messy tree. Branches die back and fall off and have to be cleared out to keep the beds looking good. The "grand lady" is always dropping something that has to be cleaned up. Its giant round leaves fall by the tons in the fall. In the spring Ms. K. rakes dead blossoms, then husks of seed pods during the summer.

Our proud gardener knows that she is caretaker of a treasure and it's worth the trouble—she's got the biggest and best tree in the neighborhood.

She tells the story of the previous owners, who were finally so fed up with all the leaf raking that they hired someone to come cut the tree down. The chain saw was actually started when two alert neighbors ran up the street literally to exclaim, "Woodsman, spare that tree!" And they promised to rake all the leaves for free, to ensure the tree's survival. All things worth having and doing take time and care. There are no maintenance-free yards. An appreciation of beauty can make your yard chores less burdensome.

CASE STUDY #2: BIG MESS— SMALL MESS

I went on a consulting job last year to a young woman's home. She was beginning her second year there and didn't know where to begin. The garden had been planted by a plant lover (phytophile), but it had been let go for several years. Grass was coming up through most of the plants in the back. Some previous homeowner had sheared the camellias and escallonias. Many things were overgrown, running into each other, over sidewalks and steps. Some plants were looking leggy and sick because they were finally being shaded out by trees that had gotten big. Unfortunately she had hired Maul-and-Haul landscapers before she reached me, and they had managed to malprune several of the trees and shrubs.

It is unfortunate that one of the first responses to an overgrown yard is to go out and cut everything back, thus creating a smaller mess rather than a big mess. It also makes the final solution more difficult. It will often take years to sort out some types of badly pruned plants.

In this case the perpetrator had topped a young spruce. Not 100 feet away on a neighbor's property sat a previously topped conifer that now boasted an ugly double leader.

Also, sad to say in this yard, the same fellow had topped her little dogwood. In this crowded area a skimmia was reaching up into the dogwood tree, and her dogwood was a little out of sorts as well. What should have been done was to redefine the areas between plants, pruning to lower the skimmia (selectively pruning, of course) and visually raising the dogwood by removing some of the limbs hanging too far down into the skimmia. The dogwood needed to be selectively pruned and thinned to make it look cleaner, clearer, and much more beautiful, in such a fashion that the casual observer could not see where it had been pruned.

Because of the topping, her dogwood suckered back in the next year—the Hydra effect—and looked really awful. It will take years of patient restorative work to get it back in shape. If it had been done properly just once, the amount of upkeep would have been minimal in successive years. Oh well, this is one of those stories repeated endlessly everywhere. Don't *you* make the "cut-it-all-back" mistake.

THROWING THE BABY OUT WITH THE BATHWATER

I get so nervous when I drive by beautiful old land-scapes that have been ignored for ten to twenty years. I know they're in for it, especially the big ones. There's a parking lot in the neighborhood I grew up in that I'm very worried about. It has lots of wonderful old plants, including one thing I can't identify (thus making it doubly rare and wonderful) with big pink fuzzy blooms in the late summer. (No, I don't think it's a tamarisk.)

Frequently, when homeowners' or business owners' landscapes get out of control, they just remove them totally. EGAD! You drive by one day and thirty years of Mother Nature's work is gone to the dump in one day with a backhoe! Maybe an old pine or something is left to hold down the fort. It's sort of like a person who didn't do his or her housework for fifteen years, then just guts the house and rebuilds the inside. Well, that's one way to do it.

Frequently, some truly thoughtful and beautiful landscapes that have looked good through years of neglect get replaced with amazingly dull "low maintenance" landscapes. These are called "juniper-and-bark" places. They are just a cut above a parking lot, esthetically speaking. If you are thinking about tearing out your landscape and replacing it with all new plants, don't. First go to a nursery and start pricing new shrubs, noting the lack of anything of a full-grown size. They're all babies! (Could it be that that's why it's called the "nursery"?) If you replace your landscape with new plants it will cost a fortune, and if you find some full-grown plants they will be astronomically priced and twice as likely to die the first year. When you get your new babies home you will be tempted to plant them too close together so that the yard looks good now. That is sort of like building a playhouse the right size for your two year old and expecting him to live in it forever.

Plants must grow and get bigger (most of them, anyway). You cannot successfully stop their doing it. Some people ask for "fast-growing" plants in an effort to get a good landscape sooner. The bad news is that fast-growers don't stop once they get to where you want them. So now you've paid a fortune to take out a landscape that had probably maxed-out in size, and you've replaced it with a new, expensive one that is designed to be a mess in half the time. So what is the alternative?

A typical overgrown corner of the yard.

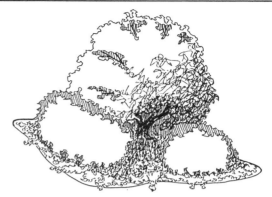

Knowing the mature size and pruning limits of your plant will guide you in making decisions. The young conifer is removed because its size is not controllable (wrong plant, wrong place). The small tree will not get much larger, but the tree-like shrub crowding it from below will be difficult to keep down, so it is transplanted to another location.

The groundcovers are cut out of the shrubs. The mound-type shrubs are pruned and lowered. They will be relatively easy to keep at a given height. The small tree is thinned and pruned to give it more definition. A few of its lower limbs are removed to keep space between it and the shrubs below.

To complete the picture, we enlarge the bed and add lower story plants. Minimal pruning will keep this bed looking good for many years to come.

SORT OUT, RENOVATE, REHABILITATE, EXTERMINATE

You can think of the renovation process as the "this old house" of landscapes. In renovating a house you learn how to replace the knob-and-tube electrical wiring and what to do to refurbish the leaded glass windows and hardwood floors. In our yard renovation, we kill the laurel, keep the dogwood, move the rhody, and renovate the forsythia.

SUMMARY

Common errors are:

❏ Cut it all back and make it smaller.

❏ Remove it all and plant a new yard. The first doesn't work and the second is too expensive or takes too long to look good.

❏ Pruning is one tool to use in renovating the overgrown yard.

❏ There are no maintenance-free yards. Your goal should be to eliminate unnecessary work while maximizing natural beauty.

Sorting Out

A good starving gardener could renovate your yard in the opposite order to the one I'm about to give you, but his or her eyes have been trained for years to see what's wrong. The order you get here is the one that will give you the best chance of not removing any great plants and will give you the best possible yard.

The first thing you want to do is get the garden uncluttered of weeds. Weeds dull your judgment and make perfectly good plants look awful. Cleaning out an overgrown shrub bed full of turf can be backbreaking work. Let it be a lesson to you never, never to let it get this far out of control again. While you're at it, prune out the dead wood and rake out the dead leaves. Start forming judgments about individual plants, and start seeing where plants are running into each other. Your choice with each plant will be to get rid of it, move it, or prune it. If you run across any plants that have never been mistreated, prune them according to Part 1.

THE GARDENER AS REFEREE

When I go into an overgrown garden I don't see plants that are too big. I see plants that are too thick or too crowded. The concept of "too big" is meaningless by itself. A sweater cannot be too big in and of itself. It must be too big for, say, "my body." The same sweater may be too small for yours. Since you can't simply make all your plants younger and smaller again, you will need to use different solutions for the different "too crowded" situations you find.

When you are pruning your garden, you are rarely working on just one tree or shrub; you are more commonly working on two or three, trying to get them to fit together nicely again. But first you need to identify your problem areas. Walk around the yard and look at the interfaces between what I call the "top," "middle," and "lower" stories of your garden. Also look at the areas where plants meet structures like houses and walkways.

By "top," "middle," and "lower" stories of your garden I mean the trees, the shrubs, and the groundcovers. When these layers become too enmeshed with one another, homeowners start to complain that their plants are too big.

Alone, it's too big.

The concept of "too big" is meaningless in itself. The two biggest shrubs in this illustration are the same size, but only one seems "too big."

Spend most of your pruning effort on redefining interface areas. Get the weeds and groundcovers out of the shrubs. Get the shrubs out of the trees. Redefining the areas between the three stories is a lot like creating shadows, by making more space between plants.

Sometimes this space is a foot; sometimes sufficient definition is created by getting plants a little more out of each other, though not necessarily without touching at all. Suddenly you can tell that a deciduous azalea is nestled inside two large rhododendrons.

Work at areas where plants and hardscape interface. If a limb is headed into the pathway, cut just that limb off. You needn't reduce the entire side of the plant. You don't need to keep trees lower than the roof either. Instead of trying to make your tree shorter, increase the space between the roofline and the trees lowest limbs. It isn't essential to keep shrubs totally off your house walls, but spend the time to keep it looking less crowded there. And, if you can, make the plants round down to the wall. No branches should touch windows.

YOU'VE IDENTIFIED PROBLEMS, NOW ATTACK THEM

Now that you have identified the major problem areas, you know the goal of your pruning and renovation choices. Go out there and start clipping and yanking the groundcovers out of the shrubs and ferns (remove whole patches if need be). Your taste may be compulsive; in which case, you want all the groundcover trimmed straight with the edge of the shrub beds or walkway, and ivy sheared tidily around the bases of trees. Or, your taste may run to the wild, like mine, where I let my ivy run up the trunk for a year because I like the way it looks, and then I rip it back.

You can also selectively prune ivy, kinnikinnick, and many other groundcovers along the walkway so that they look natural. You do this by reaching under the top layer, perhaps lifting it up like a rug, and cutting the longest strands way back. Then let the shorter top strands fall back down so that it looks as if it just hasn't grown clear out to the edge yet. It makes a softer, more natural-looking border. If your hypericum (St.-John's-wort) is long and leggy, over-

coming your small shrubs, fear not—you can, and should, cut (with hedge shears) or mow it back in the early spring to 2 inches. Really! It looks like a mess for a month, but it comes back low, even, and tidy looking. It likes to be pruned back hard, like a lawn.

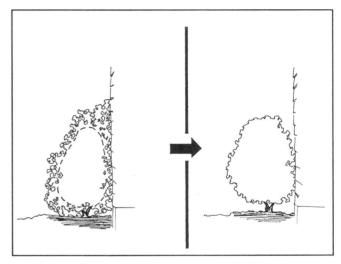

Round down shrubs to the house and to where they meet each other. It is often useful to prune up slightly the limbs touching the ground. This will make plants seem well-adjusted to their sites and not overgrown.

Cut the strands of ivy or other groundcovers that crisscross in the crown or base of your shrubs. Pull the cut strands back and either tug them out or, if they are rooted, shove them away from the base and push them flat to the ground. Otherwise ivy or other vigorous groundcovers will slowly submerge your shrubs and cause you great esthetic discomfort.

Don't let ferns and other plants grow up in the base of your low shrubs. The same fern 6 inches to 2 feet away is great, but inside a low, compact shrub, it's a weed. Under a tree or tall, leggy shrub, it provides good visual contrast, not competition.

CROWDED SHRUBS

Now that we have the groundcovers out of the shrubs, let's look at the shrubs themselves. Are they too crowded?

It's good, even desirable, to have your shrubs run into each other a little, especially similar shrubs

Too much   Too little   Just right

Often plants are too crowded, not too big. Getting some space around them, but not too much, will help the yard look tame again.

such as three rhodies of the same type. We don't want to make the mistake of having a tombstone yard or a row of soldiers where no two shrubs touch each other. But sometimes they are too, too crowded and tangled, and if you reduce both a little, they'll look much better. Locate the most interfering, longest reaching limbs on each of the two crowding shrubs. Thin those off and see if just that does the trick.

However, sometimes you may have to pick one shrub to stay and simply move or get rid of the other. As noted before, a good thing to do while you are taking out dead wood is to take off branches that actually touch the dirt, sometimes back to a side branch hanging a quarter inch above the dirt. This small definition will improve the looks of your yard more than you might imagine.

PRUNING LOWER TREE LIMBS

Now you want to redefine the area between shrubs and the next level up, either taller shrubs or the trees. You will have to make some value judgments, so stand back and imagine. Gradually you train your eye. It may be appropriate to take a few limbs off the lower part of a tree, if a tree is crowding some shrubs. There is some magic that gardeners do. It's actually common sense but easy to forget. If a big old limb is hanging down into your shrubs, first try selectively pruning only a portion of it. Take off a few lower side branches or (less desirably) cut back the end (selectively, of course). The branch, with less weight to drag it down, may now rise above the shrubs. If this doesn't work, you may have to take the branch off entirely, cutting back to the branch collar at the trunk. This removal of lower branches is called "limbing up" a tree. Trees naturally shed

their lower limbs in the forest and are well adapted to having them pruned off.

The other alternative is to lower your shrubs, depending on their type. Mound types (those with small leaves and supple limbs) are easiest to reduce. Others, like stiff-branched tree-likes, are not. But remember you don't have to have a 3-foot space between trees and shrubs. Start by taking things down (or limbing up) a little and see if it looks better. If you have a large shrub planted under a small tree (say a camellia under a plum tree), you should remove the shrub and plant a smaller one or a groundcover.

LEANING AND CROWDED SHRUBS

Another common problem occurs when the top, middle, and lower layers in your yard are all leaning and pushing each other over. Competent pruning will make them stand straight again.

You can accomplish this by cutting the lower limbs off the tallest plants, and you can head back the branches, starting with the worst oppressor. More effective, however, is picking out the one, two, or three longest and/or most leaning branches in each plant and cutting them out completely. Here again, this technique does not make sense to the logical mind, so you must just follow the recipe and cut out these most leaning branches, then you'll see the difference. You stand back and suddenly, while it doesn't even look as if you touched the plants, they stand upright again. Don't expect to make everything perfect this year, though. The increased sunlight will help the plant to round out over the next year. Just make it better for now.

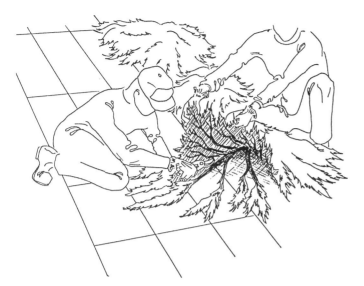

Reduce the width of junipers and other plants by removing only the lowest, broadest branches. Let the top fall back down. This is a useful way to control heathers and groundcovers too.

After pruning, the junipers look natural and you can walk by on the sidewalk easily.

JUNIPER REDUCTION

Another bit of advice. What about those junipers or evergreen azaleas hanging over your walkway? You may wish to prune selectively by taking branches back to inside the shrub, using the grab-'n-snip method. But you may achieve your goal more effectively by reaching under the base and cutting some of the lowest branches off back to the main trunk. I don't really understand it myself, because it won't look any smaller to you, except that now you will be able to walk by it.

STRIPPING

Stripping is a term I use to describe taking off all the inside branches or all the lower branches of a tree or shrub. It is one of the three major forms of bad pruning. Whereas tree topping and shrub shearing are the result of non-selective, wholesale heading cuts, stripping results from the misuse of the thinning cut. For example, some people often strip out their ornamental cherry trees. I assume that they are trying to imitate the gaunt, artistic look of some fruit trees. Perhaps they were inspired by Japanese-style pruning, which highlights the beauty of branch structures. A great deal of bad pruning is an unsuccessful attempt to imitate highly specialized forms

of pruning art. What our would-be artistic cherry-tree pruners fail to realize is that the next spring their trees will respond by exploding into a forest of ugly suckers which will bloom little, if at all, thus defeating the major purpose of this ornamental tree. Re-removal of all of the suckers every year is a maintenance nightmare and will eventually kill the tree.

ARBORIZING SHRUBS

Other people strip up all the lower limbs of shrubs they consider too big, making them somewhat reminiscent of lollipops or ostriches. I hesitate to mention stripping because of these common abuses. However, there are some instances when removing the lower limbs of a shrub is a good option. It will depend on the type of plant and its location. Don't strip up plants just because they seem too big. Good candidates are ones that are actually impeding foot traffic or totally obscuring windows. The best subjects are non-suckering tree-like shrubs. Usually they are broad-leafed evergreens, such as rhododendron, pieris, camellia, or strawberry tree (*Arbutus unedo*). Stripping up works best on very old shrubs. By cutting off the lower branches you are "arborizing" them. "Arbor" means tree, and you are turning your big shrub into a small tree. English laurel

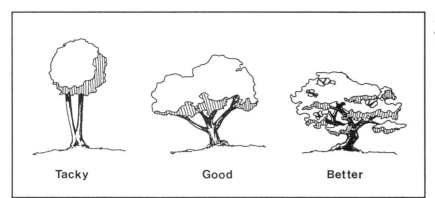

Tacky   Good   Better

Some shrubs can be arborized, meaning that they can be pruned into small trees.

is also a good subject. Instead of a giant oppressive blob, you can have an open, sort of Oriental-looking small tree. In fact, one could say that most of these plants are trees in their native habitats. They start out as shrubs and grow into understory trees in their adulthood. We just expect them to stay in the shrub-like juvenile stage forever.

Pause before you strip, though. It's a major step. Look inside your shrub and evaluate how the trunk will look when it's exposed. Is it fat? Good! Does it lean and curve gracefully? Great! If possible, endeavor to leave some branches lower down and inside to avoid the stripped or gutted appearance. To alleviate the lollipop effect, thin out the upper canopy of leaves, too. It should look a bit lacy and like a tree, not like a solid ball. Don't arborize more than a few plants in your landscape; it begins to look silly if you do too many.

Be sure to leave enough leaves to collect sunshine in order to feed the plant. Shrubs and trees vary from species to species in the degree to which they will let you put them on a diet. Trees and shrubs that have been starved by over-thinning usually succumb to death in a drought or freeze. Be sure to help heavily thinned, non-suckering plants by supplying sufficient water and fertilizer.

LAYERING CONIFER TREES AND CAMELLIAS

Some trees, such as needled evergreens, lend themselves to fairly dramatic thinning. This is called *layering* or *windowing*. Deodar cedar, Atlas cedar, and pines are examples. Pines particularly can withstand heavy thinning. Take care to avoid stripping each

limb out to a puff of green on the end. Instead, remove entire limbs alternately up the trunk. Then follow each scaffold branch and cut off the laterals (side branches) that hang too far down and those that go too far up.

Follow the same system for thinning out an oppressive camellia ball. You can either turn it into a small tree or thin it entirely top to bottom so that it looks like a veil of leaves. Through the shell you can see glimpses of the fine, clean branches inside. Here again, remove dead wood and prune from the inside out and the bottom up.

REHABILITATING SHRUBS AND TREES—SO YOU MADE SOME MISTAKES

What if your plants have all been stripped and sheared before? What can you do to restore them to their former beauty? Well, first of all, you can start by letting them grow out. Plants naturally go back to their own habit if left alone. You can help, though.

To Restore Sheared Shrubs: On your sheared cane-growers you already know what to do. Fight your way in there and saw out one-third of the canes at the base. Do this for three years in a row and you will have a nice, natural-looking shrub. You can and should always thin the tangled tops, too, by cutting some of them back to simpler side branches.

On your sheared tree-likes you will find a situation somewhat like the one shown here. Each cut branch has forked, causing a twiggy outer shell.

You can start to reestablish a more natural look by taking out the middle fork, or sometimes by cutting the whole forked end back to a simpler side branch.

Sheared plants develop a twiggy outer shell. This makes size control difficult in the long run and is hard on the plant's health.

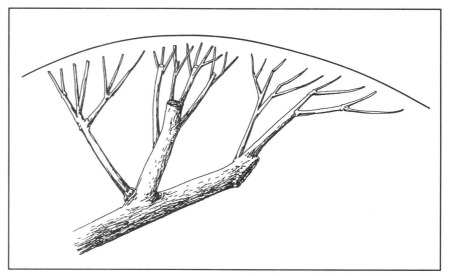

To restore natural shape to sheared plants, cut out middle forks.

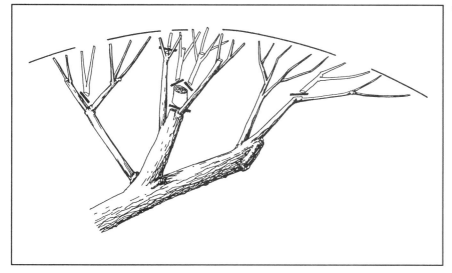

You can ease up a thick sheared shrub by cutting out some of the worst tangled branches back to simpler side branches.

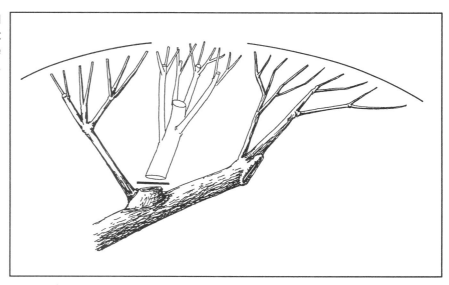

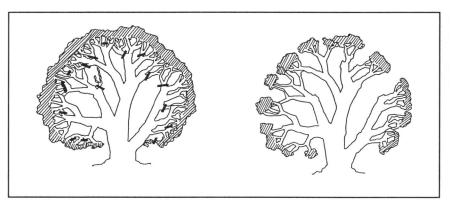

Once light reaches the interior, you may get new growth down inside. This will give you something to cut back to if you need to reduce the size of your shrub.

If your tree-like is a solid ball, you need to open it up and thin it somewhat, so that light can get to those inside branches, and dormant buds can begin to grow out and make inside branches.

If your tree-like is a small solid ball, like some sheared Zabel laurels I know, reach your gloved hand in and start shaking and tugging, pulling them apart, looking for the biggest, worst-tangled forked branches, then cut them out, back to side branches or parent stems. Right away these balls will ease up and look better. You can almost breathe easier yourself. Come back next year and do some more. It will take several years to restore them to their natural shape. Spend a majority of time thinning at the base of sheared balls and boxes.

As for your sheared mounds, let them grow out a while. Also, rummage around in the twiggy outer shell and look for the worst snarls or "birds' nests." Cut some out back to a branch or bud deep down farther inside. Also, if you are enthusiastic, crawl inside the base, and if it's semi-cane-like, cut out some of the worst canes to the base—and voila—what a difference! They're really fun to tug out! Some, like barberries, are especially challenging. Be sure to wear gloves and long sleeves.

MALPRUNED TREES AND TREE-LIKES

The question of what to do with tree-likes that have been stripped and topped is a harder and sadder one. Wherever certain types of trees have been stripped and topped, they will send back a host of suckers. Sometimes, like a car that's been in a car crash, the plant can be considered a total loss. This is then a case for removal. Others can be patiently restored. If the heading cuts were made on thick branches and the sucker regrowth is excessive and floppy, not stiff, you are in trouble. In less severe cases, you will choose some of these suckers to become the new branches.

You can restore your plant only over years—sometimes as long as ten years. If you try to remove all the unwanted suckers at once, they will simply regrow. The suckers will eventually branch out and begin to curve again, but not until the plant reaches close to its previous height. This is bad news, I realize, for people who find themselves staring at the monsters of their own creation. But you must be patient. Let the suckers grow for awhile to see which ones become the fatter, stiffer branches. After, say, three years, start taking off only a few of the skinniest, ugliest, wrong-way, crossing suckers every year, and let the others grow and get bigger. Leave several unwanted suckers in each cluster for this year; thin out some more next year. Slowly narrow down the number of suckers, to the last one that is your new branch.

Remember, summer is the best time to prune old suckers. In the spring you can just rub out brand new ones. On all previously badly pruned shrubs and trees you will find a lot of dead wood, especially dead stubs. Meticulously remove all dead wood. It will help the most in making your tree or shrub look better now.

MALPRUNED RHODODENDRONS

The very hardest plants I have to deal with are previously badly pruned rhododendrons. Often I go to a house where someone has chain-sawed off a very old rhododendron to about 5 feet. These plants sometimes reestablish quite well and look all right from the outside. Most, however, look scraggly. By the time I get there they are about the same size as before they were cut, but now, when I step inside to check things out, I find masses of skinny branches rambling and dipping down and heading all over the place. Spaghetti! It's enough to turn your hair white. There's nothing worth keeping, it seems. It is possible to help these plants look better, but it is hardly ever good. This is where the "look for the worst first rule" comes in very handy. Be sure to keep the fattest branches and any that head mainly up and out, no matter how awful. Cut off a few of the worst, skinniest branches that go long distances, whipping around other branches. These are the never-will-amount-to-anything branches. Also, you

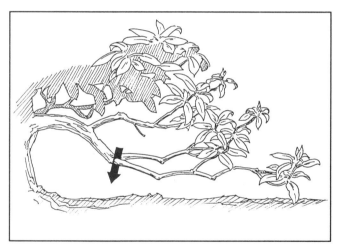

Previously malpruned rhododendrons will have daunting unruly regrowth. Cut off some of the lowest in each series of "goosenecks" to improve the looks of your shrub. Leave anything that is headed up and out.

will find what I refer to as "multiple goosenecks." With branches like these, try cutting off the lowest gooseneck. You will probably still be discouraged and dissatisfied until you step back outside. See, it looks better; not good, but better. An angry plantsman's curse on the first person who said, "You can keep on top of it." What damage he has done!

SUMMARY

☐ Get the groundcovers out of the shrubs and the shrubs out of the trees.

☐ Renovation choices for each shrub are: prune it, move it, get rid of it.

☐ Deciding how much and whether or not to thin will depend on three criteria:

1. Does it sucker easily?

2. Will it starve?

3. Will it look good (i.e., fat trunk)?

☐ I visited a house where the gentleman had grossly over-thinned his camellia. He had been told to prune it so that "a bird could fly through it." His wife commented, "They meant a sparrow, not a goose!" Take care that thinning doesn't turn into stripping, even on plants that don't sucker back.

☐ The four steps to rehabilitating previously badly pruned plants are (1) wait, (2) thin, (3) wait, and (4) thin.

☐ Remove suckers gradually over years, narrowing the number down to the one or two you want to become new branches. Do it in the summer.

Adding the Lower Story

When people plant their yards they tend to do it like putting in furniture—up against the wall, in rows along the edges. They also put things too close together but, unlike your footstool, a shrub doubles or triples its volume. After the homeowner puts in the shrub, he digs a bed around it to fit, and that's it. Even though the shrub gets bigger, the bed stays the same size. Sometimes, grass being the way it is, the bed even gets smaller. This creates the optical illusion that your shrub is too big, when actually the *shrub bed is too small*. Cutting a shrub back to fit the bed is sort of like cutting your houseplant back to fit the pot. In your yard it might be time to repot!

At the yard of one of my favorite clients, a grouping of evergreen azaleas finally became so big that they were crowding each other, and those next to the edge of the lawn were being held back by the edger going by, chop, chop, chop! It looked like water

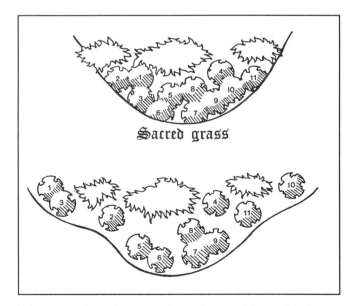

Sacred grass

When pruning alone won't work, consider enlarging the shrub beds and rearranging the shrubs. This is often the longer-lasting and better solution.

building up behind a dam. The beds simply needed to be made bigger and the azaleas rearranged so that they looked comfortable again. The amount of work was minimal compared to hacking back the azaleas every year. People don't realize how very easy it is to dig up plants and move them around. They also are wary of the idea of removing lawn. Yet, the amount of lawn removed is often negligible. Most people can't even tell when the lawn edge has been cut back by a foot or three.

SACRED GRASS: DON'T LET IT RUIN YOUR YARD

Some people are afraid that more shrub bed space will mean more weeding. This is not the case, and the effect of the larger beds on the overall beauty of a yard is quite significant. They also dread digging up turf. Do it anyway! And bury it in a compost hole in the corner of your yard. Or turn it over, and cover it with water and black plastic. Next year it will be great compost!

You should also surround your trees with dirt and mulch, not lawn. This area is called a *tree well* or tree pit. The absence of turf will make the trees grow faster. If you mulch, you won't need to weed much. Besides, tree wells are great places for bulbs, groundcovers and perennials, ferns and whatnot. Tree wells not only increase the growth rate of your tree, they greatly improve its chances of survival during drought. And you won't be tempted to girdle or injure your tree with the weed trimmer, causing troublesome suckers. Large tree wells make your tree look comfortable and help to keep it from appearing too big.

So make your beds bigger—much bigger, as big as you dare, certainly out beyond the dripline of your trees and shrub canopy. And move some plants

Use mulch to keep the area around your tree free of grass and weeds. The "tree well" should extend to the dripline.

Rhododendrons are easiest to move because their rootballs are flat, like pancakes. Dig a trench one shovel's blade deep, or deeper, around the dripline. Then dig and slice, using the back of the shovel, to make the rootball. Cutting large roots is okay.

Once the shrub is free, tilt it to one side and shove a bunched-up tarp underneath it. Tilt it the other way and pull the tarp through to the other side. Lift the plant out of the hole and drag it over to its new home.

Your shrubs may not be too crowded or too big. The problem may simply be that they are ALL big.

around until it all looks good. Good gardeners are always digging things up and moving them around. Small plants are easy to move, but even big trees are movable. Americans used to move trees bigger than we do now, with horses and wagons. The limiting factor is power lines. No tree on its side can be taller than those wires. We're talking BIG. Get over the idea that anything in your yard is or should be of a permanent size or location. Gardens are kinetic art, just very slow moving. Your job is to manage them in motion.

Some plants are easy to transplant and some aren't. Tree-likes are easiest and look good right away. Cane-growers, especially ones with mat-like roots, are harder. It's difficult to get a real root ball, and things tend to fall apart. Mexican orange, for example, can just be cut back drastically and maintained at a lower level rather than being moved. Rhododendrons are easiest because their root balls are like pancakes. I've moved rhodies 6 feet tall with help from friends. It's a fun project.

HOW TO MOVE A RHODODENDRON

First, make sure your rhododendron is healthy. Then tie the limbs up to make digging easier. Next, dig a trench around the outside as if you were planning to make a root ball bigger than you could carry. When you are down past where the roots go, flip your shovel over and start chipping the roots and dirt back with the back side of your shovel and digging dirt out from under the roots using the back of the shovel. This protects the roots and makes a clean, tight root ball. Towards the end, you flip the shovel back right side up and stomp on it under the root ball in an attempt to slice the final roots. Keep an already-dull pair of loppers to cut any big anchoring roots as you run into them. These are not the roots

you need to handle with care. They just hold the plant down and store energy. It's all the tiny, tiny rootlets that absorb nutrients and water that need special treatment. This means you 1) do not break up the root ball, 2) do preserve as many rootlets as possible, 3) do keep them in dirt, 4) do keep them moist/wet, and 5) do not let them dry out in the open air. Each minute counts.

If the plant is big, have your buddy tilt it by pulling or pushing it over while you dig and slice. NEVER, NEVER yank the shrub out or pry up on it with your shovel. Just keep working on it, digging and slicing, until you feel it get loose. You will know when that is. Now rock the plant back and slide a big tarp under it as fast as you can, then rock it the other way. Have your buddy pull the edge of the tarp on through and under the plant. Use the tarp to tug it out of its hole. Sometimes you can give it a gentler ride out of the hole using a board as a runway. If your shrub is big, you and your friends can slide it out, pull it on the tarp, and drag your plant over to its new home. If your shrub is truly huge, you can rig something up with a chain and truck, tying the rope to the tarp, which is used sort of like a diaper around the root ball. DO NOT tie the rope to the trunk. Trees and shrubs with great gashed trunks will usually die from the injury later, probably next spring or in the late summer. If your shrub is 3 or 4 feet tall or less, you won't need to go through this trouble. You can just do it by yourself. Use your shovel handle to measure how broad and deep a hole to dig. Dig it, slide the shrub into the hole, and bury it. Then, WATER, WATER, WATER! Today, tomorrow, and next week.

It is always best to transplant broadleaf evergreens when it is cool or warm and wet, not hot and dry or cold and frozen. That means spring or fall. Summer

The solution is to add lower story plants for contrast. You may choose to eliminate a few larger shrubs and replace with a new lower story.

Another solution is to thin out tree-likes and under-plant with woodland plants.

You can also enlarge beds and add a foreground of low shrubs and perennials.

is stressful for plants even if you water them. They need a lot more water than in milder temperatures. Very cold weather also dries them. It is possible to transplant things off-season, but it is considerably more stressful for them. Deciduous plants and needled evergreens transplant well in early winter when they are dormant, but do not wait until the weather is below freezing.

LAND OF GIANTS

Sometimes you have a yard where all the plants are giants, but they're not crowding each other. They're all sort of huge. Instead of cutting them back or moving them or killing them, you may just need to *complement* or *contrast* them with some smaller shrubs or plant understory.

If you have a row of giants, you may need to remove one to break up the giant wall effect, as well as generally thinning to give them definition.

A pleasing yard has a top, a middle, and a lower story, as you will recall. That is, trees, shrubs, and small things (ferns, flowers, groundcovers). Having a yard full of all mature shrubs is imposing; having one with nothing but small things looks vulnerable. A wildflower meadow alone will not protect you from the big bad street. A nice garden is balanced with all three stories. Sometimes, for a woodland effect, skip the middle story and put wonderful woodland plants inside and under your giants; try ferns, bleeding heart, trillium, hellebore, and hardy cyclamen. Under your deciduous flowering shrubs put spring bulbs that bloom at the same time as the shrubs, such as daffodils with your forsythia. Add a ring of lower plants around your giant mounds, maybe something with a contrasting color or texture or, conversely, add something tall and skinny. Add contrast to your mature shrubs and your garden will seem parklike and tame again.

Yes, I'm afraid this chapter is a plot to get you to buy more plants. Really, really nice gardens have four or five stories, starting with a few enormous trees and working down. Under every plant is a smaller treasure or bulb, and vines clamber up walls and through trees. You can find rare ferns and flowers growing from chinks in walls, and you can even find tiny flowers throughout the lawn. If you are a lawn worshiper, as opposed to a flower worshiper, as is my next-door neighbor, you may wish to forgo the lawn flowers. I thought she would have a heart attack when I proudly pointed to the English lawn daisy I had just planted. She works so hard to eliminate them from her yard.

SUMMARY

Alternatives to cutting back shrubs are:

- ❏ Make beds bigger
- ❏ Rearrange plants
- ❏ Eliminate some plants
- ❏ Make beds bigger and add more lower shrubs
- ❏ Thin out mature shrubs and add woodland understory and other smaller plants down in and amongst them.

Speaking and Understanding Gardenese

When you go out to fix a backyard that has become a jungle, you will be passing judgment on each of your plants. You must weigh many factors on whether to prune a particular plant, move it, get rid of it, or leave it alone and nurse it back to good health. This section is devoted to helping you decide what to keep and what to kill. A shortcut in this process is to hire a starving gardener and pick his or her brain. But be aware that there are a lot of plant snobs out there who have slanted judgments. This chapter may teach you how to hold your own. Perhaps it will even start you on the road to becoming a plant snob yourself.

When you look at the plants in your yard, you can start to assign them points according to the following system. This section on how to speak gardenese should be used when deciding what to add to your yard as well.

"MATURE AND IN THE RIGHT PLACE"

You can give a plant lots of points for just being the right size and in the right place. When you design your yard, you site plants by the size and shape of the plant more than by the specific kind. For example, I want a low, fat plant under my window so it doesn't block it, or I want something tall and evergreen to hide the neighbor's garage, with something in front of it that changes color or has nice blooms. This is what is meant by giving a plant points for being in the right place. Also, if you have a difficult area, say, hot, dry, clay, or sand, and something is actually surviving and doing well there, give it points. It's what most of your plants have going for them. It takes time and money to get a new plant just the way you want it. So, if you have a 5-foot rhododendron in just the right place, or a full-grown tree of any type that isn't in the *wrong* place (under wires, for example), give it some points.

ANCIENT PLANTS

Plants, just like people, get lots of points for making it from maturity into great old age, even if they were nothing special the rest of their lives. If somebody on your block has stopped and said, "WOW! that's a really old whatever," consider keeping it even if it's not a *choice* plant.

"CHOICE"

Choice is gardenese for "good." It includes many top-of-the-line plants. However, before you buy or keep a choice plant, you may wish to find out if it is choice and easy or fussy; choice and well-behaved, vigorous, or messy; or choice and perfectly hardy, tender, rare, or common.

Some bamboos are very choice, but are considered too vigorous. A snowdrop tree (*Styrax j.*) is choice, easy and not too big. Hardy cyclamen is choice and easy, but not too vigorous.

THE HEARTWARMING GINKGO STORY

The ginkgo is a choice tree that people don't plant much. Here is an excerpt from a local planting project tree list: "Ginkgo or Maidenhair Tree (*Ginkgo biloba*), grafted males only, ht. 35-50'." This is one of my favorites because it is trouble free, has nice fall color, and comes with a lot of history. (I love a good story.) Not to be planted under power lines, this tree gets big, eventually! Its slow growth habit and its very dainty, uniquely fan-shaped leaves keep it from ever becoming oppressive. It's tough and, unlike many other plants, is not prone to any diseases or pests. The ginkgo's main attraction is its fall color, which is an amazing, flawless soft yellow. Even though I don't like yellow, I really love this tree. An added attraction is that it drops its yellow

Ginkgo leaves look like tiny Oriental fans.

leaves in a week, not slowly over months, something to consider when you do your own leaf raking.

Now for the history and the story. Ginkgos are from an extremely ancient order of plant, a living link with the prehistoric tree-fern age. Technically speaking, they are conifers, that is, cone-bearing plants like pine trees, not flowering plants. They used to flourish all over the world. Petrified ginkgos can be found in eastern Washington. The story is that ginkgos disappeared from the wild and were kept alive only in Chinese monasteries. This notion caused plant explorers to go traipsing around the Chinese countrysides, and led plant historians of the past century to pore over old travel logs looking for "wild" ginkgos and arguing about whether they were really wild or just escaped cultivated ginkgos. I rather like the idea of ginkgos being perpetuated through history by Chinese monks and ending up on the parking strips of Mytown, USA.

The only drawback to ginkgos is that, in their early years, they may look a little gawky. Early years means before age thirty. But if you plant this tree, not only will you get connected to the distant future, but your ginkgo will reach maximum beauty at full maturity in 2,000 years. Wow!

The only reason you don't see more ginkgos and other good, choice plants is that people don't ask for them in the nurseries, so nurseries don't sell enough of them to grow them, so nobody buys them, and you never see them, so you don't ask for

them, and obviously, it's a vicious circle! Demand and availability! Your chain store usually only stocks those plants that are frequently requested, but your local independent nursery has some plant nuts in there who are trying to sell you some rare and wonderful things, but you have to look around to find them. Designer-architects are reluctant to recommend plants that are hard to find or that may be rare because they're difficult. But really good designer-architects will give you two or three choices for each circle on their landscape blueprint, including some rare and wonderful plants that aren't likely to die.

"UNUSUAL"

Some plants are choice because they do or are something *unusual*. Blooming at an odd time is unusual. Plants that bloom any time other than spring get extra points. I am very fond of winter bloomers and especially of scented winter bloomers. There are others that just look unusual, like bright purple berries (beauty berry), and anything that's contorted (curvy limbs like corkscrew willow) or pendulous (weeping willow). I've heard a plant of this type referred to as a "weirdness." You shouldn't have more than a few of them, but one or two can add a lot of interest to a yard. If you have two weirdnesses that are right next to each other, I suggest you move or get rid of one because they compete for attention and detract from each other.

"RARE" VS. "COMMON"

Some plants achieve choice status just by being rare. That's why a diamond is worth a lot more than ocean-washed glass even though they can look a lot alike. The flip side of rare and wonderful is the "familiarity breeds contempt" syndrome. A lot of people consider wildflowers that spring up everywhere to be sort of devalued because they're so common. The British think they're grand and rare and often take some home, work on them (hybridize them), and sell them back to us as choice British garden plants.

There may be some very good reasons a plant is rare around your area. One is that it doesn't like it there. Some plants grew up in and are adapted to different soil types, temperatures, and amounts of sun, and when you put them into your yard they will be so rare as to die slowly and meanwhile look awful. These plants are rare and difficult or *take special culture*, which means that you have to put blankets on them in winter or plant them in straight sand or put on hats for the rain. Sometimes a plant is rare and tender. As a novice, avoid these.

"TENDER" VS. "HARDY"

A *somewhat tender* plant is a plant that's likely to freeze. A *hardy* plant won't. The world is divided into climate zones. Often the major determining factor in whether a plant will survive is the lowest temperature it can take. If you have a eucalyptus in your north country yard, it may be choice and rare simply because it hasn't frozen to death like others in the city. Your yard has many micro-climates, and an iffy, somewhat tender plant will survive in one spot, yet freeze only 30 feet away. Older, somewhat tender plants have a better chance of making it through a freeze than ones just getting stabilized, so you may wish to baby young new plants for a few years with mulch and windbreaks, and then see if they can tough it out. Some tender plants are good enough to plant and then just replace when they freeze (that is, treat them like annuals). The hebe ("Autumn Glory"), for example, is such a plant for relatively moderate climates. It doesn't get too big, looks tidy, blooms in the fall, and is easy, but it sometimes freezes. When it does, I just plant a new one.

"EASY" VS. "FUSSY"

These terms have a lot to do with whether to choose a new plant or whether to keep an old one. *Easy* is short for "easy-culture." That just means that you can take it home and it will do well with a modicum of care. There will be a wide range of situations it will take: it will be happy in sun or part shade; it doesn't need more or less water or fertilizer; it won't freeze; and you can transplant it. On the other hand, some plants are fussy—maybe you'll be lucky and they will like where you put them, and maybe they won't. Sometimes you never know why.

Daphne odora is fussy. This is a highly prized ever

green plant (tree-like and it likes lime) that has extremely sweet-smelling flowers in early, early spring. Mine is doing well, but some other people's never catch on. Alstromeria is another plant that can be both fussy and too easy, baffling its owners. This is a tall perennial flower that costs a fortune as a cut flower in the shops. In some people's yards it never takes hold, while in others it's a weed. It's taking over one of my beds and actually overcoming a rhododendron. Want some?

"WELL-BEHAVED, RELIABLE, VIGOROUS, MESSY, INVASIVE"

The most important term in this glossary is *vigorous*. Vigorous may mean that you won't have to wait fifteen years for it to look like anything if you're planting it from scratch. It won't die of disease, drought, or cold. You won't have to spend your life babying it. So it may be the ever popular low-maintenance plant. On the other hand, it could be a weed. It all depends on how you look at it.

When you ask your nursery person about a particular plant that you like and he or she says, "It's rather vigorous," a little red flag should go up. Your next question should be, "Could it be considered *invasive*?" I would suggest that you don't plant anything that's considered invasive until you know what you're doing. If you have invasive plants you may even wish to do battle to eliminate them. I have an "invasive" section in my yard, but I watch it very, very closely. I call it "the woodland section"—it's where lots of choice-vigorous things duke it out. I go in every once in awhile and referee. The section is low maintenance. It has foxglove, salal, wild bleeding heart, wild iris, huckleberry, trillium, forget-me-not, kinnikinnick, ferns, Welsh poppy, merry bell, and ginger, to name only a few of the carefree inhabitants. But it has eaten up a lot of choice and not so vigorous plants like wintergreen, hepatica, lady's slipper, and avalanche lilies.

BEWARE THE VINES

Most vines are vigorous, and you have to watch and prune them regularly or they will climb onto your tree and smother and kill it. The English like to run vines through their other garden plants, but it would make me pretty nervous. Vines are simply wonderful and worth it in many, many cases. There's nothing like them for hiding your neighbor's ugly chain link fence or filling in big empty walls or for growing up arbors or standards. Many of the great weeds are vines: wild clematis, ivy, and bindweed can and will kill forest trees. So watch their city cousins carefully. The only really well-behaved vine I know is *Hydrangea anomola 'petiolarus'*, a hydrangea vine. It is very understated and tasteful.

Give points to your plant if it is *well behaved*, which means that the plant will not creep or grow huge too fast or seed a bunch of unwanted babies in your yard. Well-behaved means it's not messy either. Messy plants usually drop things like acorns, dead twigs, too many big leaves, honeydew, seeds, pods, berries that stain, bark, you name it. If your messy tree leans over a cliff or is in a woodland bed that gets raked out once a year, it's no big deal. If your messy plant drops seeds that grow into zillions of little trees that you have to pull out with pliers in two years, you may have a behavior problem.

A classic example of a well-behaved, reliable, and not too vigorous easy shrub is the pieris or andromeda. I also think it's choice because it has three good shows in that it 1) is evergreen and tidy looking, 2) has sweet-smelling spring flowers, and 3) has new growth that is coppery colored.

"HARD-WORKING, TWO SHOWS OR MORE"

Because your yard space is so valuable, you want to give lots of points to plants that do more than one thing. Some combinations are good foliage and flower, fall color and spring flower, scented flower or scented foliage with something else. Then there are good winter branch patterns plus anything else, or good flowers and interesting fruit. Give your plants lots of extra points for these.

HEALTH

Before removing any old plant or tree in your yard, or adding a new one, consider its health. I have never been a health nut, but gardening may make me into one and that's because health is what makes

plants look good or bad three-fourths of the time. You probably don't realize it, just as I didn't.

Most people develop an unwarranted prejudice against certain plants because they are either too common and vigorous, or the ones they had before were sick and badly pruned. Before you slate a plant for death, especially if it's a rare and wonderful one, you may wish to be nice to it for awhile with good weeding, watering, pruning, and fertilizing, to see if your sow's ear will turn into a silk purse. I promise you that a little care and attention can work miracles. Conversely, some plants are simply prone to diseases and are always in a state of dropping dead bits. In some cases, you just learn to live with it (like mildew on your Oregon grape or azalea), or you fight back with vigilant use of chemicals and/or good maintenance (garden hygiene and pruning), or you cut the darn sick thing out and put in A GOOD PERFORMER!

Horticulturists today are taking a lot of our old garden favorites that have disease problems and breeding disease-resistant varieties. All or most of the fruiting and flowering cherries, plums, apples, peaches, crabapples, and roses get a lot of diseases, and if you don't want to spray like crazy and can't stand to see a certain amount of damage and dead wood, ask your nursery person for disease-resistant varieties. Good roses are being invented. Also dogwoods that are prone to anthracnose are being worked on to improve their resistance. So if you love that old cherry tree but it is looking bad, consider removing it and replanting with a well-behaved, reliable, disease-resistant variety. Give points to your plant if it's *healthy* and *disease-resistant*.

"WELL-FORMED"

A plant gets further points for being particularly *well-formed*. When I was doing my backyard I wanted to take out the mountain ash tree (*Sorbus aucuparia*). It had going for it: 1) already being there, 2) providing two shows, 3) being well-formed. Lots of mountain ashes are shaped badly, but mine is a perfect globe. Against it was the fact that: 1) it's common, almost a weed, 2) it's in the wrong place, taking up valuable headroom, 3) it produces troublesome little seedlings everywhere. My husband-to-be was aghast at my suggestion of removing it (I wanted a nice disease-prone "Autumnalis" cherry). In fact, the question was a pivotal point in our relationship. (If the divorce ever comes, I know where to take the chain saw.) I grumble at the seedlings every year. I've replaced six plants that couldn't get established underneath it because of root competition. But in November, it's breathtaking in its ruby-glowing and gold color. Sometimes I get up just to look at it out the window. Anyway, if your common thing happens to be healthy and nicely formed, consider keeping it. If your rare and wonderful thing is sick and badly formed, consider nursing it back to health and doing a little corrective pruning over the next few years.

NOSTALGIA

Many people have a fondness for the plants with which they grew up. Having seen their mom's great yellow forsythia in bloom one spring day, that shrub has meant spring to them ever since. Roses and lilacs are old favorites. Every year when it's spring I stuff my nose in a lilac bloom. The olfactory trigger sends me back into some vaguely remembered distant, simpler, finer days.

Plant snobs often eschew these old-time plants. They want to turn you on to some rare wonderfuls that they know, and their own tastes have evolved from nostalgia to certain specific styles. Some have gone the tasteful, understated species route; others, the new and improved hybrid route. Sometimes they know that the plant you love is not appropriate for your setting, for example, an old-fashioned forsythia in a redwood forest. For one thing, there's not enough sun and, well, they just don't go together well. But you don't ever have to remove something you love just because it's theoretically wrong. Remember, the *only purpose* of a garden is to give you (and maybe your neighbors and their kids) pleasure. So give your plant lots of points, too, just because you like it. If a gardener wrinkles his or her nose, say, "This came from a start that came over on the Mayflower," or "This is from seed I collected at Vita's garden." (Vita was a famous gardener.) Then your snobbish gardener just might say, "AHH! How rare and wonderful!"

SUMMARY

☐ Gardenese is not difficult to learn—much of it is common sense. When you have mastered the language, you will be able to find out a great deal about what to plant where and the kinds of care your plants need.

☐ Learn to speak gardenese and then use your local Extension Agents and nursery persons for advice.

Getting Rid of Unwanted Plants

This chapter is devoted to convincing you that it's all right to kill plants or otherwise dispose of them. On the other end of the spectrum from those chain saw-happy homeowners, who want their yards to look like a very tidy prairie (and allow nothing to stand between them and their view of anything) are the tender souls who can't bear to cut anything down. These are the people for whom this chapter is written. Do not suffer a weed to live! If thy plant offend thee, pluck it out!

THE DEFINITION OF A WEED IS ANYTHING IN THE WRONG PLACE!

Weeds can often be beautiful.

Weeds can often be huge, like trees.

Weeds can often be wildflowers.

Weeds can be wonderful plants that are simply in the wrong place.

When you stop to think about it, a garden is a series of god-like choices you have made. There is no intrinsic badness in a dandelion (which was once a cultivated flower that escaped and did too well) or in any of the weeds, except perhaps some poisonous ones. People just decided that some are more esthetically desirable than others. It's okay to kill plants. When you weed, you kill. In fact, when you eat, you kill. Vegetarians kill plants and eat them. When you read the newspaper, you kill (paper/trees). Life—the proverb goes—feeds on death (unless you are yourself a plant, and then you fuel up on sunshine). I feel that it is just our job to kill wisely and judiciously, with respect and with the big picture kept in mind.

As a species we have a pretty interesting (though not exclusive) sense of esthetic value. We cherish things because they're pretty and not just because they help us survive. And we have actually formed emotional attachments to other species (pets) and sometimes to plants. I have often thought of myself as the dispenser of life and death, as on one sweep of the yard I fertilize, while on another I apply herbicides. And when you and I are gone, weeded out ourselves, what we have chosen to do in the yard will revert to that private battle for a place in the sun that those plants carried on among themselves for millennia before we arrived on the scene, and (if the planet is lucky) will be carrying on for many more millennia.

HOW TO KILL EFFECTIVELY

If you cut down your needled evergreen (say a spruce or juniper), it will just die, no problem. But guess what happens if you cut down your cane-grower or your deciduous tree-like? It will grow back. Your cane-grower will be renovated. Your tree-like may or may not grow back ugly. If you foolishly cut down an aspen or a poplar, you will stimulate scores of new saplings to grow from the extensive root systems. A nightmare!

The best way to kill effectively is to dig out the stump and/or most of the roots. If it is impossible to do this, you must treat the stump. This means to paint chemical on it to kill it so that it doesn't return. On the label for the herbicide Roundup®, the large size (glyphosate is the active ingredient), you will find directions for stump cut treatments for trees and woody brush. With trees you paint it on to cover the entire cambium. "Apply 50 to 100 percent solution of product to freshly cut surface immediately after cutting. Delays in application may result in reduced performance." This means minutes. I use Roundup because it binds tightly to the soil and therefore is not available to kill nearby plants or move through the soil to the water table. Be careful

If you cut down a fir tree (and most other conifers), it will simply die. Most deciduous trees, however, will sucker back from the stump. Some trees, such as poplars, will respond by suckering up from their extensive root systems.

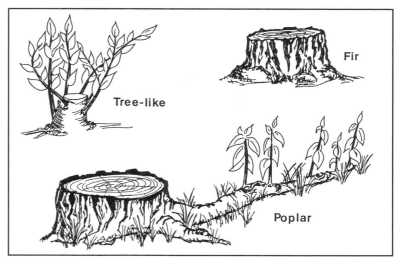

that the roots of the treated stump are not grafted (connected) to a same species tree next to it. Dissimilar species rarely graft to each other. (See more about herbicides in the section on maintaining your yard.)

Sometimes it is best when you saw or cut your plant to leave some room between the stump and the ground (2 inches to a foot), paint it with herbicide, and wait to see if it survives next spring. If it grows back, it will do so just under the cut. Let it grow all summer, putting all its energy back up above the ground, then just before fall when it's going to draw energy back down into the roots, cut it again below the first cut, including all the new suckers, and paint it again; let it suck the poison back down into the roots. After a year goes by with no activity, you may remove the ugly stump by cutting it to the ground. Or you can put a tasteful vine on it to cover it until it rots out. My clever neighbor put an open-ended whisky barrel over her stump, filled it with dirt, added some more barrels and flowers and put a shrub bed around them, too. It looks great!

If you really, really don't like any chemicals, there is hope. You can hire someone with a machine called a stump grinder to come and chew out the stump. Or you can rent one yourself. These are pretty amazing. Stump grinders just turn stumps into sawdust. You do need sufficient access to wheel it in, and you should dig down and get as much dirt away from your stump as you can before the stump grinder arrives. Then fill in the hole and plant some

thing you really want, something that—according to your definition—is not a weed.

A clever way to hide a stump. Use an open-ended whisky barrel and plant it with flowers.

SUMMARY

☐ Don't be afraid to eliminate unwanted or hopelessly unhealthy plants from your landscape. Even trees can be cut down and stumps removed.

☐ Some things can be killed by cutting them down, but others will simply regenerate. The stump or roots must be dug out or treated with chemicals to make sure they do not return.

Radical Renovation

What the guy down the block did to his rhododendron is criminal mutilation. What *I* did to mine is radical renovation. That's how I explained it to my wedding guest who stood aghast at a rhododendron stump that had been cut back to 4 inches from the ground.

In another case of radical renovation, the subject was a 5' x 16' x 8' sheared, ugly, never-blooming deciduous mock orange (*Philadelphus sp.*) hedge in a local park. I remember the look on the caretaker's face when Lisa, a consulting gardener, and I told him of our plans to cut it *all* back to the ground. These types of radical renovative pruning are perfectly all right if you know what you're doing. It is, however, a lot like surgery, and hence recommended only in otherwise hopeless cases.

Cane-types, as I have mentioned before, can generally be started over by cutting all the canes to the ground. It's often better to do it in stages over years if you can. New growth on cane-growers tends to be straighter, and there are greater spaces between flower buds. The more esthetically pleasing branches, the ones that arch, are older. On the other hand, very old branches may begin to show fewer flowers, on forsythias, for example. So you need to weigh the factors of height, number of flowers, and arching habit when deciding how much to prune. This is why removing one-third of the canes for three years is a good idea, if you intend to renew your shrub. In the case of the giant sheared hedge, it would have been unrealistic to do it this way. You couldn't fight your way in with loppers. So, if it is appropriate, get out the brush blade or chain saw and have at it. Be nice to your renewed shrub and give it lots of love, old manure, and water to help it hit the comeback trail.

You can usually radically renovate most mound-type shrubs by cutting out one-third of the growth each year, as with cane-growers, or by cutting them totally to the ground as well. On stiffer branched mounds, it is sometimes better to reduce everything to 2 or 3 feet below the height at which you want them eventually to wind up, and to do a lot of thinning down inside as well. Escallonia is a good example of such a plant. Once the plant regrows to the size you like, you may "grab and snip" to keep it there.

RENOVATING/RESTORING TREE-LIKES, NON-SUCKERING TYPES

I redesigned my own yard as a novice gardener and made nearly all the possible common errors. One of them was that I wanted full-grown plants to begin with, so I spent a lot of extra money on several very big (4 to 5 feet) rhododendrons instead of being cheap and patient. These shrubs were thin and leggy because they were grown too close together back at the nursery. Usually a leggy plant, when put in the sun, will fill out naturally. I was impatient, and I began working my own terrible experiments. As it turns out, even many tree-like shrubs can be radically renovated.

You will have the best success in renovating rhododendrons in the early spring. Some horticultural specialists say to start as early as February, when it's getting warm and dormant buds are fat. These are the tiny (pencil-tip size) buds, usually hidden on the branch or trunk, ready to grow if natural disaster breaks out the top. It's better to cut the tops back all at once on some broadleaf evergreen shrubs like rhododendrons—not in thirds as you do with cane-growers. If you cut back just one branch, the plant will choose to let this branch die totally, and meanwhile it puts its energy into the other fork. But if all the branches are equally cut back, they must all break bud.

To stimulate a bud to grow out and eventually become a branch, nick the bark just above the bud with a razor blade. Make your cut about the size and depth of a fingernail clipping.

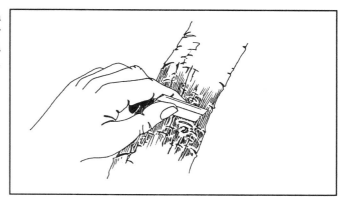

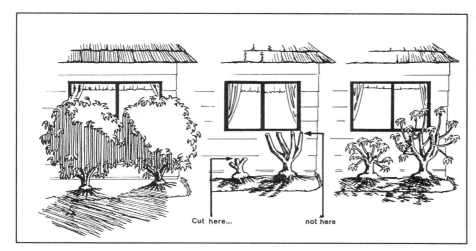

Cut here...   not here

The most common error when dramatically reducing plants is not cutting back far enough. Leave enough room for your shrub to grow back for several years, perhaps several feet. By then it will have reestablished its natural form.

After cutting back a tree-like, take care to help it regrow a good new framework. Cut out too crowded, too spindly, and wrong-way shoots.

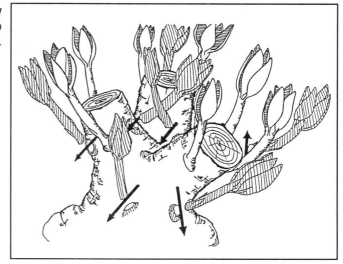

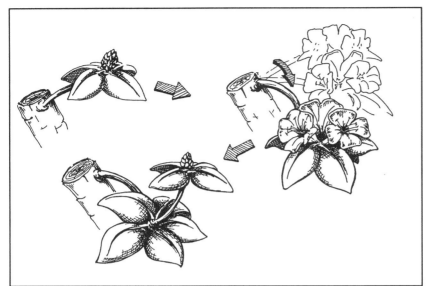

The strange regrowth on radically pruned rhododendrons is due to the flower truss, which weighs down soft new shoots. The shoot "hardens off" in that position. Next spring, growth heads up again.

Be sure you are not working against a plant's natural habit. Your type of rhododendron or other broad-leaf evergreen plant has a size and degree of openness that is characteristic of its species. A large-leaved Loderi-type rhododendron wants to be 12 feet tall and open. You cannot prune it into a hybrid-Jean-Marie-type 5-foot ball. It will simply grow back in an open form. Tree-likes that lend themselves to renovation are naturally growing compactly with small, closely spaced leaves. Inquire seriously, "Why is my rhododendron leggy?" It may need water, not pruning.

What about my own rhododendron stump? The original plant was too ugly for too long, and I have a deep need to test the outer limits of pruning. So I cut it to 5 inches from the ground. It's coming back now in great shape.

Most people can't bear to cut back the entire top of tree-likes radically. Another option is to thin the top, so that light reaches the interior, and then to score or nick the buds. Take a razor blade and make a 1/8-inch deep cut about 1/4 inch above one of the tiny dormant buds as they plump up in the early spring. This will trick the bud into thinking the top was broken out and it will begin to grow. These buds exist clear down to the base of your rhododendron, by the way. When you have enough growth below (in one to three years), cut out the top. Nicking buds works on other types of shrubs and trees, too.

Other kinds of tree-likes that can be successfully renovated by severe pruning in addition to some TLC (Tender Loving Care) are camellias, pieris, aucuba, laurel, photinia, Rose of Sharon (Hibiscus sp.), laurestinus (Viburnum tinus), and evergreen euonymus. Don't try it on the types that sucker back, particularly dogwood trees, magnolia, or witch hazel (see helpful lists in the Appendix).

Things to remember: when you saw your non-suckering tree-like back, it will look for all the world like plant mutilation. Be sure you cut it way, way back, not just to where you want it to be. That's because it's going to have to grow back for three years before it looks like anything, and by then it will be 3 feet taller. After cutting, train the new shoots and suckers to prevent the roller-coaster effect we will soon discuss, and to build a nice framework.

One difference between a mutilated rhododendron and a renovated one is how it looks six years later. The hardest plants to restore, you will remember, are old, badly pruned rhododendrons. When you step inside one of these, you see a roller-coaster ride of skinny branches going every which way. Squiggles, zips, and wows! Retraining regrowth is important in renovation. Cut or rub off the new suckers or buds that are too crowded, or those that face back through the center, or those that are too, too straight up and ugly on any and all renovated plants. Also in the case of rhododendrons you find that the nice flower blossom is the culprit in your roller-coaster. The nice, green, soft, new shoot that charges out from a chain-sawed stump will get a big fat whorl of leaves or a big flower head on it that will weight it down. When the branch hardens off in that position, you have the beginning of your roller-coaster ride. I remove the flowers or cut back new branches to a node or whorl of leaves to help keep this from happening. After three years, you may let it bloom.

Some types of rhododendrons won't break bud; they'll just die. They are the smooth-barked kinds with *Thompsonii* blood in their veins. Most of the hardy hybrids won't give up this easily, but if you do radical restorative pruning on tree-likes, you must be prepared to have them die. They don't usually, but it's very stressful for them. Be sure to water them and avoid high nitrogen fertilizer, which would encourage too much wild regrowth.

CAVEATS GALORE

I almost omitted this section on radical renovation for tree-likes, because I have nightmares of what people will do with a little bit of knowledge. I've already seen what they do with none at all. Radical renovation is appropriate only when:

1. You have all the room you need for the plant to grow back to its mature (not necessarily its ultimate) height.
2. It has been previously malpruned and is therefore too ugly to be thinned out or opened up.
3. It is actually blocking a pathway or window and doesn't just *seem* too big.
4. It has a naturally compact form, not open and tall.
5. It is of mature age (fifteen years old or older).
6. It is healthy and well watered.
7. It is not a suckering or finely-branched plant.
8. It is not a conifer or needled evergreen (except yews).
9. If the only other alternative is removal, and you are prepared that it may die from surgery.
10. If you know that it will take two to five years for it to look good again.
11. If you do not use radical renovation to keep plants small, but only to start them over.

SUMMARY

❑ Radical renovation is a way to start plants over by cutting them nearly to the ground.

❑ It works best with cane-growers and mounds.

❑ It is possible but rarely appropriate with tree-like shrubs.

My Tree's Too Big

The good news is *your tree is not too big*. The bad news is you can't make it smaller. It is exactly and perfectly the correct size for its age, genus, and species. Now, wait. Don't put this book back on the shelf! There *are* alternatives. Your tree may be 1) a big weed, 2) inappropriately placed, or 3) too oppressive, in which case you may prune it, move it, or kill it, but under no circumstances is it appropriate to torture it. Topping is torture, and it will make matters far worse in the long run. Topping, you may recall, is ugly. It also devalues your tree. Trees have a monetary value that is part of the value of your property. A professional appraiser will reduce the appraised value of your tree generally by about one-third if it's been topped. An appraisal for a large, old tree might be $1,000 or more.

TOPPING IS *NOT* THE ANSWER

Topping doesn't work to keep trees small. It just stimulates rapid regrowth of weakly attached suckers. It endangers tree health. It doesn't kill right away. It kills slowly, many years later when the trees succumb to root rot, or die in the drought, or break up because they are finally rotten clear through. Topping trees is hazardous to tree health in sort of the same way smoking is hazardous to human health. People don't die from the cigarette smoke, they die from some other cause years later. For many years, people did not connect smoking with health problems, just as topping does not appear to be connected with the eventual, seemingly unrelated death of the tree. Topped trees are dangerous trees, as well; they are more likely to drop limbs or blow over. Therefore, there are few, if any, circumstances under which topping is appropriate, not even for a billion-dollar view, not for the power lines (it's better to remove the trees and replant). For people who want to make their too-big tree small again, I know this is bad news. Read on.

In nine cases out of ten the homeowner needs attitude adjustment or a good pruner. We will deal with your attitude in the last part.

WHAT A GOOD PRUNER CAN DO FOR YOU

A good tree pruner (an arborist) is an underpaid artist. He or she can transform that big, ugly old

The ill effects of topping: Shown is a deciduous tree soon after topping. The same deciduous tree one year later. At right is a topped conifer. The natural shape and therefore the purpose of the tree is compromised.

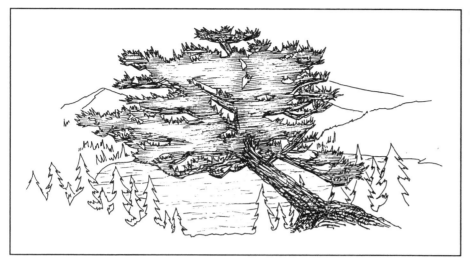

Trees should not be topped, but they can be pruned. Here is an example of a pine tree obscuring a water view.

Here is the same tree thinned or "windowed" for a view. Trees vary in the degree to which they will accept thinning without dying or suckering back in following years. Pay close attention to these parameters.

thing in your backyard into a thing of beauty. How does a tree pruner (called an arborist) do it? The highest compliment I ever got was when someone came out to his yard and said, "I never noticed how beautiful that maple was! Did you prune it?" Good pruning is invisible and truly miraculous. Try it on your tree before you opt for removal. Removal (death) is appropriate in some situations, but pause and reflect before you decide on removal because:

1. Trees are real living things. They just don't move and make noises the way animals do when you kill them.
2. Trees are a legacy. You may owe it to posterity to leave that tree even if you don't enjoy it so much. Some kid someday will want to build a tree house in it, some animal may make its

home in it, and so forth. Who are you, of a mere eighty-year lifespan, who change addresses an average of once every seven years, to cut it down? Not to mention its benefits to mankind and the ecology, like shade, wind break, making oxygen out of carbon dioxide, and cleaning particulates out of the air. Why should it die because you don't want to rake its leaves?

A good pruner can train your tree away from your gutters, can open up your tree to let in tons more sunlight, can remove weak and dead limbs so nothing is likely to fall on you or your house—really, a pruner can often tell when there's danger. If you fear your large tree, have a qualified arborist do a "hazard tree evaluation." If the tree is truly hazardous and not too big, it should be removed. A good tree pruner can make it easy for you to walk under or around or by your tree. Or he or she can just plain make it less bulky and oppressive. Depending on the species of tree, a good pruner can create "windows" for your view. A pine tree (see illustration) will take a lot of thinning. Not so, a cherry tree.

DON'T BE AFRAID OF YOUR TREE'S HEIGHT

Frequently, people decide to try to stop their tree from getting bigger as it approaches the roof line of their home. If the tree towers 30 feet over the house, they leave it alone. It's a psychological problem, an invisible height barrier. It is subconsciously disturbing to have a tree the same height as your house. The solution is to let the tree grow taller. A good pruner will help it look better for now. Trees cannot be stopped with pruning; the species of the plant determines its size and basic shape.

Most people top their trees because they're arborphobic (afraid of large trees). Trees do not fall over because they are too big. They fall over because they are structurally unsound or sick. An elephant doesn't fall over any more often than a pig—it's just more impressive when it does. A healthy tree has exactly the right number and size of roots to hold up its crown. Some types or species of trees are genetically prone to be weaker structured or shorter lived. Signs of a potentially hazardous tree are: mushrooms and white sheeting under the bark, large cracks and deep rotten hollows, old topping cuts, the ground around trees heaving in windstorms, recent construction nearby, trees that used to live in the forest but were recently left by new development or clear-cuts, trees whose roots have been cut or compacted or covered up by bulldozing, leaning trees, and trees with thinning and yellowing foliage and excessive amounts of dead wood. Wind-throw does occur in high wind areas but can be prevented by thinning trees so the wind passes through them. Topping makes trees more prone to wind-throw because the characteristic thick regrowth catches even more wind. A good motto is: When in doubt, thin it out.

Occasionally an arborist will reduce the size of a tree using selective heading cuts. This is called "drop-crotching." It is not the answer because, although it reduces suckering, it will still cause the tree to rot out.

JUSTIFIABLE DENDROCIDE

There are circumstances in which it is all right to kill your tree. A truly hazardous tree should be removed. There was a house I know where someone had planted a baby giant sequoia under the eaves. I watched for four years until it reached the roof and the owners finally topped it. It is a good candidate for removal. You cannot train evergreens around things as you can deciduous trees except perhaps some pines. Needled evergreens planted in front of windows or next to walkways may have to go because you cannot reduce their width. The city is full of people who tried to do so by cutting halfway into their conifers. OOPS! Whereas deciduous things will respond by regrowing tons of skinny, ugly, but at least green-leafed branches, your average conifer will not green up again, ever. Big trees under power lines are candidates for justifiable *dendrocide*. (*Dendron* from the Latin for "tree.") Replace them with trees that *crown-out* low.

Selectively thinning a series of overplanted trees by cutting some down is sometimes justifiable dendrocide. One of the hardest yards I ever consulted on was another plant lover's yard, overgrown with a series of huge, incredibly wonderful, overplanted rare trees—two giant katsura, an Empress tree, a Korean dogwood, and a ginkgo. But they were now competing too heavily with each other and shading out equally wonderful shrubs below. These smaller shrubs were showing signs of stress by getting too thin and leggy as they reached for the never-enough sun.

It is true that trees can be planted in groves like a forest, and even one below the other (Japanese maples are good to plant under other trees) or in groups. Birches look best this way, but sometimes there are just too many. Selective tree removal is the lifeboat theory of gardening—one must go to save the rest. Removal is appropriate when pruning alone can't cure the too-intense shade. It helps if the trees in question are not rare, old, and wonderful ones, as in the above example.

You may care to remember the definition of a weed. Common weedy trees seen in my area are big-leaf maples, Western red cedars, holly, mountain ash, and alder. Be careful, though! With a simple attitude adjustment a weedy tree could be the star attraction of your yard.

Sometimes it's all right to kill a tree if it's very, very, very sick and old. Old, heavily diseased, fruiting cherries and native western dogwoods are good candidates for death with dignity. You may have a case for wrongful placement. This means that the previous owner planted a birch—which invariably gets aphids and drips sticky honeydew—over the only parking spot; a madrona over your patio—madronas are always shedding bark, berries, or leaves (I'd rule against extermination and tell you to hire a neighborhood kid to rake); or a weeping willow over your drain pipes, making your plumbing bill exceed $300 per year.

Don't get chain saw happy on me now. Blocking your view is not justifiable dendrocide and will bring a scowl to the judge's face.

The deciduous thing in front of your window can probably be thinned successfully so that you can see sort of into and through it. As for your sweeping view of sea, lake, or mountains, it's time for an attitude adjustment.

You paid lots of money for that view, and you pay lots and lots of property taxes every year to keep it. You want to keep it a view. You don't want all those doggone trees in the way. I've heard it a billion times. But your view *should* include some lovely trees as focal points (these are called "horizon trees"). If creating a distant view requires removing more than three trees, maybe you were meant to have a "woodland" view instead. (I can hear the protest even as I write.) Well, consider the alternatives and the big picture.

It is humanly impossible to reduce the size of a tree significantly without deleterious effect. I am referring again to *topping*. When you top your trees (or your neighbors' trees below you) you have only ensured an ugly view of mutilated trees with the worst yet to come. Some trees are so healthy and vigorous that they spring back pretty well, but just observe how a real one looks compared to one you've tortured for years. Really look at its branches in the winter. You'll see what I mean. If you still top, start looking over your shoulder for the Tree Police. They're going to come to show you what it's like to be "kept small."

So you say, justifiable dendrocide. Wrong! Just imagine, for a moment, what the skyline will look like when everybody removes his or her big trees between the top of the hill and the water below. Rooftops and power lines and someone else's dirty back alley! Looks good, doesn't it? Trees break up that bleak outlook, cover up the unsightly, and soften the view for the entire community. Now start thinking in terms of the grandeur of a big tree. Look at beauty with your eyes, not your pocketbook. Think of the pretty fall colors. Now leave that tree alone or have a professional come to prune it and make it a real star! Be a real hero, be a person who knows how to treat a tree!

SUMMARY

The three options for the too-big tree:

❑ Remove it. Perhaps you want to plant a smaller growing tree now and take out the big one later. If your tree is truly hazardous, it should come out soon.

❑ Prune it. You can reduce the bulk and clutter, (not the height) of trees. Taking off lower and specifically interfering limbs is all right, too. Use a professional arborist (member of ISA—International Society of Arboriculture or NAA—National Arborist Association). Have him or her prune to National Arborist Association pruning standards.

❑ Love it. Tree lovers judge the greatness of a tree by its size and age. Bigger and older is better! To love it and leave it alone may be the best and cheapest solution.

PART III
DESIGNING
AND INSTALLING
A NEW LANDSCAPE

What Makes a Yard Look Good or Bad

Let's start by examining what makes yards look bad. The very worst ones are the yards that people have covered with concrete, so they won't have to mow them. The reason you plant a yard is, after all, to relieve you from the squareness, the flatness, and the harshness of the concrete and the buildings of our urban areas. Besides the no-maintenance "no yard" we see a second error. This is the house that you don't see because the tiny shrubs and trees that were planted right up close to the house fifteen years ago are all now full-sized and are so smashed up against the house that you can't see out the windows or get in the doors. Beyond this jungle pressed against the house you find only empty grass out to the street.

THE OVERPLANTED YARD

Another extremely common problem is the overplanted yard. People tend to space their new plants so that they look "right" when they are planted. But plants are only babies when you get them. They get bigger and bigger, and soon they are too crowded. Plant lovers tend to overplant also. In their enthusiasm to own every treasured plant that's available, they shoehorn them in, hoping that somehow more space will be found in the future. But as the plants grow larger, they inevitably interfere with each other and lose their shape and charm. A special case of plant-lovers-overplanting is the garden wherein one of everything exists, but the feeling of theme is wholly lost. This is called "fruit salad" or, if you want to be nice, you can refer to it as a "collector's garden."

THE LOW MAINTENANCE YARD

At the other end of the spectrum is the ever-popular "low maintenance" yard. These are juniper-and-bark yards you see everywhere, particularly in parking lots, condominiums, and industrial parks. Often they include rhododendron, some juniper, photinia, and mugho pine. A few larger evergreen trees are used ("we don't want any deciduous trees because we don't want to rake leaves"). These are good enough if they are really what you want. But soon, soon, you will be bored, because aside from the short burst of color from your spring-flowering shrubs, the scene never changes. After awhile you don't even see it. And if you don't see it, you probably won't weed or maintain it, much less enjoy it.

OTHER LANDSCAPE DESIGN ERRORS

The kind of yard that has always intrigued me is the one where the house is surrounded by giant trees and shrubs on the outside, out by the street. The house seems mysterious and inviting nestled back there. But if you talk to the people who live there, chances are they'll say, "You can have it!" It's dark there all the time, and they wish they could just grow enough grass to put their lawn furniture on. And nothing ever blooms, it's too shady.

Another common design error is planting individual shrubs out in the middle of the lawn every so often. This breaks up the monotony of the empty lawn that ends with a "shrubs jammed up against the back fence in rows" look. But the shrubs look to me like tiny lone islands in the sea of green. They are fussy to mow around. Better to put in a large island or peninsula and add some companions to keep them company.

Also note yards where all the plants are the same height and texture. They are oppressive and dull. People seem to think that a shrub ought to be wider than it is tall and always about waist high. A nice yard has different sizes and textures of things.

GARDEN STYLES

Another mistake to avoid is mixing garden styles. Just as with furniture and interior decorating, gardens have styles. Sometimes styles can be blended and sometimes not. Generally, you want your more intensive formal-looking areas, like roses and annual flower beds, closer to the house; then you can let the garden become more natural as you move farther away. My yard is basically Pacific Northwest style, evolving into woodland in the back garden. Lately, I've added a small perennial flower bed next to the garage. It "works," as they say. But a yard starts to look funny if you have a Japanese cloud-pruned pine *and* an English perennial border *and* some natural-looking shrubs *and* a fish pond. If you live in the woods, among towering forest trees, one sheared bush looks odd. Pollarded trees look good next to the chateaux in France; they look silly as the only two treated that way out of a row of trees on the parking strip in front of your house. Pollarded trees are the ones pruned to look like 5-foot lollipops. Some garden styles I have identified are these:

❏ Formal English—clipped hedges, roses, knot gardens

❏ English cottage—fruit trees and lots of perennials rambling around in great profusion

❏ Japanese—highly trained and maintained pines and other trees with masses of low sheared shrubs, placed rocks, and sand seas

❏ Early American—forsythias, quince, peonies, bearded iris

❏ Pacific Northwest—rocks to look like mountain outcroppings, rhododendron, pines, heather, vine maples, Douglas firs

❏ Woodland—tall trees with understory plants and groundcovers

❏ Prairie—grasses and sun-loving wildflowers

You wouldn't put an art deco table next to your French Provincial couch. Be equally careful to blend styles in your yard. A good exercise for you is to start looking at yards as you pass them. When you find one you like, try to put into words what it is that appeals to you.

You should know that people go through stages of gardening taste the way they do tastes in clothes or cars. At first people are attracted to the "riot of color" yards packed with annuals and dahlias. They also like sheared shrubs. They graduate through various styles and stages of snobbery. I know of a garden in England that is all shrubs planted for contrasting shapes and textures. But there are no bright colors—simply all shades of green. Some people become miniaturists—these are the alpine rock gardeners. A friend of mine went with her mother to buy a tiny alpine plant for her mother's friend. When they selected a plant, my friend said, "Oh, she'll love it. You can hardly see it at all!"

Other people go the "tasteful species" route. Allow me to interpret this gardenese for you. Because people like flowers, horticulturists began to breed bigger and more spectacular flowers on plants and shrubs to dazzle us. These are "hybrids." Often the plants have lost many interesting secondary characteristics like scent and interesting sizes, colors, and shapes of leaves. Hybrid rhododendrons look a lot alike most of the year, but species (those are ones existing naturally in the wild) vary greatly in size: some have giant leaves; others are tiny plants. Some species rhododendrons have blue felt called "indementum" under the leaves; others have gold felt. Some smell interesting if you rub or prune them. Some have dangling trumpets for blooms. Species plants are more likely to bloom at a different season or smell good. They look more "natural."

Anyway, there is nothing wrong with any style of yard. You may be torn among several, but eventually your own style will, trust me, assert itself. Many go full circle and come back to "gaudy" dahlias; others remain true to their first love, perhaps the rose. Still others find new styles more suited to their personality. I like things to look wild, natural, and lush, but not oppressive or unkempt. So I go for more woodland, for vigorous and species types. Take some time to look in books and visit gardens to see what type you identify with most closely.

ELEMENTS OF GOOD GARDEN DESIGN

So now, let's talk about what makes things look good. Generally, you want shrubs and trees, plus grass, to soften the hard, angular lines of your house and lot. Some people eliminate grass altogether and use a patio surrounded by beds. A flat sea of green grass does, however, add contrast for your shrub beds. Grass is good if you have kids. Cool grass on the sole of a bare foot in summer is a much savored tactile treat. A few very tall things are essential, to put your house in scale, or set it off, especially if it's a tall or big house. But you don't want so many tall things that they block all the light. A tall tree takes up a lot of space but it adds the element of "grandeur." A big tree goes on the south or west side to protect you from the blazing hot sun. It also adds habitat for kids and other wildlife, songbirds, for example. I think our urban settings are sorely lacking in grandeur and habitat.

Carve out your beds in gentle sweeps around the outside perimeter. Make them three times as big as you think you need them. The amount of grass you need is really quite small. Enough for six chairs and a picnic table or three beach towels. I like a 50/50 ratio of lawn to beds. If you are lucky enough to have a lot of land, you may wish to break it up into "rooms" with shrub bed peninsulas or fences, the path winding from one "room" to another. These rooms are not square—they're just spaces that are separated, more or less. One of the most pleasurable gardening experiences is that of mystery, as when you catch a glimpse of more garden around a corner or through a gate. To lend this inviting air of mystery to your house, plant up the outside corners with your tallest trees and shrubs and have them descend to the entry to the street. This will mean that your landscape cups your house like an open hand. The broad openings, however, will invite you in and let in light.

A good thing to incorporate in your yard always is truck access. At some point or another you will need to get a refrigerator to the back door or a cement truck or 6 yards of mulch. Even if this is a giant gate in your fence, which you open once in six years, be sure you have it. If the access is not big enough for a truck, then make it at least wide enough for a wheelbarrow. Having a hidden utility area is also a very good idea.

If your house is up a steep hill, you will want to build a rockery, which you can make special with good plant choices and stepped back rocks that leave you places to plant. If your whole area slopes steeply, then seriously consider terracing, or rock or wall reinforcements. When landscape architects tell you the groundcover will spread and hold the bank, they lie. All landscaping needs maintenance, or else the weeds will invade and prosper until you have a blackberry patch. And if it's too steep for you to walk on, this is what will happen. Also erosion occurs with undeniable regularity on steep slopes. Don't ignore it! Gravity always wins. Having steep slopes means that the summer irrigation water runs off before it sinks into the soil. Steep slopes mean that all that expensive mulch you spread to keep the weeds down will migrate down to the bottom in about a year—leaving bare spots above and a useless thick pile at the bottom. Invest the time and money to fix your steep grades now; plant your garden later.

THEME

Take measures to avoid a spotty, unplanned-looking yard. Plant in groups of threes, fives, or sevens—pairs at the very least. Plant smaller things in groups, never rows. If this rule is carried to the extreme with very broad curves and huge masses of same type plants, your yard will look institutional; if it's ignored and you plant one of everything, and beds have too many curves, it will look fussy. Groupings or masses of plants give your yard a sense of being planned. The backbone of your yard is made up of these groups. They are like the chorus line in the stage show. They allow the other, more "choice" plants to show off. They give it *theme*.

A certain sense of theme can be achieved by repeating a shrub on different sides of an area, or by repeating a plant shape, or by matching colors at bloom time. One person might plan a yard of blue, white, and pink. Another might choose yellow and white. A person might mirror similar arches in front or back, or feature the same style of crockery or benches. Or you can repeat a certain angle or curve on your beds, only bigger or smaller, someplace else.

Among these threes and fives, plant some specialties; any plant that is featured as a one-of-a-kind in your yard is called a *specimen plant*. A *specimen plant* is one that is a particularly impressive or unusual example of a species due to its size, shape, age, or any other trait that epitomizes the character of the species. Other specialty plants to tuck in include winter bloomers. Plant things that stay low or are easy to keep low under your windows and taller things in the empty wall spaces. Sarcococca makes a nice low, shade-loving plant for that skinny space between the walkway and house. It's evergreen and smells nice, too. Evergreen huckleberry is good for this skinny spot, and so is nandina. The Appendix includes a list of plants for skinny places.

SEASONAL INTEREST

An interesting yard has shows for every season. In spring all the rhododendrons and azaleas and flowering ornamental dogwood, cherry, plum, crabapple, and deciduous flowering shrubs will bloom. Maybe you have a flowering vine too, like a spring-blooming clematis. As spring turns to summer, you should carefully choose some summer-flowering shrubs and many sweet smellers to make lounging around outside more interesting. There's usually a lull midsummer, and you may wish to add some flowers, that is to say, annuals or perennials, to keep things interesting.

Choose some early fall bulbs and perennials to lead into the fall show. Add some vines, trees, and shrubs that turn colors or have interesting berries. And even though you didn't plan it that way, it will look as if you chose them to go with each other. In deepest winter you should have your backbone of evergreen plants to keep the barren feeling away. Also use things with interesting bark like London plane tree or red twig dogwood. Perhaps you will choose to highlight one of the specimen trees or shrubs that has a graceful or bold branch pattern in your yard so that it will show up penciled in frost. Tucked against some other shrubs where you hardly notice them in the summer, you can put the winter or early, early spring scented bloomers, like witch hazel. They often flower without much leaf to accompany them, which makes them all the more charming.

Winter is when your hardscape shows up the most. This means the lines of your beds, the big rocks that you might put in for interest. The stepping stones or paths, their shape, arrangement, and texture, show up. The variation in height will add a lot too, as well as how you divided things up generally. And if you

have a tasteful urn or bench that is your focal point, it will be very much the star in the winter.

FOCAL POINTS

Each area of your yard should have a focal point. This can be an ornament or an interesting tree or shrub. In my backyard it is a rock-ring fire pit. My friend, wild man Delessio, would always start a fire in my backyard during parties. I had to institutionalize it to keep my lawn from becoming riddled with black spots. So a focal point can even be dull. It's just a resting spot for your eyes so that the remainder of the yard seems to fit. That's why you shouldn't have too many focal points in one area; it defeats the purpose.

CONTRAST

Contrast is the stuff of which great landscapes are made. Gray-leaved things and purple-leaved things can add a lot of contrast to a yard; they help make contrast in *color*. Other important elements are contrast in *form* (as in round things versus columnar things) and contrast in *texture* (things that look soft or lacy versus bold or spiky). They can be placed to show each other off. People think it's flowers that make a garden beautiful, but it's really contrast.

One of the smartest improvements that I ever saw occurred in a yard that used to have an enormous bank of Pfitzer junipers and a big tree. The couple who moved in made many wonderful additions, including a perennial bed and a raised vegetable patch. But true genius emerged when—instead of pulling out the Pfitzers—they added contrasting weeping Alaska cedars. Most people, I'm sure, never consciously notice or comment. But I'll bet those trees are great laced in snow. The chevron-shaped Pfitzers are perfectly contrasted by the slender draped boughs of the cedars. The three tall trees also offset or balance the mass of low junipers. This evergreen scene provides a good solid backbone to the yard.

Make sure to plant the things that are going to get tall in the back of the bed (if the bed abuts a fence or wall) or the center of the bed if it's an island, and don't plant rows of juniper along your walkways. Don't plant rows of anything, actually. Invariably one of the plants dies, and it will be hard to find its

Balance—Before. Sometimes a yard will benefit from the addition of a plant or plants.

Balance—After. Here the addition of a bed and shrub makes the yard look more finished.

match. Also, plan your yard to have a minimum number of objects to mow around in your lawn area. I have two. One is the fire pit; the other is a tree.

One of the things that make a yard look nice is what I have called "three stories." Trees make up the top story, under them or in front of them are the shrubs, under them or in front of them are the groundcovers. It is also pleasing to spot something growing behind or under things, such as bulbs under deciduous shrubs or hellebores or ferns under tall, tree-like shrubs. Consider the "bottom floor" especially, just outside your windows and near the entryways, where you may wish to glance down at something interesting.

BALANCE

Your yard may be missing balance. By this I certainly don't mean that everything should be exactly the same on both sides. But if something seems wrong, you might need to plant a shrub or bring in a rock for that empty space to give your yard balance. I worked in a landscape where the owners wanted me to remove everything on the forest floor in a certain area. In this area there existed a small tree with three azaleas on one side and none on the other side, just the blank forest floor and low scrub back to some trees. What was needed was something to fill in, not something taken out. To add balance, plants on either side need not be the same size or type. They must just have approximately equal weight or mass. A mass of short shrubs on one side of a tree may equal a large shrub on the other side.

ADVENTURE AND SURPRISE

Adventure and surprise are other elements of garden design. Paths that take you on a journey, even a tiny one, to behind that clump of shrubs and trees, add a lot. Side yards have a lot of adventure, because you must walk through them to see what's there. Plants that come and go, like bulbs and perennials, add surprise. Some people go so far as to put in gates that lead nowhere or enticing paths that lead to the dull utility area. It's showmanship. And now you must set the stage.

SUMMARY

❑ Is your yard too dull?

❑ Is it too crowded?

❑ Are no two shrubs the same?

❑ Does it have narrow beds that follow the house, walls, and fences?

❑ Are there mixed styles?

❑ Are the plants all the same height?

Design do's:

❑ Solve drainage and erosion problems first.

❑ Include access for trucks, wheelbarrows, and daylight.

❑ Include tall trees for grandeur, shade, habitat, the environment.

❑ Make beds very large, with sweeping curves.

❑ Plant in odd numbers—threes, fives, and sevens.

❑ Plant in drifts, not rows.

Will your new yard have ...

❑ Theme?

❑ Shows for every season?

❑ Good hardscape?

❑ Focal points—not too many, but one for every area?

❑ Contrast in height, texture, color, and form?

❑ Balance?

❑ Adventure and surprise?

Map and Hardscape

Now that you know what makes a yard look good or bad, you can start improving or redesigning yours. The first thing you need to do is make a to-scale map of your yard and house. Don't skip this part—you can see things on paper you can't see looking outside. I discovered by staring at my map that I was wasting a third of my yard potential in a long grass driveway past my house to my garage. I kept trying to think of skinny plants for either side. This was rather limiting. By looking at the map, I decided to make the driveway come in from the alley in back (and then my husband moved the walls of the garage end to end) and turned that old driveway space into a side garden with a winding green path. Now it's the nicest part of the yard.

MAPPING YOUR YARD

On a big piece of graph paper, map out your house and yard. Figure out how long your stride is and pace off the footage to one corner of your house, then pace off everything else. Draw in all permanent structures in ink; try out new designs in pencil. But beware: you may find that you need to move the "permanent" garden shed or cut down the tree. It's essential to put in overhead wires and underground utilities, too. And be sure to put in North.

With a black or colored pencil, put in the features you're pretty sure you want to save. The temptation is either to keep all those big old trees because trees are sacred or, alternately, to take out everything because you're tired of the whole mess. But consider carefully. You will be spending a fortune on tiny shrubs that will take a long time to amount to anything. Saving that old camellia or lilac may give much needed height and weight to your new yard. Also many old shrubs can look amazingly good when cleaned up by an experienced pruner.

Leave out existing concrete paths and present shrub bed lines on your map. This will be a great help to you in being creative. With the sweep of a pencil you can change your shrubs, change the shape of beds, or add a giant tree. Try an outer ring perimeter of trees and shrubs and an inner ring of beds around your house. Try a mounded island bed in the middle with a path around the outside and beds on the perimeter. Try dividing the map into the different spaces (the rooms) separated from each other by shrub beds, or hedges, or fences. The shrub bed and lawn shapes on your map should resemble jigsaw puzzle pieces, with the grass and beds of about equal size. The peanut is a shape much admired by garden designers. It may help to draw in a nice shape for the lawn area first. What is left over is the bed space. Then you continue designing to fill in the empty beds.

Remember to leave truck or wheelbarrow access (with no steps) to all areas. People who are really creative get tracing paper at the local art store. On one piece of tracing paper they put the circles of the plants they will see in the winter, mostly evergreens. On top of that they overlay a sheet of colored circles representing spring color, and again one for fall color. Get as detailed or as simple as you like. Use your local copy store to make copies of your map to doodle on.

USING YOUR MAP

Your map will also help you avoid overplanting. When you draw in your shrubs and trees (as circles), draw them in full grown size or width, then purchase just that many plants. Look up the mature height and figure that it will be about as wide as it is tall, if a shrub. Many trees and some shrubs will, of course, be tall and thin. Be sure to map their mature width. When you go to plant them spaced for their

A typical yard, perhaps the one you've just bought.

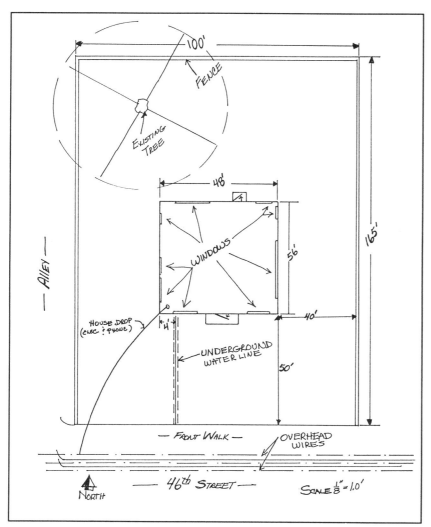

Make a to-scale map. Don't forget to put in utilities and North.

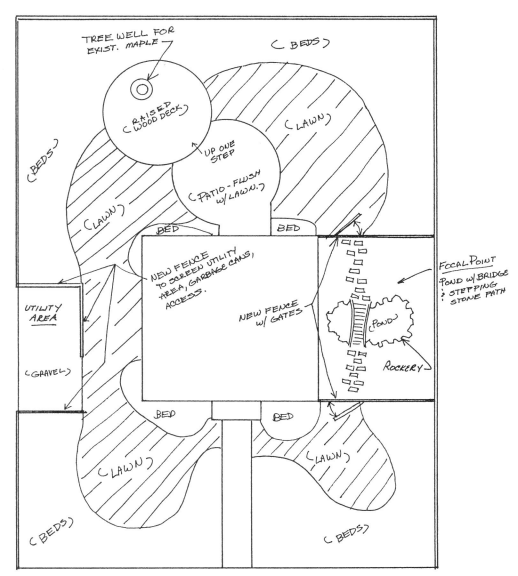

Make copies of your map. Try out different hardscapes until you find one you like. Draw in the shape of the lawn first, then choose plants to fit areas left over.

adult size, they will look too far apart—vulnerable—dumb, in fact. Do it anyway. Avoid the number one fault of new landscapes: overplanting. If you make everything look finished now, you will regret it later. In almost no time they will crowd each other and you will have to cut out those expensive shrubs it seems you just bought, or they will run into each other and look crowded and choked. We will talk more later about ameliorating new landscape owners' shock syndrome (NLOSS).

Color the circles of same-type plants the same color, connect them with a line, and then take the line to the side where you can name the plant. You need not know what exact plants you want where. Just picture something, say, "about 10 feet, evergreen, columnar—there," and draw it in. Or "a group of five small mounded shrubs, there—with a focal point at the edge." Later we will do a plant search to name that circle.

The map is good because it starts you out with a good hardscape. It forces you to look at the basic shapes of things: your walkways and paths, your patio, the vistas, the shapes of shrub beds. Also, plug in the *focal points*, one per area. Note also where your main view windows are. The most important view may be the one from the kitchen sink window.

Be sure to draw your beds three times as big as you think you'll need them; you can't have a bed too big. It will be burgeoning and billowing with wonderful things, getting bigger all the time. I have the hardest time convincing people to make their beds big enough. Even if you show them a full-grown forsythia and then stand on the spot where you want to plant three—they can't seem to visualize a bed big enough to hold them. Empty bed space must be scary to many people. To me it's a wonderful opportunity.

PLANNING TO USE YOUR SPACE

To assist you in your planning, you may wish to lay hoses or ropes out on the grass where you want your beds to be. Move them around until they look right. Imagine them planted with full-sized plants. Spend some time looking out your windows, imagining what you'd like to see. Visualize. Visualize. Visualize. You may also wish to get copies of your "before"

pictures. Don't forget to take these pictures. Especially take pictures of "nothing" areas. Later they will look great and you will want to remember how dull and empty it was there before. My local copy store can take three or four series pictures and blow them up on one big sheet—even in color. Draw on them to get an idea of how a tree or a group of shrubs would look in various places. Don't worry if you think you can't draw. Just concentrate on getting the basic shape and size.

Consider the style that is appropriate for your house, but don't be trapped by it. I thought that because my house was in a square, flat, crowded neighborhood, I should have square, flat beds. Wrong. The beds all curve and are built up as mounds. For contrast I have the flat green lawn. It works. But it would have been inappropriate in such a small lot to put in a formal yard with lots of topiary and urns and statues and rose beds. There is just not enough room. It really wouldn't match the neighborhood. And even though I love those pictures of English perennial borders, the flowers all die back to ugly dead twigs in the winter, and in the summer they are very high maintenance. So I made only the tiny one in back.

Draw in big beds next to your house; people do not need to walk right next to the house where those old concrete paths are. They will enjoy walking around a nice curved bed full of fun things. Concrete paths can be pretty easy to remove. When I tackled mine, I was amazed. I had one that went straight back from my back door to an old shed's foundation. I broke it up one afternoon with a sledgehammer and carted the pieces off to one side. I used the broken concrete as stepping stones arranged in a curve to the side garage door, the curve complementing a shrub bed curve nearby.

With your hardscape map you should note traffic paths and views from windows. And don't forget the dictates of family needs. Should there be room for a play area? A dog run? A vegetable patch? I still have my map; the lines remain the same but the names of plants have changed. As a phytophile, I've had to rotate in new rare and wonderful plants and give away last year's favorites. It's how I avoid "fruit salad."

Bad rock work. The rocks are all the same size and evenly spaced.

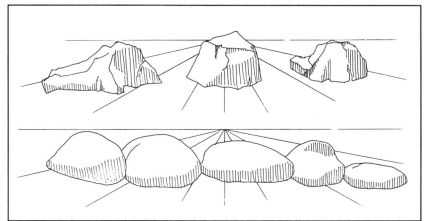

Good rock work. Use rocks in groupings. For a natural look, bury them halfway.

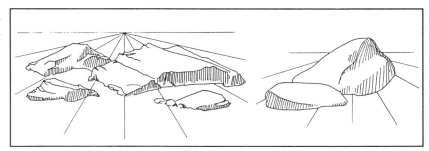

NLOSS—NEW LANDSCAPE OWNER'S SHOCK SYNDROME

Speaking of your hardscape and NLOSS (new landscape owner's shock syndrome), you should seriously consider *grade change* and *rock work* for your yard. I wish that I had built my beds up twice as high as I did (they were up about 8 inches but they've sunk). Try having terraces or mounds (but never too steep; you will find them hard to mow and, furthermore, they will encourage erosion). Constructing mounds or interlocking retaining walls adds interest by making a contrast in height. You can create the same effect by waiting for all your tall things to grow tall, your medium things to grow medium, and your small ones to get established just as they are. But we are so impatient as to want things to look good now. Incorporating height into our gardens with raised beds will help alleviate new landscape owner's shock syndrome. This syndrome commonly occurs when the homeowner spends about three times as much as she or he figured it should cost at the most, and looking outside sees all these incredibly small, widely spaced shrubs for the money. The final cure for NLOSS is, you guessed it, patience. You may wish to interplant widely spaced

shrubs with easy seeded annual flowers, ferns, or groundcovers. They may help ease the sense of emptiness until your babies grow.

CONSIDER ROCKS

Another thing you should consider for your hardscape is the addition of some tasteful big rocks, arranged either in the Japanese style or as a natural rocky outcropping. In the winter your view will be of these rocks and whatever is evergreen in your yard. These items do a lot to relieve NLOSS. In Japan there are people who professionally pick rocks; they listen to them. To the Japanese, rocks can stand for certain values. A very pleasing aspect in a yard is a rock that mirrors "the movement" of a plant or plants. Also rocks can counterbalance a leaning tree or can be nestled into a groundcover like an egg in a nest. Bury your rock halfway in the ground to give it a natural look. Always place rocks in groups of mixed sizes. Consider rocks. You can wait years to add trees and shrubs to your landscape, and you can change things around if you don't like them, but it's very hard to go back and add walls, paths, good soil, or big rocks once things get under way. Instead of poured concrete patios (so ugly) and wood decks (they get wet and rot out and become slippery in wet climates), consider flagstones and aggregate concrete bordered by bricks. Stepping stones of any sort are nice, too.

Bad rock work looks as if some giant just plunked down a rock every so often. Good rock work is art. Dry or wet stream beds can be done poorly or done well, as with all rock work. A good stream bed is dug out and will vary in width and depth. It curves and has large placed rocks as well as small ones. Bad dry stream beds look as if a truck full of same-sized rock pulled up, lifted its dump-bed, and drove off.

SUMMARY

❑ Make a to-scale map.

❑ Put in North, overhead and underground utilities, windows, and permanent structures.

❑ Take "before" photos.

❑ Have a copy store make copies of photos and the map on which to draw.

❑ Use ropes or hoses to try out shrub bed lines.

❑ Pay special attention to window views—make them interesting; do not block windows with evergreens.

❑ Blend style with neighborhood.

❑ Raised or mounded beds and good rock work make landscapes look good while you wait for the garden to mature (alleviating NLOSS).

❑ Avoid designing with shrubs spaced too close together.

How to Choose and Arrange Your Plants

By now you should have a map of your hardscape and an idea of what style you want and what will make your yard look good. Perhaps you have decided to build raised or mounded beds or add rocks. You have decided to take measures to control potential drainage and erosion problems. You may even have already penciled in some circles on your map to stand for tall trees, low masses of shrubs, a flower "cutting" bed, or focal points. Or perhaps you've just used the previous information to help you decide to run beds together or to add something to your existing landscape. Now it's time to select, transport, and arrange your plants.

THE EASY WAY

First, let's go over the easy way to pick your plants. As a novice, I invited two knowledgeable gardeners to come to my house and look at my hardscape map with me. They listed their favorite plants, and we discussed where they might go and how many to get. I got to listen when they disagreed on things, which was very helpful. Then I went to nurseries and looked at the plants they had suggested.

THE HARD WAY (BUT THE BEST WAY)

That's the easy way. The other way takes patience, which is, as we know, the greatest gardening lesson. You will have to do plant homework. You get a notebook and start making plant lists. You visit nurseries and jot down names of plants you like, you look at plants you like in friends' and neighbors' yards—perhaps you go on garden tours and ask the person standing next to you, "What's that?" Beginning gardeners spend a lot of time asking, "What's that?" Advanced gardeners ask, "Which one is that?" referring to the particular named variety of a plant. Your local nursery people have a wealth of information. You already know some gardenese with which to communicate and interpret, especially *hardy*, *vigorous*, and *reliable*. Ask your nursery people if they like the plant you are considering.

If you have in mind a certain place for your nursery plant, another good question is, "Would this be good to plant in such-and-such a place?" say, "on the parking strip?" or "next to my patio?" Another good thing to tell your nursery person is on which side of your house (facing which direction) you want to put the plant.

MICRO-CLIMATES

It is not apparent to the novice that a yard has micro-climates. Micro-climates can make a life and death difference to your shrub. The north side of your yard has less intense light and heat; so does the east side. Pay attention to where the coldest winter winds come from in your area. If you have a wall or slotted fence or grouping of shrubs, this will help protect your plants from the freezing and drying winter gales. The west and south sides have more intense heat and sun. Walls and concrete intensify both the heat and the shade. Shade provided by leaves of trees, especially deciduous trees, is less intense than shade made by buildings. A hydrangea, for example, may enjoy some light shade, but if it's trapped between condominiums, it will get leggy and may not bloom. Conversely, if you plant a shrub next to the road, the driveway, or against a wall facing south—well, it's in for a hot time. The signs of a plant that is baking to death are yellowed, curled, or crispy leaves. This may not seem obvious to you. I know it wasn't to me when I started out. I thought I could just make plants grow wherever I wanted them. Some shrubs simply love to bask in the sun. Put your rose bed, your herb garden, and your rockery plants on the south wall. It makes a huge difference if you give them what they like.

THE FIRST PIECE OF ADVICE

This brings me back to the first and most often ignored piece of essential advice. *Select plants according to their cultural requirements.* Examples of cultural requirements are the kind of light they require (sun or shade), the kind of soil they need (sand, loam, will take clay), and their mature sizes. *Verily I say unto thee: Read thy plant's tag, for by it ye shall know its name. Also ye shall know what it requireth. Yea, verily, its light, its soil, and its height. And the greatest of these is height.* In·your notebook write down the plant's botanical name and its common name. You will need its botanical name (Latin name) so that you can look it up in a gardening encyclopedia to find out more about it.

The tag on your shrub will give its name, height, and whether it needs sun or shade. You should know that "sun" or "shade" may not tell the entire story. "Shade" may mean it prefers shade, but it may "take some sun." This means it can take some sun without looking bad, but it won't like it as much as the shade. In the marine climate where I live the heat of the sun is less intense than only a hundred miles away over the mountains. Therefore, I can get away with planting my pieris or astilbe on the south side of the house. Information in your gardening encyclopedia may need further interpretation. A plant that "needs good drainage" and a plant that's "sun, drought tolerant" may both do well on the sunny side, but the first one's roots will rot in less than sandy soil; it may also take some part shade as long as it's planted in sandy or gritty soil. The latter may live in heavy (more clay) soil but will hate it if you move it into the shade. Confused? Use your nursery person. Try to catch him or her off season when things aren't too busy—this means sometime other than spring. In fact you should make a point of visiting your nursery during other seasons to see the other "shows" and get an idea of what plants, shrubs, etc., bloom together.

The "mature height" listed on your plant tag is also somewhat misleading: your plant will not stop when it reaches its mature height. It just slows down its growth and eventually stops many years later. In general, a plant's *"ultimate* height" is about twice its "mature height." As mentioned in the first section on pruning, plants vary in how much their ultimate height can be affected with selective pruning. Some types, the tree-likes, must be allowed to reach their ultimate height to serve their proper function in the landscape. Others, like Japanese holly and similar small-leaved plants, can be kept down almost indefinitely. Speaking of slow, there's a general rule about trees. You can either get fast, tall, and weak, or you can get slow, strong, and maybe not so tall. Everybody wants a tree that grows fast to 40 feet and then stops. No such luck. Your "fast" tree grows fast to 80 feet and then drops a limb on your car. Remember, patience!

In your notebook you have been collecting names of plants you like and putting down their cultural requirements, especially their heights and widths. To this you want to add the time they bloom, the color of bloom, and other notes like "scented," "gray foliage," "gets berries." Also you want to mark down whether they are deciduous, evergreen, broadleaf, or needled.

PLANT CATEGORIES

Wait! Time for more gardenese. *Deciduous* means the plant drops *all* its leaves in the winter. *Evergreen* means it stays green all year. (It sheds its *old* leaves every year though; you may not have noticed the pile of old leaves under your pine or rhododendron.) *Broadleaf* means it has a big leaf like an oak tree or a camellia. *Needled* means it's like a Christmas tree or many other conifers (has a cone, not a flower) or like a cedar or juniper. Thus your oak tree is a deciduous broadleaf, but your camellia is a broadleaf evergreen, and your fir tree is a needled evergreen. There actually exist a few deciduous needled things like the larch tree that looks a lot like a Christmas tree all summer and then turns a nice soft yellow in the fall. Then its needles drop for the winter. More than one homeowner has cut down his or her "dead" larch only to find out that it was just a deciduous needled tree.

You can divide your plants into columns according to height, S/Sh (sun/shade), E/D (evergreen, deciduous) and perhaps Fl. (flowering), and F.C. (fall color). You will use this information to plug them in on your map. It is at this point that you will feel

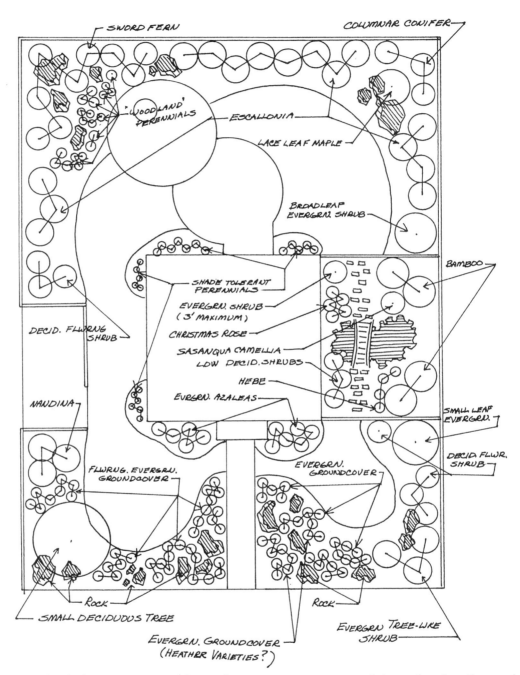

Draw in circles to represent plants, then go on a name search based on location and desired effect.

Shown is the yard not too long after planting. This design will hold up well over time.

the first pangs of phytophilia (plant lover's disease). There isn't enough room for all your favorites. But you *will* avoid overplanting and fruit salad, won't you? Name your circles, putting the evergreens in first—this will be what you see in the winter. It is "the backbone" of your yard. Also site your tall things, your trees, at the lot corners and build down. A deciduous tree can stand on its own in the middle of the yard too, especially if it has a nice branch pattern, interesting bark or flowers, or fall color. Fall color looks nice in front of a backdrop of dark needled evergreens, too. Deciduous plants are good to have because they screen you in the summer and keep things cool, but in the winter when you need more light, they let more in. You can even put them in front of windows for this reason.

Remember to plant shrubs and groundcovers in drifts. Plant in groups of threes and fives or repeat the same shrub. Plant low things next to walks and under windows and near doors. Plant tall columnar things in back, against tall walls without windows. Vary height, texture, and color. Put scented flowers near the path, scented leaves where you can snatch a leaf to crush under your nose. Don't put tall trees under power lines or broad trees on narrow parking strips where their branches get beaten by trucks or poke people in the nose. Messy trees don't belong over cars or patios. Don't plant anything prone to

diseases unless you can't live without that particular plant. Plant the shrubs on the side of your house and out quite a bit—there's no rain water under the eaves of your house. The shrubs will grow back to the wall in a year or two. When you site your plant, always look up. Will it get rain? Put special things near doors or where you look out windows.

SOME GENERALITIES

What follows is a list of a few generalities. There are exceptions to some of them, but they will help you assess plants off-hand.

1. Needled evergreens like the sun.
2. Gray things, especially gray fuzzy things, like sun.
3. Things with small leaves like the sun (big leaves like shade).
4. Flowers, especially deciduous flowering things, like the sun.
5. There are no shade plants that flower heavily.
6. Light colored or variegated (two-tone) things look good in the shade (but they do not necessarily *like* the shade).
7. It is almost impossible to grow other plants under needled evergreens. Let firs, spruces, and such grow to the ground for this reason.
8. Plants get better autumn color (such as red)

when a bit stressed and when there are sunny days and cold nights.

9. Trees get big.
10. Shrubs get bigger too.
11. Landscape architects recommend that you should have no more than seventeen different species or types of trees and shrubs in your yard (not counting groundcovers, bulbs, flowers).
12. The smaller the bed, the fewer different types of plants should be used. For example, use only three species in a 4-foot by 6-foot bed.

I also encourage you to leave some unfilled spaces or unnamed circles open on your map. This is not only because you will go broke if you try to do everything at once, but because you will surely fall in love with more rare and wonderful plants next year and you'll need a place to put them. Leave borders along the outside of beds for annual flowers, too. You will soon find out the truth about nurseries. Unlike supermarkets, all of which carry oranges at almost every time of year, your nurseries will only carry certain plants in certain seasons, and one may have a particular type of tree or shrub but not the other kind you want. That's why many people turn to catalog shopping. All this is hard on impulse, immediate-gratification types like myself. But you eventually get used to the enforced delays. And in the end you will enjoy browsing through your nursery to see what's new.

TRANSPORTING PLANTS

Now that you know pretty much the plants you want to get, you go to the nursery or nurseries and buy them. I suggest you be sure to get your trees in first, since they need the longest time to grow. If you are buying a lot from one nursery, they will deliver to your home for a small fee. If you have a pickup truck yourself and want to transport some things home, take steps to avoid desiccating (drying out) your plants. This is serious business. Plants can't handle fifty-five mile per hour winds blowing them around; the wind at that speed is also likely to break some limbs. Bundle the limbs of your tree together with twine or wrap the tree in burlap and lay it on its side; secure the pot so that it doesn't roll back and forth. Jam the rest of your pots in tightly together and towards the cab of the truck. There is

less wind just behind the cab. Invest in some Wilt-Pruf® or similar stuff that you spray on the leaves to keep them from drying out. Some say this liquid (anti-transpirant, anti-desiccant) is also useful if you're planting things in the summer, if you can't help planting in the summer.

When you get home, plant your plants as soon as you can. If you can't get them in the ground right away, keep them well watered (once a day) until they're planted. Keep them in the shade, together in bunches. If they're balled and burlapped, keep the roots buried (heeled-in) in sawdust or dirt. Many otherwise-good gardeners bring their plants home and leave them in pots for days. They're testing them, pushing them, seeing how much they can get away with. I call it the pot-requirement. Don't you do it.

ARRANGING PLANTS

When it comes time to plant, drag your plants over to where you think you want them and arrange them sitting on the ground in their pots. Stand back and imagine them full grown. The movie *Little Big Man* had a scene in it where the gunfighter showed the new guy how to shoot. He said you look at your target with "snake eyes" and imagine yourself shooting. "Snake eyes" is when you squint and everything gets sort of blurry, and you can more easily imagine with your mind's eye. I want you to look at your landscape with "snake eyes." That spindly little tree says it will get 50 feet tall. Imagine it through time, bigger, bigger, is it 50 feet yet? If you can't see it, go look at a neighbor's tree that's 50 feet tall. Now walk back and picture that tree there. Whoa! You'll have to move those other shrubs farther away to make it all fit. Use snake eyes on all your shrubs to make sure they're planted far enough apart. Also take the time to turn the best side out on your plants. Walk back and forth to see if everything fits together well. See to it that no major tree branches head into walls or out into the way of foot traffic.

Once everything checks out in all four dimensions, you may plant your shrubs. Mark the spot by pushing your shovel in where the pot was, so that you don't forget where your plant goes when you move it to take it out of its pot. Some people twist and push down their pots so they leave a ring on the dirt to mark the location to dig. When you plant a group

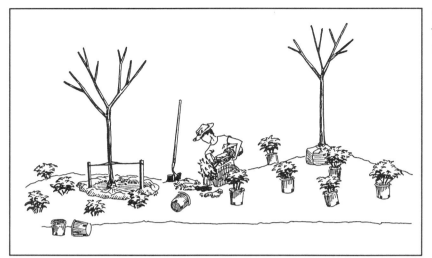

Be certain to arrange plants according to their mature size. Avoid the most common gardening error—overplanting.

This is the previous planting only a few years later.

of plants, start from the back or the inside and move out. When planted, the plants that looked so small and vulnerable before will now be about half their original size.

I have cautioned about overplanting. Some people choose to double plant and then remove some plants as they mature. But most people have a hard time removing (killing) plants, period, especially when things are just beginning to look good. But if you wait any longer, a big hole will be left when you finally must thin out crowded plants. Cultivating patience is a chore. Some people fill in spaces between tree-like shrubs with more understory plants that just get shaded out as major shrubs and trees mature. This is a better solution. I recently encouraged a yard owner to surround her new laceleaf maple with small-leaved heathers. As the maple grows she

can simply remove the heathers, which will then be in too much shade. Certain plants are much better than others for massing—planting too close together. These are not the shrubs with tree-like habits; they tend to be small-leaved mounds. The truth is, you'll probably plant a little too close now as a compromise and pay for it later. Gardens, after all, go through stages and must be artfully managed and planned wisely. A good garden manager can slow down the middle age of a garden's life, which is when it looks best, before things get too overgrown and need to be renovated.

THE NOTEBOOK

As you buy your plants, enter their names and locations in a notebook. This is your garden book. It goes with the house. Trust me, you will forget the names of things. And it will help you someday when a new young gardener marveling at your yard, looking for ideas for his or her yard asks, "What's that?"

SUMMARY

❏ Read and believe your plant tags.

❏ Critical information includes: size, sun/shade, and name—common and Latin.

❏ *Ultimate* height of a tree or shrub is about twice the mature height listed in books or on tags.

❏ Be careful that your new shrubs and trees do not dry out during transport or while waiting to be planted.

❏ Arrange plants according to how they will look in ten years. Set them where they will be planted while still in their pots and rearrange them until you achieve the look you want.

More Unheeded Advice

You should now have a map of how you want your yard to look and most, but not all, of the plant names determined. You should also have a fair idea of how to plant everything.

You have received the first of three always ignored, most important pieces of advice. This advice is to choose and place your plants according to their cultural requirements, especially mature size, light requirements, and soil requirements. Now that you've ignored those, let's get on to the other two, which are: *amend your soil* and *plan for irrigation*. As soon as you price these, you will be tempted to ignore them as well, if you haven't already.

IMPROVE YOUR SOIL

You should probably improve your soil now before everything is planted, and while you're considering building up mounded beds anyway. It's sort of a once in a lifetime opportunity to do it right. Very few people are blessed with a good, rich, sandy loam soil naturally in their yard. If you do have this or have inherited good soil from previous owners' obsessive use of compost, you should take some time to gloat in the knowledge that you are the envy of less lucky gardeners everywhere.

I would guess that 80% of the pests, disease, death, and general lack of good looks in gardens is due to bad soil, either too sandy or with too much clay. Sand doesn't hold nutrients and it dries out instantly, so plants starve and die of thirst. Clay soils alternately drown their victims when wet and bake them when dry. It's also hard for roots to push through packed clay. Clay additionally tortures gardeners by breaking their backs; it's so hard and heavy to dig, and it will increase the time and difficulty of weeding by at least threefold. The heavy clay soil has to be pried up or forked up, just to get

at the weed roots. The roots tend to break off, and the weed will rise again as soon as your back is turned. Or if you manage to get the whole root, you will get a giant mass of clay glop attached to it. Clay is the absolute bane of a gardener's life.

You solve both of these problems, clay or sand, by mixing in generous amounts of organic soil amendments. Organic, of course, means anything that used to be alive; for example, sawdust, bark, old moldy leaves, peat moss. *Compost* is, of course, the best. In addition, organic fertilizer, such as powdered dry chicken manure or steer manure, which you can buy in bags at a local supermarket or by truckloads from the nursery, is great. Blood meal and bone meal are also used. These additions not only improve the soil structure and texture, they will slowly release elements. Use these fertilizers along with organic amendments to improve the soil structure.

My former partner swears that powdered dry manure cures just about every garden ill from chlorosis to moles. I suspect she's right. The organics also encourage the natural web of organisms that combine to create a healthy, lovely yard. We will discuss these at greater length in the section on maintaining your yard. The "topsoil" you bought will still be woefully lacking in wonderful organics. The good old topsoil stripped from old farms is no longer available. They now build "topsoil" out of sawdust and poor dirt. It's better than clay or sand but many still refer to it by various epithets. These "store-bought" topsoils, as well as bark and sawdust mulches, will actually rob your soil of nitrogen as they decompose for a few years, so be sure to add some fertilizer, organic or chemical, every year. If you have a layer of *very* clayish soil, called *hardpan*, you should forget mixing in amendments and just build raised beds of good soil above it. To see if you have hardpan, try digging a hole. If you have to jump on your shovel with both feet to get it in, you are in deep trouble. To see if you have a drainage problem, dig a hole and fill it with water. If it takes a day to drain—more bad news. Perhaps you want to design and build a "bog" garden. Seriously.

If you buy "soil" from the landscape supply company,consider turning in generous amounts of organic matter and composted manure. Your plants will love you for it. It is said that when the gardener enters Paradise, the first thing he says is, "Ah! Just smell that humus!"

PLAN FOR IRRIGATION

The other always ignored, most important piece of gardening advice is to plan for irrigation. I ignored this one and I'm so tired of dragging hoses around my yard I could give up and die. Hoses look ugly, especially in summer barbecue pictures; you have to move them to mow every week; and you have to put them away in the winter. I know of a humorous description of a man battling with a hose like a giant snake. It's said that an elephant hasn't a memory to compare with that of a coiled hose.

Here in western Washington folks say, "But it rains here all the time. Anyway, I can water the whole lawn with just one sprinkler." This reveals two common misconceptions. One is that only lawns need water. Shrubs and trees need water, too. It just takes longer for them to brown up from drought than grass does. Whereas grass can green up again in the fall rains, your pieris won't; it will be brown and dead for good. Lack of water usually stresses plants and it takes several stresses over time to kill,

but just a few will make your new shrub prone to leaf drop, disease, freezing, you name it! I, who usually am pretty good about watering, watered even more last year to encourage my bedding annuals to grow and be beautiful in time for my wedding. I was shocked to see how much better everything else did, too. It was magical. People just don't believe the difference good, deep, regular watering makes to the *looks* of plants.

The other misconception is that it rains in western Washington all the time. Statistics *prove* that a one-month drought is the norm in this region. We call it summer. It will cause lots of hardship on trees and plants. This is, incidentally, the season residents of this area are vacationing, not dragging hoses around. An automatic or semi-automatic irrigation system will solve your problems. And you won't have to roll it up and hide it for the barbecue, either.

Now that we know the three pieces of essential advice and can ignore them, we can go on to the nuts and bolts of planting your yard.

SUMMARY

The three pieces of most-ignored, best garden advice:

❏ Meet your plant's requirements: mature size, light, and soil needs.

❏ Improve the soil with organics or truck in new soil.

❏ Put in automatic irrigation.

Installation How-tos and Tricks

By now you have a map of how and where and what you want everything to be. You also possess the three great unheeded pieces of gardening advice. Now we can go on to plant everything.

The first tip is the work party. It's a great invention. You invite all your friends and their wheelbarrows over and provide food and drink. It's especially important to tap the goodwill of your friends if you intend to wheelbarrow in 15 yards of soil, mix it with 8 yards of manure, and shape it into tastefully mounded beds.

Perhaps you have had one friend take out the dead tree one weekend, and the next weekend the work party digs sod, pushes dirt, loads up branches, and hauls out old shrubs with chain and truck. You may find that, after you have removed the sod and unwanted plants and structures, you can visualize more easily. This is because you have created the blank canvas on which to paint the picture of your yard. If new ideas or desires arise, don't be afraid to change your plan. You shape your beds (the pros come in before and after to put in patio, fences, retaining walls, irrigation, and tasteful big rocks). The approved order of events has you planting your plants, biggest first. Then put in irrigation so that the lawn is watered separately from shrubs and the irrigation heads are correctly placed, not blasting into the trunk of a tree or something. Then put in the lawn (if you're doing that). Then mulch your beds.

SMALL CONSTRUCTION

In your effort to fight gravity with terracing, or in order to build up some tasteful mounded beds, it may be necessary to make walls. If your wall is over 3 feet, have a professional do it. Be sure he or she accounts for drainage so that water doesn't build up

behind the wall or the weight of dirt pull it over. An easy small wall or terrace can be made out of the chunks of broken concrete left over from where you took out the old paths. When you go to stack them, be sure to stagger them and tilt them slightly toward the dirt-filled side. In this way, the wall will catch water and let it down between the stones. You will have made a "dry wall" suitable for planting with wonderful plants like wallflowers and alpines. Or you can plant groundcovers to flow over the wall from the bed above. Avoid straight lines—your house has enough of those.

Other walls can be created from railroad ties or what are called "landscape timbers." Stack them also in a staggered pattern, like bricks. Attach them to each other and to the ground with spikes. A spike can be made of ½-inch rebar or with old pipe. Your plumbing shop or lumber store can cut the pieces for you. Drill a hole through your timbers with a super long drill bit (called a ship's auger) the same size as the spikes. Or, to do it the hard way, you can try to pound pipe on either side of your timbers. You use a sledge hammer for this exercise. And believe me—it's exercise. You can also use timbers to define areas. Bury them so that they stick up only an inch or two, just a bit above the grass blades.

Between the shrub bed and the grass you should just leave an empty space. People often edge their beds with bricks or wood strips called bender board, or with plastic strips. These never seem to work well. I do believe in hard borders elsewhere: for example, sunken timbers between your shrubbery and your neighbor's grass, or between your grass and your gravel driveway. They make things look tidier and then the areas are easier to maintain. The tool to use for digging your timber trench in clay, or for any hard digging, is the mattock. The sheer weight of it allows you to cut through hardpan. The vertical blade on the other end is designed to slice through roots, if you're cutting out a plant.

You can also use ties or timbers as steps. Make your outdoor steps very long if you can, and wide too. Use pipe or rebar to hold them. Fill in with dirt or crushed rock behind. While working for the Parks Department we actually bolted two ties together (using all-thread cut off with hacksaws and counter-sunk) and stacked them on top of each other.

Railroad ties used to be cheap. Not so any more. Creosote, that black stuff, is what they use to treat the wood so that it won't rot—at least not for a long time. But creosote is nasty stuff. It's murder on the chain saw blade. And it oozes sticky stuff in the summer, which is not nice to sit on, and it gums up your shoes. The alternative—landscape timbers— should be treated with preservatives to keep them from rotting out quickly (all wood in dirt rots even-tually). But be careful, a common lumber preser-vative—pentachlorophenol—is death on plants.

PATHS

If you decide to make paths, you can use materials such as bark or crushed rock. Crushed rock is not gravel. Gravel is whole rocks. Crushed rock is crushed, it's flatter; it packs down and is easier to walk on. The size of crushed rock is measured by its biggest pieces: ³/₄ inch minus means the biggest pieces are ³/₄ inch long and "minus" are the ones that are smaller. "Fines" means fine particles. It's good to have a lot of fines to pack down. I avoid "pea gravel," which is little round pea-sized rocks, because it rolls into beds and smashes down when you walk on it. I never use it near concrete. It's like having a pile of marbles nearby, and it could cause a nasty fall. When you make a path, you use your square point shovel, scooted flat to make it level, but not quite level. You want the water to run off to the sides, so make a slight hump in the middle of the path. Rake your path a lot with the hard rake to get out big rocks, and with the fan rake to make it smooth. When you put down your covering mate-rial, rake it back and forth, back and forth with these rakes, using them upside down. In fact, I find that I'm using my rakes upside down to level mate-rial more often than I'm using them right side up to rake out debris. Then fill up the rented roller with

water to make it heavy and flatten your path. We're having some fun now.

If you're using stepping stones, lay them in a flat trench of sand and fill in around them. Be sure to make the trench level high enough so the grass blades will grow up ³/₄ inch to meet the top of the stones, not go over them.

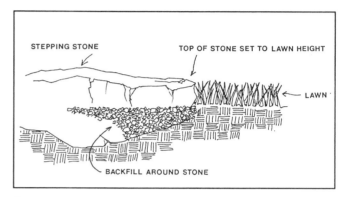

A common error when laying stepping stones is placing them level with the soil. Then the grass grows up and buries the stones. Proper placement shown here allows for the turf to grow up to meet the stones.

SOME ROTTEN ADVICE

When seeking advice on how to plant your trees and shrubs, you will run across several great gar-dener's misconceptions still advanced by profes-sionals who should know better.

1. *Amend the backfill* is a common admonition but a wrong one. It means adding good soil or peat moss or something else to the planting hole you just dug for your new plant. You wouldn't even be tempted to do this if you had followed earlier good advice to amend the entire yard with good soil and manure. But research has shown that plants' roots like to stay in the nice soft dirt they grew in, in their pots, so instead of reaching out and getting firmly established in the cold cruel world of native soil in your yard, they will just circle around in a tangled mess looking "pot bound." An amended planting hole works the same way. And thus, they never really take off. Still pot-bound trees fall over in winds, and still pot-bound plants die easily. As a gardener, I of-ten take out dead plants whose roots are in the

characteristic shape of the pot they came out of two years ago.

Do not amend the backfill because it causes uneven irrigation. It is difficult for water to pass between *layers of unlike soils,* and it makes no difference what order (clay over sand, sand over rocks) they are in. Yes, I know this is hard to believe, but it's true.

To repeat this crucial information: even if you have a layer of sand over a layer of pebbles, water poured on top will finish filling up the sand area before it begins to drop down to the pebbles. The pebbles do not enhance drainage. So when you amend your backfill in the planting hole, you have created a second barrier or difficult interface for both plant roots and water to overcome. No matter what you add to the soil in the hole, you will create uneven moisture on either side of the interface and the roots won't like it.

It is quite desirable, on the other hand, to just break up the soil to soften it for your new plant's roots. To loosen soil, you use your shovel or bash the dirt clumps with it or your garden fork. On very hard clay soil, use the mattock.

The phenomenon of "roots staying in the pot" is the reason for a good practice of cutting off already circling roots and of scratching up the sides of a root ball. In the case of very, very clay-like root balls, it is sometimes considered advantageous to split the ball base and spread the roots out in butterfly fashion.

2. Along the same line as "amend the backfill" is the very common notion that it's okay to *leave things wrapped* in burlap, and leave trees in wire baskets. Mostly this idea is promoted by landscape installers who know that otherwise it would add to their planting time to unwrap everything. Burlap is just another barrier for your plant to overcome, even if it does rot in time. And a root might not be strangled by a wire basket until ten years later when it becomes the same diameter as the wire hole. The mechanized digging of plants has made life easier for nurserymen, but perhaps not for the plants. The wire baskets that some of these nursery trees come in will be impossible to get off. If you have them, use bolt or wire cutters and at least cut

the wire. On wrapped root balls, take off the plastic ties around the trunk and remove the burlap. An exception I've found is plants dug in the wild, with small, barely held-together root balls, which might be endangered by removing the burlap. In this case it's okay to leave it on. Just untie the top and peel it back a bit.

3. Another common bit of rotten advice is to *cut back the top growth of your new tree to balance the lost roots* from when your plant was dug. Some nurserymen and landscapers still say you should cut back all the tips. (Plants are either grown in pots, dug from dirt and wrapped in burlap "B&B," or sold without dirt at all—"bare root.") Recent research shows that plants do better if the leaf area is left on; they use their leaves to make the energy for new root growth. They need their branch tips to send grow messages to the roots. If some branches die back next year, cut them off then, not now. Let the plant be your guide. You can, if you like, do some minor necessary pruning as described in previous chapters, and to remove broken branches resulting from the transplant move. After all, you have the perfect opportunity as you are now handling the plant. But avoid pruning "to balance with root loss," especially by using heading cuts.

You may also be interested to hear that plants bought small and established early in their lives will later catch up to and out-strip plants that were bought big. I didn't believe this one either—being the immediate gratification type. But I've seen the waste of my money as the inexpensive tiny trees I bought seven years ago presently outstrip the expensive "specimen" trees on the other side of the yard.

4. Another common gardening mistake is heeding advice to *stake plants, especially trees, "very securely".* Research has shown that *less* is better. It may be necessary for some little saplings to have help so as not to fall over in the wind until their roots take hold. It has been proven, however, that plants grown to rely on stakes will topple over in that big wind 10, 20, or 50 years later, when the same plant, left on its own, won't. It is the waving in the wind that sends the message

to the plant to put on thicker trunk and more roots. So stake your plant gently about one-third of the way up, between two stakes, using two figure-eight ties (don't use straight wire); rubber straps are good, so that the tree can wobble in the wind a bit. Big trees with big, heavy root balls that you would find difficult to push over yourself don't generally need any staking help. The practice of staking is left over from when most plants were sold "bare root," that is, without any dirt on their roots. They had to be staked.

You will remember to untie your tree from the stakes as soon as possible, in one year at the longest, we hope. Ties left on trees will strangle (girdle) them, causing disfigurement and sometimes top death. You may leave the stakes themselves in if you choose to protect the young tree from car bumpers and they seem to have some deterrent effect, psychologically, on vandals who like to snap saplings in half. Do remember to remove the stakes too, eventually. Arborists frequently find stakes embedded in old trees they are cutting down. It is like finding the forceps sewn up in a surgery patient.

THE NICEST THING TO DO

The nicest thing you can do for your new plants is WATER, WATER, WATER. Soak them as soon as you get them planted. Minutes count! Then water them a lot for the first year. Remember not to work or compress wet soil. Tamp the soil down before you soak it. If you dig or work water-soaked soil, you will destroy its structure, making it something akin to concrete once it dries out. (I like to put the hose on at a bare trickle and prop it on the trunk for thirty minutes to an hour, once every other day for a week.) Water *deeply, gently.* Then water once a week for a month. And always water during a drought. It is more important to water long and deep than frequently. Long and deep watering encourages deep root development, which is good in times of drought. Also there is a phenomenon called "surface tension." Surface tension means that although the top layer of soil seems wet, the soil just underneath is powder dry. It will actually repel water sending it off trickling down the street while the roots dry out. It's the same phenomenon that keeps

a glop of cocoa dry on the bottom of your cup, or floating on top. You must put on A LOT of water to break "surface tension" in the summer. Sometimes two hours or more of water are needed. Test this out by digging down an inch or two to see if the soil is damp down past the mulch layer. This is the only safe way to determine whether or not your plant is getting watered.

Remember when planting to take the time to turn your plant to show off its good side. If it doesn't look right where you planted it after you step back, dig it up and move it. It's like arranging the furniture, but the plant will be in that spot a lot longer than a chair, so take the time and trouble to do it right. Remember how big the plants get, as you space them.

PLANTING TREES AND CARRYING THINGS

What about that big tree you picked out at the nursery that is being delivered tomorrow? Well, have truck access to where you want the tree to go (you remembered to do this), dig a big hole where you want to plant ahead of time, and invite your brother-in-law over to help. Dig the hole deeper and larger than you think you'll need. You can always raise the big tree by rocking it and shoveling in more dirt. It's difficult, maybe impossible, to get it back out to dig the hole deeper. Have the driver back over to the hole and plop it in, or slide it down on a board. If a truck can't get there, use a long pole to lever it over. If it's a smaller plant, you can use a dolly or drag it on a tarp. Take your time. A smart thing to do is to take a moment to spin your tree so that a main branch is not headed into the pathway or a window.

An interesting Japanese practice is to plant a young sapling at an angle; I know it looks funny at first. But the top will right itself naturally, after which you will be left with an interesting, curvaceous trunk that your kid can climb.

Don't break your back carrying heavy plants and pots around. Use a wheelbarrow (or a dolly is sometimes easier because you don't have to lift up), or a tarp on a wheelbarrow, or use your little pickup truck—go ahead and drive on the grass, it's okay.

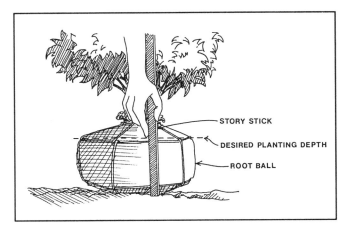

Before planting, use a story stick to measure the size of the rootball.

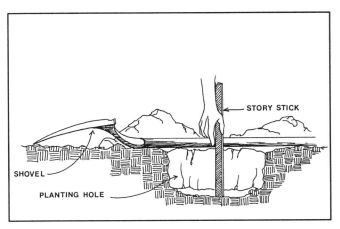

With the story stick, check to see if the planting hole is deep enough.

It's easy to fix a lawn but hard to repair your back. If your wheelbarrow sinks, lay down boards to where you want to go. Professionals will sometimes carry a heavy pot on a piece of flat fire hose held between two people. It's useful to tie your gates open for the day, too.

PLANTING TIPS

When you plant, be sure to wear your holster with a pair of hand pruners in it and have a root scratcher —a claw-like hand tool—also. Use the pruner to cut off circling roots and burlap ties on root balls. Use the scratcher to scratch up roots along the root ball so they will interface readily with the new soil. Don't ever PULL your plant out of the pot by its trunk. NEVER, NEVER, NEVER. You will rip off all the most important rootlets from the root ball. Turn the pot over, even if it's a big one, and let gravity pull it out. If you have to, cut off the plastic pot or metal can (use rented tin snips). Root-bound plants can also be helped out of their pots by using a long knife to slice roots from the side of the pot. For small (4 inch) pots, a vigorous whack of the bottom of the upturned plant with your trowel will pop it out. A surefire way to get a plant out of its pot is to turn the pot over and tap its rim on anything hard, a nearby rock or window ledge will do. That tough clinging plant will fall out as if by magic. If it's very big, be sure you have a friend ready to catch it.

As you fill in the planting hole, stomp or compress it firmly with your hand or foot, or tamp it down by pushing your shovel handle repeatedly down into soft soil. Use water to settle the fluffy dirt at the end. Remember to wait until the water is totally drained out before adding more soil. Make a dirt rim or "saucer" around your plant, so that when you water it fills up and will soak your new plant and not run off. This level saucer is especially important on slopes so water doesn't just run off down the hill. Be sure to remove this saucer in a year, though. If you wish, you may add a light (low-numbers) fertilizer in the planting hole or on top. My husband always admonishes the new plant to "grow and do well" before he moves on.

STORY STICK

When you are digging a hole for a shrub or tree, measure the depth of its root ball with your shovel handle. Walk over to your hole and see if it's deep enough. Sometimes you need to lay a tool handle across the hole's surface to get a fix on how deep your hole is. Using your handle or anything like this is called using a "story stick." It tells the story of how deep to go.

Do not be surprised to find that even though you put something big in the hole, you do not have enough dirt to fill it back up. Where did the extra dirt go? Nobody knows. It's a gardening mystery. You can make things go better and cleaner if you take the time to put a tarp on the ground under your dirt pile from the hole. Better yet, have a tarp for each side. Then when you backfill and you get down to the bottom of the dirt, you can just dump it back into the hole and your grass looks fresh as a lawn daisy. Here again, you can check the level of your plant against the soil level by running a board or tool handle across the hole. Be sure the cross stick is on the real ground and not on the dirt piles. Don't plant too low or too high. Bury it at the same level as before. This is very important. Burying a tree or shrub just inches too low can kill it. The ill effect of planting too deep may not be seen for fifteen years for a tree.

MULCH

Now that all your plants are in and they look too small and too far apart, and you are broke, I want you to spend more money. Yes, I do. It's very important to *mulch your beds*. This may be the fourth most ignored bit of essential gardening advice. You need 2 to 3 inches of mulch over all your shrub beds—now, not next year. A manure-based, weed-free compost is good. Mulching will cut your weeding time in half. This time is not such a big dent in your life this year, but weeds increase exponentially; next year, I promise, you will break down and mulch if you don't take this advice now. So save 50% of the weeding you would have to do next year, and mulch now. Think of it this way. Next spring you can either spend a morning weeding on Saturday, or you can spend Saturday morning and afternoon and Sunday morning. Got the picture? Mulch now.

SHRUB BED CREATION

When you have decided where your new beds are going to be, you may wish to kill the grass by spraying it with glyphosate (trade name Roundup™). Just spray the grass inside the rope boundary on a sunny day and wait for it to brown out in two or three weeks. Then you can easily dig it up or rototill it into the existing soil or just bury it with 6 inches to a foot of topsoil. Roundup will not leave a toxic soil residue. Dead turf isn't nearly the bear to work with that live turf is. If you hate chemicals, even Roundup, you can rent a tool called a sod cutter. It will cut your sod out like a roll of carpet. Be sure to put it on the deep setting, so as not to leave roots that would come up in your new beds.

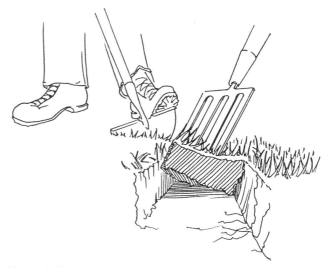

Use a half-moon edger and garden fork to edge the shrub beds. The edge should be 1½ to 2 inches deep and 2 to 3 inches wide.

To rent sod cutters, rototillers, stump grinders, and the like, you need to borrow (1) a pickup truck; (2) a strong back or two; (3) some long boards to use as ramps. Don't be scared. The nice man at the rental shop will show you how to operate these machines and give you a can of mixed gas to go with them. He will load and unload them for you at the shop. These machines are really not so difficult, they are just new to you, and they are noisy. Ear protection helps make them seem less intimidating.

As you prepare your dead grass area to become a shrub bed, you will want to use the half-moon edger. Use it to cut the border between the grass and the bed. Or perhaps you prefer a power edger. Getting a nice curved or even a straight shrub bed line is not as easy as you might think. People run string between two stakes or screwdrivers to indicate a straight edge. For curved lines, use loose rope or just eyeball it. If you've previously sprayed with Roundup, you simply follow the brown-green border. A half-moon edger slices more easily into semi-moist ground. If it's summer, it is wise to soak the lawn thoroughly a day before. When you slice along the line, try to use just one foot and scoot the blade along without ever lifting it up totally from the ground. Slice along the entire line first, then go back to cut the turf into bite-sized pieces. Then pry the pieces out with your spading fork. Make a *big* trench between the grass and the bed—as much as 2

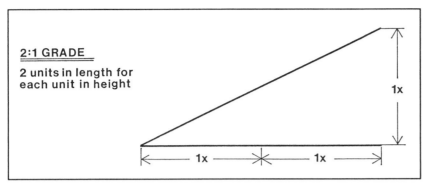

2:1 GRADE

2 units in length for
each unit in height

Avoid building slopes steeper than two to
one. They will be difficult to mow if the
area is lawn. If it is a bed area, it will be
prone to erosion problems.

to 4 inches deep and wide. This will help keep the grass from encroaching into your beds. Do this before the store-bought soil arrives, even though you may have to fill some spots back in to give yourself wheelbarrow access.

ORDERING SOIL AND OTHER LANDSCAPE MATERIALS

It can be very traumatic, also very exciting, putting in a real landscape, especially if you do your hardscape all at once. The work party has removed all the structures and plants designated for destruction or as gifts to friends. And perhaps you have dug up shrubs that you intend to replant once the grade has been changed. (They should be "heeled in," that is, temporarily planted, in some soil or sawdust in a shady area. Don't forget to keep them moist.) You have the outline of your beds dug. Now comes the soil and composted manure, perhaps, if you've decided to amend your soil or build up mounded beds. There is nothing quite as thrilling as the sound of the big truck when the soil arrives. But first you will need to know how much to order. You order dirt and bark from nurseries or other places that carry these items. In my phone book it's under "Bark," and some under "Landscape Materials." These materials are measured in "yards," which is shorthand for cubic yards or 3' x 3' x 3'. My ³/₄-ton pickup holds 3 yards of mulch with my side boards on. It's pretty light stuff, though. My truck couldn't hold 3 yards of soil. To estimate the amount of soil or mulch you want to order, pace off your beds to find out how big they are. I know they are not square, so just rearrange them in your mind's eye until they are. Then pace it off. My pace is 3 feet. Then multiply the width, the length, and the height to find out

how many cubic feet you have. Divide by 27 (3 x 3 x 3) to get the number of cubic yards. An average mounded bed is a foot high (or sometimes 6 to 8 inches), depending on how wide it is. Try to avoid slopes of more than two to one. They erode and/or are hard to mow.

For mulch I use these figures: 1 yard will cover 160 square feet to a depth of 2 inches, or 1 yard of material will cover about 110 square feet 3 inches deep. One yard only covers 80 square feet at 4 inches. If you order soil for making beds, you can figure that 1 yard of soil will cover 27 square feet to 12 inches deep.

DELIVERED DIRT

As for your store-bought soil, have the truck driver get as close as possible to where it's going. It's okay to drive over grass as long as it's not so soggy that the truck will get stuck. Even if the driver leaves some ruts, these are quicker and easier to fill in and overseed than it is to wheelbarrow yards and yards and yards of soil. A good driver can raise the truck bed and zoom off leaving the dirt spread out, or he or she can leave it in a big pile if you prefer. Your driver can also "split" the load, leaving half in front of the house and half in back. It's sort of a challenge to dump just the right amount. Be sure to ask nicely. If you can't get the soil exactly where it's meant to go, just put it as close as you can. If you put a big tarp under a pile of soil, it will be a help toward the end of the job. Simply lift up the tarp ends to force the scattered bits into a nice, big, easy-to-shovel pile in the center.

To move soil and other material, you use wheelbarrows. If the ground is muddy, or if you need to go down stairs or up curbs, use boards to run the wheelbarrow over. If you can't get a wheelbarrow into the site, carry soil in plastic 5-gallon buckets, the kind spackle or paint come in. Second best for toting is the use of tarps slung over your back. On a big bucket hauling job it helps to hum the theme of the "Sorcerer's Apprentice" and sometimes the work song of the flying monkeys from *The Wizard of Oz*. Local teenagers are a good resource for dirt hauling projects. They have been allocated an unfair amount of the world's human energy resources. Use them to your advantage.

Where I live, the big sawdust company will send out a machine with a long, long tube to "blow" on bark mulch. It takes two people. It's fast. It's easy. It's not cheaper, though. And it won't blow sawdust because the particles are too fine. It is great for hills and rockeries.

When you spread your soil, start at the back and move forward, just like painting a floor. Finish up using your hard rake to make things smooth and even. You may wish to do what I call "the Bristol stomp," stepping repeatedly to pack down places that are too high and to compact the soft edges of your beds. Or you can just let the rain settle the dirt for you.

To mix soil and manure or soil and other organic amendments, you can use a rototiller or, to go deep, dig with a shovel or a spading fork. There is also a method called *double digging* that the British invented. It starts with a trench. Next to it you dig out another row of dirt and mix it with "amendments" like manure, leaves, or compost, and fill in the first trench. This leaves empty the area you just excavated. You repeat with the next bit of land. When you're through, you have an empty trench to be filled with a pile of dirt clear back where you started. Sounds like hard work? It is.

I just thought you'd want to know the depths to which some people will stoop to ensure a beautiful garden. I just build mounded beds on top of existing soil or herbicided sod.

SUMMARY

❑ Throw a work party to clean out your old yard and spread new soil in a short time.

❑ You can make small walls, paths, and steps yourself.

When planting:

❑ DO NOT amend the backfill of your planting hole.

❑ DO NOT cut the tops off your new trees when planting them to compensate for root loss.

❑ When staking trees—less is better.

❑ DO take off all ties and burlap.

❑ DO WATER, WATER, WATER.

❑ DO make sure your plants will not stay "pot-bound" in the ground—ruffle the roots.

❑ DO mulch the soil surface.

❑ DO amend the soil (not just the hole) with manure or compost.

❑ DO break up tough clay soils with shovel and mattock, but DO NOT attempt to work such soils when they are wet.

PART IV
MAINTAINING YOUR YARD

Taking Care of Your Yard

Maintaining your yard takes work—cursed work. As a professional gardener, my cohorts and I cringe at the customer's request for a low-maintenance yard. A "low-maintenance" yard is either the deep woods or a concrete lawn. Gardens are, by their very nature, living, moving, growing, changing systems. Once you decide which plants you want and which you don't (one definition of a weed being anything in the wrong place), you have drawn the battle lines.

Dandelions, blackberries, morning glories (bindweed)—these are the enemy. Grass, mountain laurel, Shasta daisies, these are the innocents to be protected, nourished, enjoyed. And even some of these can become the enemy if found in the wrong place: grass in the lawn is good, grass in the shrub bed is a weed.

Daisies may be fine unless they overcome their neighbors in the perennial border. I can always count on the fact that the same customer who wants the low-maintenance yard will, in the very next breath, ask for a perennial bed—the epitome of high-maintenance landscaping.

LIFE IS MAINTENANCE

Without maintenance, the universe, the entire universe, succumbs to the third law of physics—entropy. This law states that everything that *is*, is falling apart. I'm sure you've noticed. In fact, with a few notable exceptions, LIFE is MAINTENANCE. Your body, its cells and molecules, is in constant change and motion, but it is maintaining a reasonable sameness over time—albeit more wrinkled and tired. Work is maintenance. We maintain the house, the car, the boat. Even on vacation we try to maintain perfect comfort and peace, or we maintain the level of activity we call fun. Too much is stress; too little, boredom.

The maintenance work in your yard can be kept at a minimum. When I went into the gardening business, the best advice I got was, "Don't work hard, work smart."

The good news is that by being smart you can reduce garden work to a manageable minimum that is not too physically taxing. Like the dentist, the professional gardener strives to put himself or herself almost out of business—leaving only regular brushing, flossing, and checkups. In this section we will go over the smart ways to beat weeds, to water, and to fertilize your plants and the strategies and philosophies behind pest control.

You know many of these already. A well-planned yard—one that takes into account the mature size of plants—takes more patience but less pruning work. Using selective pruning is wise because, unlike shearing and other forms of "bad" pruning, it stays done longer, although it takes greater initial investment in learning how to do it. You eliminate the need to "weedwhack" when fences, trees, and lamp posts are surrounded or bordered by shrub beds, not turf.

Automatic or semi-automatic irrigation will save you from most of the drudgery of watering by hand. And mulch will cut your weeding time and effort by half or more. The combination of sufficient water, smart plant choices, and good soil will give you the healthy plants that resist most pests and diseases. No huge pesticide or plant replacement costs here.

In gardening, as in taking care of your teeth, you avoid those big, painful, costly fixups by adhering to a strict preventive maintenance routine. Weeding (which comes in after mowing, trimming, and edging in actual maintenance hours spent) is the same way. Whereas all gardening teaches patience, weeding actually instills vigilance, humility, and tenacity.

GARDENING IS AN UNNATURAL ACT

Weeding can be as much of a challenge as any well-matched contest. Many people think of it as un-skilled labor; most people are distressed by the fact that, like housework, it won't stay done. But weeding is skilled work. You need to know your enemy, the weeds: their types and their strategies for surviving in your beautiful garden. Then it becomes a game of strength, stamina, and wits. Each month is a rematch, and your gratification can be to vanquish the opponent faster and with less effort each time. You can never, however, defeat the opponent utterly and completely. As gardeners, we are imposing a halt on the natural succession of plants in the backyard. The fittest will always succeed in crowding out and overpowering our less vigorous ornamental plants if we choose to cease our intervention. Gardening is an unnatural act. Because, you see, we are endeavoring to construct a false plant community and then we keep it from changing according to the laws of natural succession by weeding and pruning. Furthermore, we rake out leaves, and then (silly us) have to add fertilizer and mulch to make up for it. And weeds are, themselves, strangely enough, created by humans.

Weeds generally do not exist in old, long established plant communities. In these old ecologies we find that plants have just divided things up fairly and in a balanced fashion—they demonstrate an interlocking harmony that inspires awe in those humans who glimpse the incredible interwovenness of nature.

But those pioneering, greedy, tenacious species we call weeds follow only receding glaciers, landslides, and humans. They like disturbed soil. Most weeds in North America came from Europe, stowaways in the hulls of ships, as seeds in dirt ballast. Others were foolishly imported by heedless Pandoras who brought them over for sentimental reminders of home. These plants, well behaved in their natural habitat, run unchecked through new ecosystems, displacing and destroying the balance of centuries because their natural population checks were left behind.

Kudzu in the southern United States is a famous example. It is a vine that was imported from the Orient to help curb erosion. It took off immediately, infesting farmland and countryside alike.

People make jokes about kudzu vines strangling them in the night and burying lazy dogs. So successful is this plant in its new home that, whereas the "climax" ecology of the Southern states was once a forest, the land left to its own battle now will end up as monotonous flat fields of kudzu alone.

Ralph Waldo Emerson said, "A weed is a plant whose virtue has yet to be discovered." But gardeners know that beyond this notion is weeds' staying power, their ability to defy eradication, and their propensity to overcome their neighbors. They eliminate the variety and the diversity in the garden that is the essence of its beauty.

All gardeners become philosophical after awhile, and most come to a quiet understanding that our own creative, intelligent, magnificent species, Homo sapiens, is in the truest sense a "weed"—or pest species, the most dangerous weed on the planet. Humans out-compete almost all other species. We even eliminate total ecosystems. We reduce the bio-diversity of nature, cultivating instead for sameness, threatening to create a world filled with exact replicas: cornfields, white chickens, brown cows, and one kind of tomato. Some say that intelligence was an experiment in nature that didn't work. At what point did Homo sapiens cease being simply "vigorous" and become "invasive"?

The natural checks of our population—disease and war—have not been successful, nor have we, in keeping the population within manageable bounds.

But back to the weeds that intend to overpopulate your miniature world. The mistake most people make is that they take weeds personally. They are personally offended that these plants are trying to take over and won't go away. I take weeding seriously but not personally. It's a game. I decide who the good guys and the bad guys are and the object of the game. Nothing stays done in this life and nothing stays the same—especially gardens. So, with that understanding, weeding then becomes something to do, not something to get done. It is while weeding that you gain the intimacy with your garden that bonds you to nature. Because you have to be out there, crawling around on hands and knees (humility being the lesson here), you are forced to feel, smell, and touch nature. There are, for example, many plants whose leaves smell if you brush

Many fragrant and small delights are missed by people with dull gardens or those who have the work done for them.

them, and only because you are out there weeding will you discover this. And many fragrant and small delights and wonderments are missed by people with dull gardens or who have their work done for them.

SUMMARY

The smartest ways to reduce maintenance costs:

- ❑ Plan for mature size of shrubs and trees.
- ❑ Prune selectively; don't shear.
- ❑ Reduce grass-trimming time by designing beds (not lawn) around structures.
- ❑ Install automatic irrigation.
- ❑ Have good soil and good drainage, and eliminate steep slopes.
- ❑ Choose appropriate plants for the site.

Weeds: Hand-to-hand Combat

Weeds, weeds, weeds! I love some of their names. They sound so much like the ingredients in the witches' brew or the lady of the castle's sachet:

Fiddleneck	Madwort
Common lamb's quarters	Shepherd's purse
Tumble mustard	Catchweed bedstraw
Pigweed	Mayweed
Witch grass	Heal-all
Henbit	Toadrush
Prickly lettuce	Bouncing bet
Lady's thumb	Green foxtail
Spotted cat's-ear	Goldenrod
Wild oats	Smartweed
Dodder	Toadflax

I am not as amused by the colorful names of more familiar weeds in my region—horsetail, morning glory, chickweed, fireweed, shot weed, and nightshade. Weeds vary in species according to climate, zone, and geographical area. But all weeds of all areas share one or more familiar strategies to overcome your yard. When you understand their plans, you can best choose your tactics and tools.

Most weeds are one of three types: annual, herbaceous perennial, or woody perennial.

ANNUAL WEEDS

Many annual weeds are small plants in such large numbers that they form a mat like chickweed or shot weed. Others can grow quite tall—pigweed, lamb's quarters, and prickly lettuce. These annuals have shallow roots and are generally easy to pull or hoe out of the ground. But watch out! These easy weeds make up for their puniness by reproducing quickly. I schedule my visits to clients' yards for once a month, because this is all the time it takes for these tiny villains to germinate, grow up, set flowers, and—egad—go to seed! And watch the seeds, for *one* plant can number its seeds in the hundreds, some even in the many thousands! For example, pigweed numbers 117,400 seeds to a plant and shepherd's purse, 36,000 seeds to a plant: each one a potential new plant to plague you next month. The new homeowner or yard owner is often gratified after weeding the garden plot just outside the front door, because it was so painless and looks so clean. The same owner is discouraged to find the exact same mat of thick weeds reappear in but one month's time. Using chemical contact sprays like Roundup (glyphosate) to try to control annuals is silly. Seedlings will soon replace their dead parents. Besides, it's like using a chain saw to cut butter.

USING MULCH TO CONTROL WEEDS

The cure? Mulch. Mulch is both a verb and a noun. One mulches with mulch. When you mulch, you are covering the soil with a layer of material. This material—called mulch—can be rocks, peanut shells, straw, shredded newspapers, bark, sawdust, leaves—you name it. You use mulch to smother germinating weed seeds or keep them from "seeing" daylight and thus prevent germination.

My clients think of me as a steer manure compost junkie. The mulch I use is made of one-third steer manure and two-thirds sawdust composted for eight months. The fact that it is "hot-composted" means that any weed seeds it may have contained have been destroyed.

There are things you should know about mulch. It helps your soil retain water, but it takes extra irrigation to get the water down to the soil. Often times the homeowner will water the mulched beds for fifteen minutes to an hour—it looks good and wet, but wait, the shrubs are wilting. You must water a lot longer to get that water down to the plants' roots.

To be sure, dig down with your finger. Is the soil moist at the roots? If the answer is yes, then you have watered enough.

Not only does mulch retain water, smother tiny weeds and weed seeds, and make it easy to pull new weeds, it is also harder for new wind-borne weed seeds to get a foothold.

Mulch can be spread anywhere from 1 inch to 4 inches thick. The thicker it is, the more effective and longer lasting. Spread it thick in big empty spaces. Spread it thin around the root zones of shrubs to allow for sufficient air exchange, especially around shallow-rooted plants like azaleas and rhododendrons. And never let mulch stay mounded up in the base or the "crown" of a plant. It can cause crown rot on some shrubs and can kill them, even a year or more later.

Use the back of your fan rake and sometimes your feet to spread mulch out. Rake back and forth to get it nice and smooth and level. Then do the next load. After a while you will be able to tell how far apart to put your wheelbarrow loads. Be sure to go back and check to see that mulch is not smothering the crowns of shrubs or trees. Push the mulch away from the base of the plants with your gloved hand.

Speaking of the gloved hand—one of the advantages to using sawdust-based products instead of bark (besides looking better) is that when you spread it or weed it you don't come away with a handful of tiny slivers. These painful microscopic slivers found in bark will even get into your gloves to plague you later when you're not working in the beds.

The bigger the pieces of your mulch, the more effective it is, and the slower it is to decompose and disappear. Smaller particles look nicer, however. Composted manure mix is very fine—it looks like good, dark garden soil. And since gardens are for looks, I use it and just apply it more often. Finer mulches can also be used around tiny plants like flowers, where large-particled bark will not work well. The smaller the plant, the thinner the layer of mulch should be.

Fine particled mulches can sometimes develop a hard crust on top that repels water. To get water back down to the roots, fluff the mulch up with a hoe or hand cultivator and rake it flat again.

Mulches, especially ones containing wood products like sawdust, will rob the soil of nitrogen as they decompose, so it's wise to fertilize with nitrogen, especially on newer plantings.

Depending on the type and thickness of mulch, you can expect to reapply it once every two to six years. I generally do a little spot section in the yard every year to keep up on it and avoid having to do a big project.

Mulch will work to smother seeds, and if perhaps you left the carcasses of some hoed-up annual weeds behind, the mulch is usually enough to keep them down. It will not, however, keep your perennial-type weeds down if you haven't gotten rid of them roots and all. Those dandelions and grass will just grow taller to find their place in the sun. And they will be harder to dig out after they've been mulched over.

WEED SEEDS AND FLOWERS

Recently I was quite distraught with the irrigationist at a client's home. I spent the winter weeding and carefully mulching every square inch of barren ground, including the 2-inch strips between the concrete paths and the edged grass. The irrigationist laid new pipe and very carefully eliminated the extra soil by spreading it over my mulched strips, thus infecting the area with newly uncovered weed seeds. ARRGH! I'm sure he thought me quite crazy to kick up such a fuss.

Weed seeds themselves are by definition incredibly tough. They can lie dormant under the soil for years, until you inadvertently dig them up, to plant new shrubs or perennials and then, in classic horror story fashion, they come alive. Weed seeds have been known to stay viable for decades. Some seeds frozen for millennia in glaciers have been found viable!

If you catch *annual* weeds before they flower, you can sometimes kill them by hoeing or chopping off the tops, or knocking them out of the soil with your hand cultivator. They will dry out (desiccate) and die on a nice sunny day. But if you have automatic irrigation, or if it rains, they can, and do, sink their

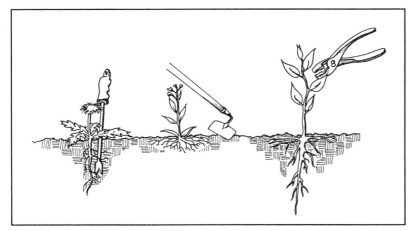

Match the tool to the weed type. Annuals can be knocked down with a garden hoe and raked out. Perennial weeds must have roots dug out either with a hand cultivator or a dandelion weeder. Some tenacious tree and shrub seedlings can be pulled out with pliers.

roots in again and head back up in a day. And the bad news continues, for both annual and perennial weeds. If they have set up flowers, many have the capacity to turn their flowers into seeds after they have been uprooted and are basically dead. That dandelion flower head you snapped off when it was but a yellow flower had better go into your pocket because if you drop it, it will turn into a thousand fluffy seeds that float across the lawn and start anew. Professional gardeners always watch weeds out of the corners of their eyes. Their anxiety level rises sharply as the weeds go into flower, and they begin to twitch at the sight of ripening seed heads.

Hoe during dry weather; dig or pull out weeds after a rain. Moist ground gives up plant roots with much greater ease. You may choose to water your shrub beds deeply the day before to ease your weeding chores today.

But really, annual weeds are easy. Hoe them down and rake them out, then mulch. Catch the new little guys before they go to seed, and the population will stay in abeyance.

PERENNIAL WEEDS

Tougher to control are perennial weeds. Perennial weeds, like morning glory (bindweed) or horsetail, often die back in the winter and the roots stay alive underground. Others stay green all winter, like grass and dandelion. To eradicate these you will need to get their roots out. Roots come in several types: fibrous, creeping, and tap-rooted. A fibrous-rooted

weed has a matted clump of roots—like a grass clump, or a clump of clover. Some plant roots hold on tighter than others. Loosen the soil with your hand cultivator, or for bigger jobs with your spading fork, to get out as much root as possible. Jam your spading fork into the ground and rock it back and forth. Do this several times until the plant gives up easily and comes out with all its roots. If you just yank off the tops, the plant will simply regrow from the roots below.

More dangerous yet are tap-rooted weeds like dandelions. Their roots are like a carrot's—and go straight down. Use the knife-like dandelion weeder for these in order to dig straight down and pry them out—deep down. If you do not take the extra time and effort to do this, you are simply wasting your time, as these plants grow back lickety split from tiny bits of root left. If you can't get all the root, get as much as you can, in order to start starving the weed.

A truly accomplished weeder knows how fast to go and how much time to spend on each type of weed for the best kill-per-minute-spent ratio. He or she may whiz through a patch of annual weeds like chickweed but slowly dig out a fair amount of the roots of a perennial dandelion, red clover, or horsetail.

Speaking of horsetail, many plants have the added strategy of "rubber" roots. You discover that as you pull they simply snap off leaving enough root behind to rise again. Horsetail and morning glory fit into this group. Many of these you must control using sheer tenacity and vigilance. Dig down with your dandelion weeder and get some below-ground root of horsetail. An inch or two will make a significant difference in its ability to regrow. It does come back, but slower and smaller than before. Doing this also starves them out by never letting leaves show long enough to manufacture food from sunshine. Eventually, you find that you are winning the battle, though it may never be won.

Morning glory and some grasses and various other plants also fit in the category of weeds that have stems or roots that creep along just under or above the surface soil. They send up new plants every so often. These plant structures are called, variously, *stolons* or *runners* and *rhizomes* or *creeping roots*. (These modified plant structures can send up new plants every so often or, when broken up, say with a rototiller, each piece may become a new plant.) Morning glory and horsetail roots have been known to run 30 feet underground before re-emerging perhaps on the other side of the concrete road. You can chase these roots as far as you dare, though you will find total eradication is difficult as they break off and disappear under concrete pads and rocks, leaving a nest of hiding roots to creep back out later. Curses!

Mulch will help you check growth of the runners. In clay soil it is nearly impossible to pull up runners, as they will break off. But in nice, soft mulch they simply lift out with a light tug. For horsetail and morning glory, I sometimes resort to judicious use of herbicides. More on them later.

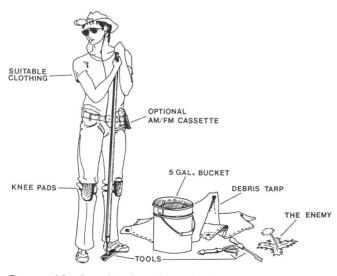

SUITABLE CLOTHING

OPTIONAL AM/FM CASSETTE

5 GAL. BUCKET

KNEE PADS

DEBRIS TARP

THE ENEMY

TOOLS

Dressed for hand-to-hand combat.

PERENNIAL WOODY WEEDS

The third type of weed is a perennial woody plant. That means that it is brown-stemmed, not green and supple. It's woody and tough like a tree or shrub. These are often trees or shrubs that "volunteered" in your yard. That means that no person planted them. Birds that eat berries often deposit pre-fertilized seed packets in your yard. Common woody weeds in my area include holly, cotoneaster, blackberry, laurel, and hawthorn.

I also include wild clematis vines and various unwanted trees such as maple, mountain ash, Douglas fir, alder, and willow. You can dig these out using a shovel and mattock or, as discussed in a previous chapter, you can cut and paint the stumps of these and other woody brush with glyphosate (Roundup). Look up the cut stump treatment instructions on your Roundup label. It says, "Apply a 50 to 100 percent solution of this product to the freshly cut surface immediately after cutting." Delays reduce performance. Don't get dirt in the container or on the brush. This also reduces efficacy. I use an old rubber cement jar, having cleaned it out with rubber cement remover. It has a built-in brush and fits nicely into a tool belt pouch I wear. The tool belt also holds my dandelion weeder and my claw-like hand cultivator.

I find I worry less about using herbicide this way than by spraying an entire berry-laden bush in which some child or animal may care to forage. And I get better results. With blackberries, say growing out of a patch of wanted ivy groundcover, I carefully cut the cane about 3 inches above ivy level. I leave my red handled clippers lying over the blackberry cane stump to mark it as I reach for my jar and brush to paint the cut stem. If you don't leave a marker, you surely will lose track of your victim once you turn your eyes away. Carefully recap your brush killer, pick up your clippers, and move on. This is painstaking and time-consuming work, but it beats cutting down the same blackberry patch or cotoneaster bush ten years in a row. The cut-and-paint method of brush control is most effective in late summer and in fall. Cut stump treatments, with Roundup or another herbicide labeled for that use, generally mean less chance of problems due to drift and overspray to desirable plants. When applied carefully there is also less chance of surface and ground water problems. *Be absolutely certain to wear gloves and eye protection when working with herbicides as a cut stump treatment.* Be sure to return your brush killer to a proper storage container at the end of the day, as it is illegal to store herbicides in other than their labeled containers.

SMART WEEDS

There are some other weed control strategies of which you should be aware. As you can see from the earlier list of plant names, there is a weed called smartweed. Personally, I think they are all pretty "smart" and, of course, tough. But the smartest weeds are the ones that hide inside your ornamental plants and groundcovers. These are the ones you are likely to miss when going through your yard. I have trained myself to peek under and inside all shrubs to see if there lurks the would-be parent of a whole new generation of weeds. These smart weeds can be difficult to dig out because their roots are entwined with your shrubs. Do whatever it takes, using dandelion weeder or fork to get as much out as possible. Even if it means sacrificing some roots on your shrub, get that weed out! As a pruner and as a weeder I have also trained my eye to pick up any and all variations of leaf type in a given setting. As practice, you should stare at yours or a neighbor's group of low shrubs and—like a kid's game— spot the leaves that don't fit. Amongst the small rounded

Smart weeds hide under and inside shrubs. Train yourself to search for them. Look for any variation in leaf type, texture, or color. Search and destroy.

leaves of the evergreen azalea, find a big heart-shaped morning glory. In a spirea with many tiny leaves, find a long, narrow fireweed. Look for the telltale shiny dark green leaves of a volunteer laurel or holly, or the grayish leaf of a cotoneaster. Search-and-destroy is the name of the game. An especially tricky one is fireweed, which looks remarkably like phlox out of bloom—only the reddish stem gives it away. Don't be fooled by smart weeds.

PRETTY WEEDS

And don't be suckered by pretty weeds. Many of these are wildflowers out of place. Although charming in the woods and fields, they can be a detriment to your garden. Or maybe not. Many of these are weeds by definition only. In one yard a client may curse the wild, stinky geraniums. Other clients may ask me to transplant some to a new area, they like them so much.

A list of "wildflower" type weeds in my area that I would eradicate:

Buttercup	Stinky geranium
Wild sweet pea	False bamboo—
	(*Polygonum C.*)
Lady fern	

A list of sometimes okay, sometimes not:

English ivy	Foxglove
Bleeding heart	Forget-me-not
Bead-ruby	Wild iris
Bluebell (scilla)	Money plant
Aegeopodium	Oxalis—some types
Violets	Ribbon grass
Bamboo	

Most of these are weeds by definition because of their vigorous growth habit. A few may be considered among the Great Weeds.

GREAT WEEDS

The Great Weeds are the ones that have a reputation for utterly destroying gardens and defeating gardeners. I would put on this list some types of bamboo (running), horsetail, false bamboo, blackberry, morning glory (bindweed), and wild clematis. Your area may have others on the "most wanted" list, including loosestrife, witchweed, kudzu, and nutsedge. Check with your local extension agent for help. Be vigilant and thorough with the great weeds. It is with these weeds that I most often resort to chemical warfare, though I have seen all of them beaten in hand-to-hand combat—it just takes a lot longer.

WEED CONTROL ERRORS

Common weed control errors that people make are: trying to deprive weeds to death by withholding water or fertilizer; and limbing-up shrubs to make it easy to get to the weeds.

In the first instance you will merely give weeds the competitive edge over your shrubs and groundcovers. Weeds are—again by definition—able to withstand extremes of heat and drought better than your desirable ornamentals. Prostrate knotweed growing in the crack in the sidewalk is known to withstand temperatures in excess of a hundred degrees. You must intervene to keep the weed population down, while watering and fertilizing your groundcovers and shrubs long enough to give them the competitive edge.

There exists a common misunderstanding that your newly planted groundcover will somehow choke out the weeds that are taking foothold. Impossible! You must—in those first years of establishing a new garden—keep your area pristine and weed-free until such time as the groundcover is so thick that the new seeds blowing in from the lot next door land on leaves, not soil, or if they find their way to the soil, the leaf cover is so thick that the light is insufficient for them to germinate.

SHADE

This is the error in raising the limbs of your shrubs to make weeding under them easier. It simply lets in more light and enables weed seeds to germinate. Shade is one of the best strategies of the good gardener. It keeps seeds from germinating and slows down the growth of those that do. Bare, clean beds can look nice, but for low maintenance fill all those spaces with healthy, vigorous trees, shrubs, and groundcovers.

STRATEGY

When tackling a yard overrun with weeds, first clean up a small section—we'll call it section A. Next time (next week or next month) re-weed A, then clear out a new patch B. Next time re-weed A and B and clear out new section C. Get the idea? When you are finally done you have a yard that is totally controlled instead of looking back to find A re-engulfed in shotweed.

SUMMARY

Strategies for dealing with weeds

Annual	puny but reproduce fast
	easy to hand weed or hoe out
	mulch to smother seeds
	vigilant removal of potential parents before they set seed
Perennial	use proper tools to dig them out
	mulch
	repeatedly cut off tops to starve
	hunt hidden, would-be parents
Woody brush and weedy trees	dig out roots; use stump grinder for trees
	cut-and-paint with herbicides registered for such use
	shade
	mulch

Herbicides

In the following section on herbicides, I often use trade names as well as the chemical names. I have done this to simplify presentation. No endorsement of brands is implied or given.

While working for the Seattle Parks Department, I took care of an urban park sandwiched between the freeway and a porno theater. It had become so overgrown and nasty it deserved not the name of "Park." This park had perhaps fifteen years of grass, morning glory, horsetail, fireweed, and you name it growing unchecked on sun-baked clay soil. The shrubs were suffering Zabel laurels, rhododendrons, a row of great, 10-foot double-file viburnums and some beaten and baked trees. During one group project we dug up and pulled out the weeds, found wine bottles, litter, and syringes left by prior users of the park, and had to dodge rats as we went. Then we sprinkled dichlobenil (Casoron®) granules and covered them over with bark mulch. In addition, the antique water system was repaired and revived and the area fertilized. It stayed neat and tidy that entire year, and with a modicum of regular hand weeding, with water and fertilizing, it became a pleasant place to sit and eat lunch. Casoron lasts in the soil for about six months, preventing new seeds from growing and preventing tiny bits of roots (like morning glory) from re-emerging.

SUCCESS STORIES

Here's another tale of hope. The second year of working as a private gardener, I had occasion to estimate the cost of restoring a landscape that was being overcome with weeds. Others had tried and failed. Most discouraging was the grass coming up through the vinca groundcover. Vinca, or periwinkle, grows as a mat of crisscrossing threadlike strands. The grass, its stalks protected by the groundcover and its roots entwined with the vinca's, was tough to weed out by hand thoroughly. I vividly recall hours of weeding in the rain, the strands of vinca cutting at my cold, sore hands, with a rematch scheduled for next month. I estimated a day and a half a month to keep this yard looking good—for the first year, anyway.

Then I heard about sethoxydin (brand name Poast®) a chemical that kills just grass. Sprayed over non-grass plants (those listed on the label), it would kill just the grass. Expensive as it was, I decided to give it a try. In the spring as the new shoots of grass, as thick as turf, emerged among the vinca, I applied the new herbicide. I came back next month to find little, if any, grass with which to continue the fight. Maintenance dropped to one-half day a month immediately. Poast does not kill all species of grasses or grass gone to seed. Still it is a powerful weapon.

A rockery overgrown with morning glory, grass, vetch, dandelions, and others defied hand weeding because the roots were too tightly crammed under and protected by the rocks. With our weed trimmer we mowed down the grass to encourage soft, tender new regrowth. Then as it grew back we sprayed the whole area with glyphosate (Roundup). We let it bake in for a week or two, pulled off the dead yellow tops and replanted. Glyphosate (the active ingredient in Roundup and Rodeo) is used as a contact spray. This means it kills what it touches. The treated weeds translocate (move) the chemical throughout the plant to roots, stems, and fruit. It interferes with biological-chemical processes specific to plants. According to a June 1986 registration standard, the Environmental Protection Agency considers glyphosate to be relatively non-toxic to most non-plant forms of life. According to the same report, glyphosate shows little tendency to "bio-accumulate." Data indicate that it does not cause mutagenic (mutations), teratogenic (birth defects), or reproductive effects.

Roundup binds tightly and quickly to the clay particles in soils. It is not, therefore, available to poison adjacent plants or leach through the soil to the water table. It decomposes by microbial activity in about two weeks. The soil is then ready to replant with desirable ornamentals. Many otherwise organic gardeners will, on occasion, resort to Roundup for these reasons. Since Roundup does not "poison" the soil, remaining weed seeds will germinate.

Be sure to spray Roundup on young, healthy, growing weeds. It doesn't work on old, dusty grass and weeds. Dirt inactivates it.

Roundup is good for the un-pullable dandelion in the sidewalk crack. However, it does not kill horsetail or clover, and it has a tough time penetrating the waxy leaves of ivy and holly. Oddly enough, creeping jenny is unaffected as well. It is still a very powerful tool for the gardener. Be sure to spray only target plants.

Some nastier chemicals exist for other weeds. For moderate success on horsetail, there is Amitrol-T®. (NOTE: Because of its potential carcinogenic hazard, Amitrol is now a restricted-use pesticide available only to licensed contractors.) For false bamboo, also called Japanese knotweed (*Polygonum cuspidatum*), dicamba. Dicamba can also be used on bamboo (or Roundup can be used instead). Dicamba is known to move through the soil and kill roots of nearby desirable shrubs. It is very soluble. Its residues are persistent (two months to a year). Be careful not to contaminate ground water and don't use it when rain is likely.

Other tales of hope include the lawn herbicides, which if used correctly (that is to say, applied at the appropriate time and carefully following all label directions, sprayed on a shaggy lawn area and not washed off for two days by the irrigation system or mowed off), will eliminate broadleaf weeds from your lawn (moss and annual grasses have to be dealt with separately).

I once saw a fearless gardener spray the steep slope just adjacent to a new area with Trimec®, a potent lawn-type formulation of chemicals. This treacherously steep slope was a maintenance nightmare of blackberry vines that shot up to obscure the view of the city, which park users expected to see from the bench above. Each year we were forced to use hand tools and screaming brush blades, at great risk to life and limb, to clear the bank. The Trimec curled and killed the young vines in a matter of days, leaving tall grass to stabilize the slope and look nice for the public.

TALES OF HORROR

Tales of hope always come with tales of horror. Once a ballfield attendant applied Casoron to the freshly weeded dirt area of the baseball field. A rainstorm followed, washing the granules onto the grass and down onto a neighboring lawn. The resulting dead grass and the affected dirt beneath had to be replaced by the city at taxpayer expense.

In another old city park, several beds that once contained beautiful old rhododendrons now lie empty. A maintenance laborer who was sent out to apply Casoron to the freshly weeded bed, tripled the rate of application to make *sure* the weeds stayed down. This circumstance, in combination with the fact that rhododendrons (as well as pines) are somewhat more susceptible to damage by Casoron than other plants, caused them to die.

Casoron, when properly used, can be a useful tool. More often than not it is abused by homeowners and landscapers. Usually excessive application rates just stunt the plants, causing telltale yellowing at the edges of the leaves. One sees it everywhere.

Another tale of horror. A lady determined to rid herself of morning glory, including the vines covering her rhodies, sprayed them with Roundup—killing both vine and shrub. Roundup is non-selective—it kills whatever it touches.

And another: A fully mature and particularly beautiful maple in a yard next to a prominent viewpoint overlooking the city simply failed to leaf out one year. Indeed, it was dead. Overuse of lawn weed killer was the cause. The ingredients in lawn herbicides work on all broadleaves, be they dandelions or trees, leaving only the grass unaffected. Since most of a tree's roots are in the top 18 inches of the soil, and they extend far beyond the dripline, trees are far more susceptible to chemical damage than one might suppose.

POTENTIAL DANGERS

The potential dangers of all pesticides (herbicides and insecticides are both pesticides) are assessed in several ways. Scientists evaluate the relative toxicity (how much it takes to kill 50% of the test animals), whether it collects in the food chain, whether it degrades quickly or slowly, how it degrades (digested by microbes, decomposed by light), whether it is likely to move through the soil to adjacent plants or to the water table, whether it causes particular kinds of physical damage to the test animals (cancer, birth defects, kidney failure, etc.) with either a single exposure or through repeated exposures.

Sometimes a particular pesticide will pose a serious threat to some non-target species. For example, geese and other birds have died browsing on lawns treated for cranefly with incorrect application of Diazinon.

You should exercise caution with all pesticides and herbicides. The fact that home and garden chemicals appear on the shelves and are registered with the Environmental Protection Agency (EPA) does not mean that the EPA guarantees their safety. In 1983, of the 600-odd chemicals in common pesticide formulae, only four had successfully submitted all the test results required to indicate relative safety to humans and the environment. At that time the EPA estimated that it would take twenty more years to fill the data gaps.

Many test results are based only on analysis of the "active ingredient." The majority of a bag or bottle of herbicide is made up of "inert ingredients," which are sometimes other chemicals. Chemical combinations are unpredictable, and two chemicals that alone may be relatively non-toxic can be dangerous when combined. No testing is done on these combinations. The term "inert" can be misleading. In 1986, sample testing of registered pesticides turned up "inerts" that were themselves pesticides. An EPA staffer discovered DDT—outlawed since 1972—listed as an inert ingredient in some registered pesticides. A secondary ingredient (POEA) found in some glyphosate formulations is three times as toxic as glyphosate itself.

There are several tales of horror concerning the validity of test results submitted to the EPA by chemi-cal companies, and about loopholes that enable a manufacturer to sell pesticides before all the required tests have been completed (i.e., conditional registration).

So don't assume that any pesticide, or any chemical for that matter, is safe. We simply do not know. Treat them with a healthy respect but without paranoia. If you choose to wage chemical warfare with either herbicides or insecticides, you need to adhere religiously to several common sense rules and procedures, whether or not they are comfortable or convenient.

USING CHEMICAL WEAPONS SAFELY

First, do your homework. Unlike other do-it-yourself projects, *do not* read the instructions only when all else fails. Plan to spend some time reading and understanding the label. Bring it inside, sit down, use good light, perhaps take notes on mixing instructions. Take your time. The label is a legal document. If you spray pesticides other than according to label directions, you are breaking the law. Anything and everything on the label is there for a very good reason. They don't make up application restrictions just to be on the safe side. Label instructions are serious business. Home and garden pesticides can be as

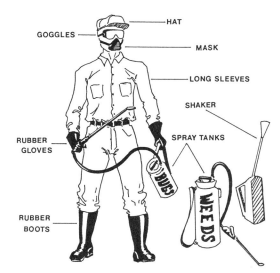

Suited up for chemical warfare. To use chemicals responsibly you must dress correctly, whether or not you find it comfortable or convenient.

much of an ecological or health danger when abused as any of the so-called industrial chemicals.

If you do your own spraying, use two well-marked (nail polish works well) spray tanks, one for "bugs," one for "weeds." This will help you avoid a serious, potentially dangerous mixup. Keep all chemicals in well-marked (original) containers. Never, ever, ever store chemicals in old food or drink containers. Keep all such materials locked in a safe place—like a garage cupboard—and include with them all mixing paraphernalia like measuring spoons or cups. They should also be well-marked and used for that purpose only. Do not use aluminum gear and avoid storing chemicals in spray tanks—they can be very corrosive.

Wear protective clothing, rubber gloves—solid ones, not just kitchen types—but not ones with cloth linings that may absorb pesticide residues. Safety glasses and a cloth face mask are in order. This is especially true when mixing and pouring materials, and when cleaning equipment, which is when most accidents occur, usually involving higher volumes and concentrations of chemicals. This may seem obvious, but people easily forget to "suit-up" when mixing or will absentmindedly take off their safety glasses just before opening the pressurized lid to the tank. Your eyes, nose, and mouth absorb fumes and particles most readily. This is followed by the palms of your hands, soles of your feet, and your forehead. So a hat may be a wise addition.

Mix small amounts so that you run out on the job. It's unacceptable to return to the spigot with a tank of unused material. Spray it all out in the yard. Don't dump it next to your spigot and never, ever, ever pour excess chemicals down drains, toilets, or sewers. These chemicals are considered hazardous waste. You don't want them to turn up in your clam chowder. If you must dispose of them, contact the regional office of the Environmental Protection Agency for guidance.

After you are through, wash your gear and your clothes and yourself—right away.

Don't ever mix two chemicals together if it's not allowed in the instructions. It could be a very big mistake. Don't ever, ever, ever use "extra for good measure." Know what plants you're spraying and/or what pests or weeds are the target. Be sensitive to

conditions that affect your spray. On very hot days liquid pesticides will vaporize into a fine mist and can drift quite far. Be sensitive to even small breezes. Big droplets from the spray nozzle will not drift as far as fine mists. With herbicides, keep that nozzle close to the plant—not waving around up high, as is commonly shown in TV ads. Buy a shaker for your granular herbicides to ensure even coverage and so you don't get it all over yourself and down in your sweaty rubber gloves. Be sensitive to the presence of pets, wildlife, children, pregnant women, waterways (even if they just look like an old ditch), and foraging bees.

My own policy is that chemical intervention should be considered an option only when it is absurd to employ cultural methods (hand weeding, mulch, etc.). Sometimes chemicals are used during an initial cleanup. Avoid using herbicides for regular, basic shrub bed maintenance. I guarantee that truly responsible use of herbicides is at least as time consuming, physically demanding (the discomfort factor alone), and expensive as mechanical control. The potential for disaster is, needless to say, considerably greater. In the vast majority of situations, weed control using hand-to-hand combat is equally as effective as chemical warfare. There are specific weeds and certain situations that may be considered exceptions, but exceptions they are. Pesticides should be the weapon of last resort.

There are dozens more commonly used herbicides that are available to homeowners. I've just told tales of hope and horror about ones I have dealt with or will use as a last resort. The tales of horror are worse for many other chemicals, especially soil "sterilants" (as in, I don't want anything to grow there ever!). Herbicides are tools to use, not abuse.

Think of hand weeding as a game, not a chore. Once everything is cleaned up, mulched, and under control, weeding is not time consuming or arduous —it just needs to be done *regularly*. It helps me to sing the weed song — to the Kenny Rogers tune, "The Gambler." It goes:

"You gotta know when to hoe 'em
Know when to pull 'em
Know when to walk away
Know when to run ..."

HERBICIDES CHART

	BRAND NAME	ACTIVE INGREDIENT	FORM/TARGET/RESIDUAL	COMMENTS
	Roundup, Rodeo, Vision, Accord, Kleen-up	Glyphosate	Liquid; kills what it touches; little or no residual effect.	Ties up in the soil; can replant in sprayed area; new weed seeds *will* germinate. Long shelf life. Certain formulations bad for fish, fry, eggs.
	Banvel, Trimec	Dicamba	Liquid usually or granules found in lawn weed killers. Kills broadleaf weeds; does not kill grass; kills what it touches (spray form). 3-12 week residual effect.	Will move through soil in rain—be very careful.
	Casoron, Norosac, Dyclomec	Dichlobenil	A gas housed in kitty-litter type granules. Inhibits stem growth and seed germination. Lasts 6 months to a year.	Keeps weeds from regrowing for a while; eventually decomposed by microbes. Apply after bed is weeded out; good under mulch. Don't get it on turf, keep it 1-2 feet away from bed/turf interface. When used in recommended doses, will not significantly affect existing trees and shrubs but will preclude use of bulbs and inhibit growth of newly transplanted shrubs and groundcovers. Signs of abuse: yellow leaves, especially the edges. *Do Not Use More Than Recommended Amount.*
	Poast	Sethoxdim	Liquid—mix with water and a liquid "sticker." Kills *just grass* that it touches, not broadleaves. 7-day residual effect.	Has not been tested for all plants yet. Read updated labels. Short shelf life. Expensive.
	Amitrol-T, Amino-Triazole, Amizole, Weedazol, Cytrol	Amitrol	Liquid; kills what it touches; turns it white. Low residual effect.	*Restricted use:* Must hire licensed person to apply it.

HERBICIDES CHART (cont.)

APPLICATION	For soft green "herbaceous" plants (i.e., dandelion) spray on tender foliage. On woody perennials, cut and paint stem in late summer, fall.	Spray on weed, plant, plant stem. Sprinkle on grass in dry form. Don't use around trees and waterways. Spot treat lawn weeds when possible.	Sprinkle on soil surface using "shaker" after bed has been weeded out.	Use when no rain is expected for 1/2 day. Spray on tender grass, not old, tough brown grass.	Spray on plant victims.
WEATHER	Sunny days; no rain (washes it off); early morning best, then sun bakes it in.	Dry days.	Vaporizes in hot weather; apply in moist, cool weather. Good to water it in or rake it into soil.	Warm, dry days or hot days.	Sunny, dry days.
USES	Kills almost anything (read label) except creeping jenny, horsetail; waxy-leaved things (i.e., holly) resist absorption.	Good for tenacious, great weeds: false bamboo, clover, real bamboo.	Good to check regrowth of horsetail, morning glory, also for pathways and places where hand-weeding is precluded. Useful under morning glory-ridden fence lines and bases of thorny shrubs. Use in weed introduction areas (places that border a weed patch).	Good for grass growing through groundcovers, or entwined in roots of shrubs.	Included here because it affords some relief from horsetail—little else does.

1. READ THE LABEL — AND FOLLOW IT.

2. DON'T USE EXTRA.

3. DON'T MIX & MATCH CHEMICALS.

4. DON'T STORE IN FOOD CONTAINERS.

5. DON'T DISPOSE OF DOWN DRAINS OR GUTTERS.

6. WATCH OUT FOR POTENTIAL BEE KILL.

SUMMARY

❑ Read and believe the entire label on all pesticides.

❑ Follow instructions to the letter.

❑ Wear protective clothing whether or not you find it comfortable.

❑ Use chemicals as the weapon of last resort. Non-chemical weed control makes good sense economically in the long run and you will rest easier.

Fertilizers and Organics

The biggest difference in the health and looks of your shrubs and trees is, once again, going to depend mostly on whether or not you have poor soil, poor drainage or too little irrigation, or plants that are ill-suited to their sites (i.e., shade lovers in the sun). Fertilizers cannot make up for deficiencies in these areas any more than pruning can. Fertilizers can, however, make a significant contribution to the overall robustness and health of your garden subjects, once their basic needs are met.

N-P-K

Plants do not eat fertilizer; they manufacture their food from sunshine. They also "breathe" air not only with their leaves; the trunks of trees and their roots need access to air. The base of a tree is apt to smother if covered over with soil during construction. Plants use the carbon dioxide in the air and give off oxygen as a waste product (lucky for us). Plants take up water and elements and simple compounds from the soil to complete biological activity. Plants use, in order of most needed, Nitrogen, Phosphorus (P_2O_2), and Potassium or Potash (K_2O), or N-P-K as they are usually called. The three numbers on your fertilizer bag always stand for the *percentage* by weight of these three elements in that same order in the bag. If you have all three numbers, then you have what's called a "complete fertilizer." Plants also use minute amounts of what are known as micro-nutrients. A deficiency in one of these may affect your plant, though this is rather uncommon. Mostly, it is said, plants want nitrogen.

Fertilizers vary in their relative amounts of N-P-K and in the specific form of each element. But it's all the same stuff, basically. You don't "feed" your roses something different than you put on your lawn, it's just in relatively different amounts. The N-nitrogen of N-P-K is primarily known as good for producing leafy green growth. The P and K are used to assist in making bigger flowers and better roots, for winter hardiness, and for disease resistance. Your grass fertilizer will be heavy on nitrogen; your fertilizer for flowers or vegetables will have more P and K. Bigger numbers on the bag simply mean it's in a more concentrated form. People who understand math will use these numbers in a formula to compare prices of different bags of fertilizer to find out which one gives you the most bang per buck. Also, they calculate application rates for their fertilizer. The general rule is 2 to 6 pounds of actual nitrogen per 1,000 square feet per year for lawns, less for shrub beds. Adjust your fertilizer spreader to distribute fertilizer at the correct rate. Go to an empty lot, pace off 100 feet by 10 feet (1,000 square feet), put on 2 pounds of real nitrogen (a percentage of the bag according to the label), and adjust it until it comes out right. The same method can be used to adjust the rate of application for liquids, except you can use water during the trials and also calibrate on an easy-to-measure concrete surface, like the driveway. When measuring liquids it is useful to remember the adage, "A pint's a pound, the world around," thus converting weight into volume.

FORMULATIONS

Fertilizers come in different formulations. Some are simple enough to be taken up by the plant immediately but won't hang around long in the soil—a shot in the arm—needing to be reapplied more often. Fertilizers with more complex compounds break down more slowly, releasing their goodies to the plants over time, and these are less likely to burn roots. Some, like Osmocote®, are coated with an ingredient that allows the fertilizer to be released when the weather is hotter and the plant needs it more. It is often used by nurseries for potted plants and for annual flower displays (marigolds, impatiens, etc.).

Fertilizers can be as complicated a subject as you care to investigate. You can load up on the various types and investigate the best time for each plant. No doubt your plants will additionally benefit from the tailored care and attention. Or you can do as I do. I use a general, all-purpose shrub fertilizer in the late spring, and a grass fertilizer for my lawn in the late fall. Fertilize, if you can, when it's going to rain soon or water after fertilizing. Chemical fertilizers can burn leaves or roots if applied too heavily. People often burn up their lawns by applying too much fertilizer and then not watering it. Fertilize in moderation. Running your plants at full steam ahead can damage them just as much as letting them starve for a little phosphorus. Use too much nitrogen and you have too many green soft shoots at the expense of flowers; fertilize too late and your plants may not harden off for the winter and get caught in an early frost. People, as always, get into trouble by using too much of a good thing. Give them what they need to be healthy but don't push them.

AVOIDING OVER-FERTILIZING

To avoid over-fertilization I usually play it safe and get the lower-numbered sacks (numbers under twelve). To spread your fertilizer, you can put it in a bucket and broadcast it. This means that, with your rubber-gloved hand, you just randomly throw it around, up in the air in a sweep as you walk. Avoid clusters of fertilizer pellets on the ground, which will cause burning or yellowing of grass blades. Then go back and "bang the bushes" to knock off excess pellets. Others may choose to sprinkle a light circle of fertilizer carefully at the dripline at the base of the shrubs. You can also, for large areas and for more even coverage, buy a plastic broadcast spreader. By turning the crank it just flies out at a relatively even rate.

USING SPREADERS

Drop spreaders are those carts used by lawn worshipers to fertilize their lawns. Use a drop spreader when applying a weed-and-feed containing a broad leaf weed killer. If you put that in a cyclone-broadcast spreader it would go flying off into your shrub beds, killing broadleaf shrubs as well. Drop spreaders are trickier to use for getting even-looking green grass. You have to divide your fertilizer into two parts and walk very straight lines—back and forth one way and then the other way. If you inadvertently over-fertilize or miss a section, the lawn will tell on you later, showing either streaks of lighter green or scorched yellow grass.

Be sure to wash yourself and your spreader after fertilizing; chemical fertilizers can be quite corrosive. Be careful with compounds containing iron (used for quick greening) as they can stain your concrete paths.

CHEMICAL VS. ORGANIC FERTILIZERS

Plants are not damaged by giving them "chemical" fertilizers, but the long-term fertility of the soil may be degraded if it receives no other help than this. There are serious concerns that the over-application of nitrogen in chemical fertilizers is leaching down and contaminating groundwater. This concern has been directed mainly to the agricultural use of fertilizers but can reasonably be considered to apply to urban use as well. The longer I am in the business, the more I tend to throw my hand in with those of the organic philosophy.

All plants take up N-P-K in the same form; however, organic fertilizers have to be processed down into simpler compounds for the plants to take them up. Worms and entire communities of fungus, bacteria, and protozoa do this work. This is good. They are attuned to the rhythms of nature. These microorganisms can't multiply and do their work until the ground warms up sufficiently in the spring. This keeps plants from growing before the time is right. With chemical fertilizers, on the other hand, all nutrients are readily available and can be used immediately, perhaps before they should be or when the plant should be slowing down in the fall.

Organic fertilizers are generally safer to use because their concentrations are much lower. The only common trouble I've heard of is that utilizing uncomposted manure—especially chicken manure—can burn plants. This is why garden books always refer to manure as "well-rotted manure." Straight from the stables, manure can also contain unwanted weed seeds, and we know about them! Properly composting manure will eradicate most seeds, and the powdered stuff you buy in bags at the hardware or grocery store or nursery will be steamed or heat-treated to destroy seeds. It's great stuff!

Dried powdered manure can be spread just like chemical fertilizers. Some people go back and hoe it in or use a cultivator to scratch it in. The fresh stuff, and especially if it gets wet, will stink for a few weeks. If you can, apply it when it's cooler and raining a lot for this reason. After a week you'll no longer notice the smell. I don't mind the smell. To me it is "the smell of victory!"

Many insist that manure and compost are not fertilizers at all, since the actual quantities of nitrogen, phosphorus, and potash available to or readily usable by the plants are small. They are, however, very good at feeding and sheltering the bacterial organisms and earthworms that do indeed create fertilizer.

Not all so-called organic fertilizers are organic (meaning once alive). Some are mined, like lime or phosphorus. Others, like blood and bone and fish meals were once certainly alive. The discovery that crop production could be increased with the addition of crushed bones to the soil allowed a hungry Europe of the late 18th century, with a new, expanding city population, to continue to be supported by limited farmlands. England was accused of widespread pillaging of the soldiers' cemeteries of Europe to supply their farmers. The reliance on bone meal ended when it was discovered that the same nutrient-building compounds could be mined in rock form.

Nitrogen fertilizer in its first, most basic form—urine—is still used by organic gardeners. Some gardeners even use their own—diluted. Wood ashes are another classic source of useful compounds; also cottonseed meal, kelp, and sludge (another human "fertilizer").

What is it about these organic compounds that causes gardeners to talk about them with the same sort of glee that a chocoholic uses in describing a new dessert bar in town? Organic gardeners have experienced the joys of building up the perfect, healthy, living, thriving, fertile ecosystem we call "soil."

Good soil is not just dirt. And the fertility of soil is more than the amounts of N, P, and K it contains. These elements must be available to the plants, and this availability depends on a host of other factors like the pH (acidity or alkalinity) of the soil, the cation (pronounced *CAT-eye-on*) exchange capacity, the water holding capacity of soil, the size of soil particles, the texture, and the air spaces. It does only temporary good for a sandy soil landscape to add chemical nitrogen, as the sand cannot hold it. The nitrogen will sluice through—perhaps polluting the water table, whereas adding organic material will allow the soil to "hold" nitrogen and release it slowly to the plant. Organics not only add nutrients to the soil; they give it *good soil structure*. Furthermore, *humus* will act as a stabilizer for organic life.

MORE GARDENESE

We are now moving from organics as fertilizers to organics as amendments. We will need to interpret some of these new gardenese verb-nouns for you backyard neophytes.

AMEND—To add something to your soil, usually by digging it in.

AMENDMENT—The stuff you are digging into your soil. Your soil amendment could be organic (leaves) or inorganic (sand).

COMPOST—The noun means organic material that has been wholly decomposed by microbial activity. Compost is usually made of green stuff (grass clippings) and brown stuff (autumn leaves, twigs) that's been kept in a heap for anywhere from three weeks to one year, whereupon it turns miraculously into dark, clean, earthy-smelling crumbly particles that look like dirt. People who compost love the fact that they have taken a troublesome waste product and turned it into "black gold" that you can't even buy at the so-called soil-sellers' yards. The verb means the process of turning organic material into compost.

HUMUS—Organic matter that has sat around awhile and has been partially decomposed by bacteria. Leaf mold fits nicely into this category. It's just that old pile of leaves that's falling apart, but you can still tell it's leaves.

MULCH—The verb means to spread a layer of something over your soil; the noun means the material you put on top of your soil. Mulches can be organic (sawdust) or inorganic (black plastic, ick!).

ORGANIC—Material that was once alive.

ORGANIC MATTER—The fresh stuff, like leaves, grass clippings, shredded bark, peat moss.

Now let's see if you can use these terms in sentences. One can mulch with compost or amend with compost. Or one could mulch with mulch, compost, or inorganic material, say red cinder rock. But one could never compost inorganic material; rocks just take too long to decompose.

COMPOST

Building good soils by mulching with compost or humus becomes an obsession with most good gardeners. Unlike chemical fertilizers, compost feeds the whole ecosystem, not just the plants, and keeps it healthy. I have done a little reading on compost, and its virtues are too numerous to explain here, but its most engaging quality seems to be its ability to solve totally opposite problems or imbalances in the garden. Soil too sandy? Add compost. Too much clay? Add compost. Soil is not fertile enough or has too many heavy metals? Add compost. Compost seems to have a stabilizing effect in nature and its benefits are long range. Besides, the plants love it, it looks good, it smells good, and it feels good in your hands.

A fairly easy compost program entails making a 4-cubic foot pile of leaves layered with grass clippings. Ideally, you use two parts grass to one part leaves. If you have a lot of room and a lot of organic material to get rid of, you can graduate to a hot compost system. There are several good books that explain hot composting. The heat generated by decomposition of the organic material is great enough to kill most weed seeds and disease organisms. So you can add more and different things to these piles, like weeds.

Composting, like most gardening, and even most of life, I guess, can be as simple or complex as you like. The mother of a friend of mine is a devoted gardener. My friend visited her one day and she proudly showed him her new three-bin compost system. Then she nipped inside to get a packet of something she sent away for in the mail—Compost Starter. Adding water to it, she then poured it reverently into one of the bins. "Good grief, Mother!" exclaimed her son, "That's not a hobby, that's a religion!"

If making your own compost seems like too much trouble, you can buy it in bags or have a pile delivered to your house in many cities now. Commercial material is probably hot composted, and the possibility of spreading weed seeds and plant disease is not a concern.

WORMS

Even more fascinating, I find, are worm boxes on display at my local Tilth Association demonstration garden and at local nurseries and garden fairs. These are boxes in which you place special starter "worms" and shredded newspaper—to these you add your table scraps. Miraculously, the worms multiply and the scraps turn into worm castings to be applied to your garden. Castings need not be broken down further for plants to use. Castings *are* fertilizer. They are, if you will, the straight poop. The reason robins can pick worms off so easily is that worms, being clean-living organisms, return to the surface to leave their castings. Don't underestimate the worms in your yard. Worms constantly mix and stir the soil, aerating it perfectly for roots to push through easily. They create vast and incredible quantities of fertilizer for your garden.

When you have good soil, you have worms, and often when you have worms, you have moles that love to eat them. I was at a nursery recently when a customer asked how to get rid of moles. The nursery person recommended a product that when applied to the ground would gas all the worms to death, thus removing the moles' food source—presumably causing the moles to leave. Kill all the worms? Horrors! Although occasional moderate use of chemical fertilizer is by all means acceptable, I encourage people to avoid over-reliance.

To sum up my own feelings about fertilizers and organics, I quote from the Washington State University Cooperative Extension Service bulletin #0648, Organic Gardening: "Your Long Range Objective should be to build your garden area to a high fertility level and then to maintain fertility through composting and mulches, reducing reliance on commercial and organic fertilizers."

SUMMARY

❑ Fertilizer bags all have three numbers on them that stand for the amount (percentage by weight) of Nitrogen (N), Phosphorus (P), and Potassium (K). Nitrogen is, generally speaking, good for producing green growth. Phosphorus and Potassium are for better roots and blooms, disease resistance, and hardiness.

❑ Don't overuse chemical fertilizers. You burn roots or leaves with overapplication or if you fail to water. Lower-numbered (numbers under twelve) sacks are less concentrated and therefore safer. Don't fertilize too early or too late, too often or too much.

❑ Use organics—mulch, weed seed-free compost, or dried manure—to improve the long-term fertility of the soil.

❑ People always try to use pruning and fertilizing to make up for bad planning. Remedial pruning and fertilizing can only help to a certain point.

❑ Think of chemical fertilizers in the same way as vitamin pills. They are no substitute for a healthy diet. Your soil will benefit greatly from a regular feeding of organic mulch.

Watering

The most common mistakes I see are made by those people who do not water enough or by those who water too little too often. This encourages roots to stay on the top layer of soil instead of going deep to where the water is stored. When these people go on vacation they are surprised to find that their grass has browned—all in a week—and they may not get the connection between drought stress and the fact that their shrublets succumb to root weevil or die in the freeze.

Deep, infrequent watering encourages deep root systems on grass and on all your shrubs and trees. If you start early in the year and water your lawn for an hour or two once a week, it will be able to take it when you go away for your summer vacation.

AUTOMATIC IRRIGATION

Another error occurs when people—including city bureaucrats—"save" money by omitting automatic irrigation systems for parks, public facilities, or commercial landscapes. The money spent paying the crews to drive to public parks and lay out, move, and turn off sprinklers every day soon (within two years) exceeds the cost of putting in an automatic system, plus the cost continues forever. Automatic systems are more reliable than people, and they can water at night or early morning so they don't interfere with sunbathing. Automatic systems make for low maintenance and save money in plant replacement costs, too, if they are properly run.

When you put in a new automatic system, pay the extra costs for durable materials. Be sure every inch of your yard is covered even if there is no plant to water there now—you may wish to put one in there later. When digging to put in irrigation, avoid cutting off all your tree's roots on the trenched side. You will kill it. Where necessary, it is possible to dig or auger straight under the tree roots near the trunk to avoid cutting them. There are even auger bits that will go through solid rock. An old-fashioned way is to drive the irrigation pipe under tree roots with a sledge hammer.

Another thing to remember about your irrigation system is to have your shrub beds and lawn on different control stations. This allows you to turn off your shrub sprinkler so it won't wash off your Roundup, say, or to conserve water by shutting down your lawn sprinklers if there is a water crisis.

If you are installing an irrigation system, put your hand-turned water spigot up high enough to get a bucket under it. When you plant your yard, the temptation is to hide the spigot with a shrub directly in front—don't. You want to have easy access to your spigot. A thorny shrub—like barberry or pyracantha—is to be especially avoided.

An automatic irrigation system comes with a controller box, which you or your irrigationist will set or program to come on at certain days and times. Some are simple, almost like kitchen timers; others, the more intimidating push-button types, remind me of the cockpit of a 747. You may choose to put a little map of which stations are where inside the controller box lid, and perhaps some instructions. Or maybe you just want to memorize where the "off" switch is and then write in the phone number of your irrigationist.

SEMI-AUTOMATIC IRRIGATION

Semi-automatic systems are those old-fashioned ones that turn on with a key that looks like a forked stick. Unlike automatic systems, you will have to be at home, and you must remember to do it.

People commonly kill their trees or cause them to blow over as a result of severing major roots when installing irrigation.

The contractor can safely auger under major roots near the trunk.

CHECKING OUT THE SYSTEM

Things to remember to do with automatic irrigation systems are: start early in the spring, and look for trouble. You will need to have your irrigationist out in the spring, to de-winterize and repair your system and then again in the fall, to drain it for the winter so that the pipes won't freeze. Be sure to call your irrigationist as soon as winter is over. Don't wait until the weather gets hot and dry. They will, by then, be in great demand and you may be unable to get them out soon enough or long enough.

You may choose to go over the system yourself. Turn on each area separately and in your rain gear (or in your swimsuit on a hot day), go see that no heads are broken, leaking, or clogged and not spraying. Also, look for ones out of alignment—meaning that the water sprays out to the sidewalk instead of the grass parking strip. Check for coverage—sometimes shrubs grow up and block the water from reaching its intended area. Then you either lower the shrub with pruning or have the irrigationist add a section of pipe to raise the head. There are limits to how much the heads can be raised—it depends on the available water pressure. Heads that aren't putting out water are often clogged with tiny bits of rust or debris. A penknife, paper clip, or screwdriver can be used to clear the opening

easily. Turning the tiny screw on the top of the head will adjust the amount of spray from your sprinkler. You can even take a head off, if you're bold, using two wrenches. Run water through the pipes to flush out any debris.

Poor lawn coverage often results when turf grows over your sprinkler heads. In the spring, use a knife to cut the turf away from the heads.

Once the system is in good working order, it's easy to forget it. Don't. I spend a certain amount of time training my customers to spot trouble before it's too late. Old irrigation systems will, from time to time, break. Usually, the only ones that the customers notice are the broken heads in the middle of the lawn because a giant brown patch develops in the middle of the green field. There are often fairly obvious signs that are overlooked until very obvious ones, like dead plants, catch the homeowner's eye. If you are weeding through your bed and the soil goes from moist to bone dry—notice it. You may have a station or head not working. An eroded hole developing around a head indicates a break at ground level or below. If you see what looks like a dry rivulet of mulch or dirt particles on your sidewalk, it may mean that you have a midnight "gurgler" or "gusher" or "geyser," terms for broken heads or pipes, causing minor flooding as you sleep. To

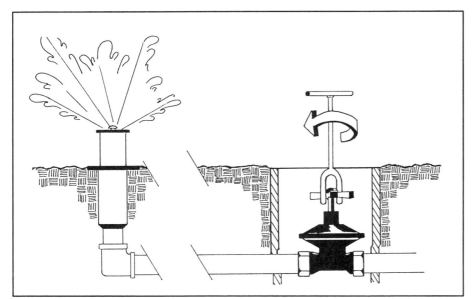

A semi-automatic irrigation system.

Sometimes shrubs grow up and block the water from reaching its intended area.

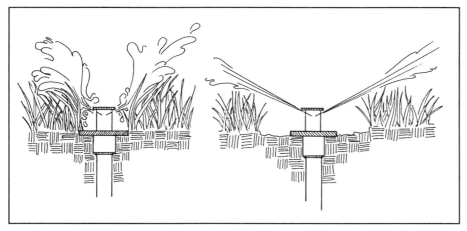

Poor lawn coverage often results when the turf grows up over the sprinkler heads.

check this out, just turn your system on "manual" and go through the stations and take a close look at what is happening. When you find the break, turn that station off and call the plumber.

HAND WATERING

If you are too poor or too foolish, as I was, to pay for automatic irrigation, you will find yourself stuck with hose and sprinkler. Even here you will find there are ways to ease your maintenance workload. They, too, are unfortunately directly correlated with initial financial outlay. The most useful of these gadgets is a mechanical timer for your hose. It looks and works much like a giant kitchen egg timer. It attaches to the spigot and then your hose screws onto it. Part of the great hassle of hand watering is that you have to hang around to turn it off. And you have to remember how long it's been on before you move the sprinkler. With the auto-timer, you simply spin the dial to the desired time (actually it measures gallons of water), and then just drive off to the grocery store, or go to sleep, or clean the house until you hear the water shut off. Then you will remember to go move the sprinkler. There is even an electronic-type timer for hose and sprinkler watering that fits between the hose bib and the hose. You can program it to come on for, say, an hour every third day.

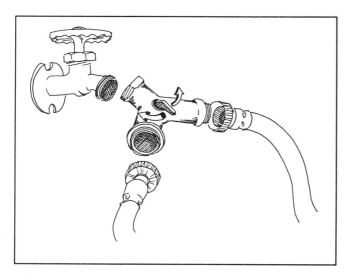

This handy irrigation device allows you to put two hoses on one spigot. A similar device allows you to shut the water off at the hose end.

Another handy device to put on between your timer and the hose will *split* the water. You can now attach two hoses to the same faucet. This is useful if—like me—you need to run one hose to the front and one to the back. This way both hoses stay in place; you just flip a tiny lever to move the water from one to the other.

HOSES

The garden hose—now there's an instrument of the devil. Just try to coil them neatly—they won't stay that way. Try to lay them flat—they curl and kink. Move them, they catch on corners, rocks, or tree trunks. Or, after you drag them to a new location, you find that you have flattened the flower beds or knocked over the flower pots. One help for this latter problem is to place rocks or stakes strategically, at the leading edge of flower beds to keep the hoses in their proper paths. And the most frustrating experience of all is when you try to attach the hose end to the sprinkler only to find that someone has driven over it and squashed the metal end, rendering the hose useless.

Buy the heavier hoses for your yard. They kink less and reduce the frustration quotient. When a hose is "kinked," if you are not familiar with this term, it is folded over, stopping the flow of water. When you turn on the faucet but find that no water is coming out of the sprinkler, you must trace the hose to find the kink. Kinking a hose with your hand can be useful if you are hand watering and you want to temporarily stop the flow of water. You just bend the hose back into a loop and squeeze it together. This, however, can predispose the hose to kink at this spot later on. A new gadget in the hardware store is a hose-end manual shut-off. No more back and forth to the spigot to change sprinklers or reconnect hoses.

The worst hoses for kinking are soaker hoses. These are the ones that act as sprinklers because they have holes in them. They are used to water long, skinny places or to run under trees and shrubs in order to get the water down to their roots. Soaker hoses are good for plants that are prone to fungus disease on their leaves, like roses and dogwoods. They water the plant's roots without giving the disease organisms the damp leaves they love.

Until recently, soaker hoses were built flat with holes on one side. As a gardener, you spent a lot of time making sure the hose was resting perfectly flat, no kinks, hole side up, usually walking, or more like skating, on it to get it right. What a device of torture. A great new type is now available called Spray and Soak®. It is made of a soft material that collapses when not filled with water, and it has holes all the way around. It is tube-like when full of water, and flat when empty. This makes these hoses a relative dream to move, store, and lay out. In my yard I leave a network of these laid out in the shrub areas where they are half hidden and never have to be moved to mow. These soft Spray and Soak hoses are not to be confused with Leaky Hose®, which is stiffer and not designed to spray, just to soak. For the large grass area I use a standard oscillating (back and forth) sprinkler.

SNAP SYSTEMS

The final investment you may choose to make is to buy snap-on type ends for all your various hoses. Once you have all your various hoses and sprinklers in place you will find that you spend the bulk of your time screwing and unscrewing hoses to hoses and hoses to sprinklers. The Gardena® system will convert all this to an irrigation system that works a lot like pop-beads. Hose and sprinkler ends just snap together.

CORRECT AMOUNTS OF WATER

I get into trouble from people who are concerned about water conservation by recommending more water. They have a good point. One way to cut down your water needs is to plant drought-tolerant plants. A well-planned garden will also group plants with similar water and soil needs together.

Exactly how much water you need to use will depend on numerous factors. Sandy soils need more water and more frequent watering; raised beds require more water; plantings on the sunny south side or exposed to wind require more. Intelligent use of mulch and increasing the water-holding capacity of your soil by adding organic amendments is a very, very good idea. Small plants, like annual flowers (marigolds, impatiens, petunias), require more fre-

quent water but not so much, because their roots are nearer the surface. A big old tree may only need attention once during the drought. Leave a hose on a trickle in the root zone, perhaps all night. This is a surprise to many people—trees can and do die from drought, succumbing as much as a year or two later.

COMPACTION

If the water doesn't seem to want to percolate down into the ground, you may have compacted soil. This is a common condition in very old and very new homes. It is the result of fifty years of foot traffic, rain, and tree roots without the relief of organic matter, in the former. In the latter, compaction is the result of bulldozers and other heavy equipment driving all over it. It is especially easy to compact soil by driving on it, walking on it, or working it when it is very wet. Compacted soil has had all the air spaces squashed out of it. It's hard to dig, like clay.

Moss in your lawn, especially if it's a sunny lawn, is often the sign of compaction. The cure for compacted soil in your shrub bed is, you guessed it, amending with organics. To help alleviate compaction in your lawn, rent a power tool called an aerator. It looks like a tiny steam roller with hollow spikes on it. It cores out hundreds of small holes. To get water or fertilizer down to the roots of your big old tree, it may even be necessary to drill holes with a power drill and a big, long auger.

SIGNS OF STRESS

The most important information in this chapter is the advice to *water when it is needed*. Some automatic systems have a sensor that will keep your system from coming on when it's been raining. Really neat, huh? For you hose and sprinkler waterers, learn to read the signs of thirsty plants. Professional gardeners commonly anticipate the time of year to start nagging their customers to water. This is because we see plants start to dry out long before homeowners do. Rhododendrons, in particular, fairly scream their heads off asking for water. A very happy rhododendron's topmost leaves on each branch will point up. A contented rhody's top whorl of leaves is more or less horizontal. A stressed-out plant, from cold, drying wind, or no water, will hold its leaves down. When it's in big trouble, they even curl inward.

On other plants, signs of drought stress are leaves that look dryer and lighter in color, feel crispy to the touch, or whose leaf tips or edges are uniform light (or dark) brown in color. Light rain during the summer can lull you into a false sense of security. The best test, as you know, is to dig your finger down into the soil and see if it's damp. Another tip-off is high temperatures, high winds, and many days without rain. Oh, the poor plants, so many die needlessly through their owners' neglect of the obvious.

LESS WATER

On rare occasions your plants may benefit from withholding water. These are ones growing in areas known to contain root-rot organisms. Often, but not always, these plants are in poorly drained soils. Some junipers and maples get root rots fairly often. Madronas and native western dogwood will benefit if their roots are not kept moist, say, by being in a regularly watered lawn area. They are adapted to dry summer conditions in their native habitats. Put these with other plants that like it dry, and water less in that area.

SUMMARY

❑ Insufficient water is a major cause of plant death, even from seemingly unrelated causes.

❑ Water deeply but infrequently.

❑ Invest in manual irrigation aids: water timers, heavy hoses, soaker hoses, water splitters, snap-together systems, hose end shut-offs.

❑ Invest in automatic irrigation systems and:

1. Activate your automatic system early in spring.

2. Take the time to check each station visually for trouble. Use a paper clip, penknife, and two wrenches to fine-tune your system.

Look for trouble:

❑ Plants dying of thirst have dull, yellowing, crispy leaves.

❑ Is your soil moist 2 inches down? Use your finger to dig down and be sure.

Factors affecting water needs:

❑ Is plant a drought or heat lover species? Less water.

❑ Is plant a shade- or water-loving species? More water.

❑ On a slope? More water, slowly.

❑ On the south or west side? More water.

❑ Windy out? Greater water need.

❑ Soil have a lot of organics? Good.

❑ Mulch used? Water deeply.

❑ Tiny plants? Shallow roots? Less water more frequently.

❑ Big plants? (trees) Deeper roots, deep water less often.

❑ New transplant? (Year or two?) Needs more water.

Pests and Diseases

The "eekstomp syndrome" is what our local Extension Agent, Sharon Collman, calls it. The homeowner sees a black beetle on the sidewalk—EEK, he STOMPS it dead. Those black beetles are valuable predators in your yard: they eat the bugs that eat your plants. People hate bugs. They assume that all bugs are bad bugs. People think that if they get a powerful enough spray—one that gets everything—they can put an end to what they think are invading insect hordes. They fear that if they don't do something, the bugs will proceed unchecked to decimate everything in the yard.

PREDATOR/PREY RELATIONSHIPS

The truth is that the vast majority of insects and other critters in the yard are doing minimal harm, and many others are doing a lot of good. Another little-appreciated fact is that nature, even in your backyard, is, for the most part, self-correcting. The miniature world of bugs is an entire ecosystem. Some bugs reproduce fast and eat a lot—like rabbits in the world of bigger animals—and other bugs are predators—the wolves. When you have an outbreak of plant-eating insects, they reproduce much faster than their predators. It takes awhile for the predator population to catch up. For example, aphids may become quite numerous before the wolves (ladybugs and lacewings) reach numbers sufficient to destroy their population. Refer to the accompanying graph of typical prey-predator population cycles. Usually the homeowner panics just as the predators really start to get going. Pesticides often wipe out the predators as well. This leaves an open field for the prey, the aphids (some of which always escape or hatch later or fly in from next door), now totally unchecked, to reproduce like crazy. You will get a rebound, a population explosion. And then you will have to spray again, and again, and again.

The adage to remember here—and it works in all nature—is, "If you kill the predators, you inherit their work." There are lots of predators in your yard. Some are nice looking and easily recognized, like birds and ladybugs. Others look just as icky as all those other bugs—spiders, wasps, flies, beetles, and the impressively grotesque praying mantis.

Other natural checks on pest populations include their own collection of yet tinier parasites and diseases. A good example of this is the tent caterpillar. It doesn't taste good enough for most birds to eat, but a very specific fly likes to lay its eggs on their bodies. The larva from these eggs eat the guts of the caterpillars. You can see it for yourself. Find some tent caterpillars and look for the distinctive white dot or dots—those are the eggs. A dotted caterpillar is a doomed caterpillar.

People *will* panic. They should know that most healthy plants can withstand a fair amount of damage. A healthy broadleaf tree can even be totally defoliated for a year by tent caterpillars or whatever, and return just fine. One-fourth of total leaf surface damaged is considered the rule of thumb for human intervention in an ornamental landscape, though.

WATCHING NATURE AT WORK

At the time this book is being written, my area has entered the second year of tent caterpillars. Last year they were so severe that entire groves of alder trees stood with branches as barren as in winter, but in mid-June. It was then that I realized I was seeing "natural selection" in progress. The trees that would actually die would be the ones that were already weakened. For whatever reason, the defoliation would simply polish them off. The fittest would survive. Nature was thinning the alder grove, just as the farmer thins the row of young carrots, leaving the

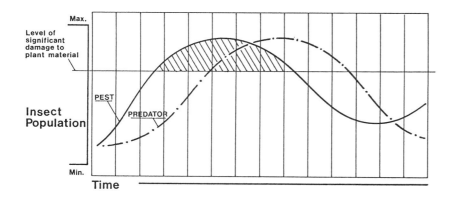

TYPICAL PEST/PREDATOR POPULATION CYCLE

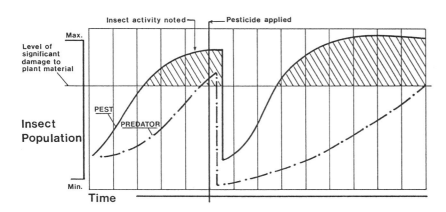

Note: Increase in significant damage

POPULATION CYCLE INTERRUPTED WITH PESTICIDE APPLIC.

Pesticides are often non-selective. They kill both the predators and prey alike. This results in an unchecked population explosion of unwanted pests. Your yard has become chemically dependent.

most promising ones. This year, the nests or tents were fewer, and in the city just simply failed to produce vast quantities of adult caterpillars. Nature, not chemicals, checked their progress. (There is evidence discovered by Drs. David Rhodes and A.B. Adams that the plants change chemically and become less tasty.)

Mankind is becoming increasingly skillful at eliminating species of plants and animals. We are best at destroying birds, but we do well with mammals and reptiles, too. However, try as we may, we have never been able intentionally to eliminate a single pest species of insect using chemicals. The common reliance on large quantities of pesticides has, however, had the alarming result of selecting for pesti-

cide-immune bugs! Malaria, a disease carried by a certain type of mosquito, was all but beaten by the use of DDT to destroy the bug. Because of the insect's rapid rate of reproduction, however, we now have breeds that are not affected by the commonly used pesticide. Farmers are finding out these hard facts about "controlling nature" now, too. Some continue to cover spray and hope that chemists will be able to invent new weapons as fast as the insects can mutate. More and more farmers are selecting pest- and disease-resistant plant varieties, while encouraging natural predators and parasites, and becoming tolerant of low levels of damage. These are looking like wiser and wiser alternatives. They are wise choices for you, too.

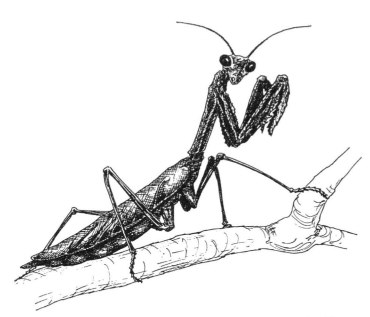

Ninety percent of the bugs in your yard do no significant damage to your plants. Many are beneficial insects like this praying mantis.

HOST-SPECIFIC PESTS

Something not commonly known is that most pests and diseases have only a few favorite plants, and many plants have specific pests that especially like them. In my area, I know, for example, that if you have a birch tree, you have, or will soon have, aphids and honeydew. If you have a native or Eastern dogwood, it is likely to have a fungal disease that scorches leaf tips, called anthracnose. Your weeping cherry probably has blossom brown rot, and your rhododendron has root weevils munching little notches in the leaves; your blue spruce has spruce aphids that are causing all the inside needles to brown and fall off in the summer, long after the aphid itself is gone. Your deciduous azaleas and Oregon grape have something that looks like powder on them (powdery mildew), and your old deciduous azalea has a grayish lichen on the branches and stems, which isn't actually hurting the plant at all, it just lives on the plant.

Other organisms can even be "symbiotic," which means they actually help their hosts. A common, thread-like type of fungus called *micchorizae* lives in association with the roots of some trees and plants. It takes nutrients from the roots, but in return it helps the roots absorb water and elements from the soil.

Knowing that most pests are fairly "host specific" (they like only one or two kinds of plants) may keep you from panicking and spraying your whole yard for fear that what your dogwood has is going to spread. It will also help you to diagnose your plant's problem. Accurate diagnosis and good timing are keys to effective treatment.

The numbers and types of pests that want to lunch on your trees and shrubs are vast. They can be divided into several large categories that determine what you can spray to stop them. There is no one chemical that gets them all. There are the so-called "broad-spectrum" pesticides that get whole subgroups of insects. However, they often get the beneficial insects as well. Reliance on broad-spectrum pesticides will also hasten the day that the bugs become resistant to them. Horticulturists now advocate using as narrow and focused a product as you can get in order to reduce the impact on the rest of the environment as much as possible.

DISEASE CATEGORIES—PEST DIAGNOSIS

General categories of insects and diseases are as follows:

Plant disease organisms:

❏ Fungus and bacteria (including root rots)

❏ Viruses—little chemical cure available

Insects and mites:

❏ Chewing insects: caterpillars, beetles, and sawflies, for example

❏ Piercing-sucking insects, such as aphids and scales

❏ Mites

You must find out what you have in order to treat it. The insecticide you used to kill a caterpillar won't work on a fungus disease. And chemicals will not kill a virus. Many insecticides used to kill caterpillars on your tree will, if they get on the clover flowers in your grass, poison foraging honeybees, which will take the poison back to the hive and kill all their buddies and larval bees, too.

For caterpillars you may be better off to use Bt. Bt

is short for *Bacillus thuringiensis*, a naturally occurring disease that kills just caterpillars. It is the active ingredient in several brands of sprays and dusts.

Bee kill is a big problem. Bees are the gardener's friend. We must have them to pollinate our fruits and vegetables. Environmental precautions are listed on pesticide labels. Once again, the label on any container of pesticide is a legal document—it must be *read* and the *instructions followed*. It will tell you if it can kill bees or poison fish. It also lists the exact plants and bugs or diseases the chemical will get.

You must take the time to sit down with your magnifying glass and read and understand it ALL. Then, FOLLOW THE DIRECTIONS. If it cautions you to avoid spraying plants in bloom, then AVOID SPRAYING PLANTS IN BLOOM.

TIMING

Just to make matters more complicated, it is a simple fact that proper timing is crucial to good pest control. Not only must you diagnose your pest, you need to know the vulnerable point in its life cycle. The window of spray opportunity for some species of scale is, for example, only a couple of weeks in the spring when they are in their crawler phase.

COVER SPRAYS

Does all this pesticide information seem pretty complicated? Well, it is. I guess this is why people resort to general sprays. Some chemical spray companies provide cover spray service to homeowners by coming four to six times a year and blasting everything in sight with a barrage of different chemicals. Because this kills all the beneficial organisms as well, the homeowner is locked into the pesticide treadmill. When weaning chemically-dependent yards from cover sprays, one often experiences a small explosion of pests because the beneficial organisms are absent—sometimes confirming in the mind of the homeowner the need for spraying.

I suggest people avoid becoming chemically dependent on cover sprays. Just say NO! Not only are we pouring gallons of poisons into the environment (reread the tales of horror in the section on weeds) that do who-knows-what to beneficial insects, birds,

pets, people, and the groundwater, it's also a terrible waste of money and chemicals. Often these companies spray for pests that are long since departed or, because of poor timing, their sprays miss the target. It hastens the day when the pests develop resistance to the sprays, and then we will be in even worse trouble. It's as if you treated your own health by having a doctor come by four times a year and give you massive doses of penicillin, pain killer, and radiation therapy, just in case, whether or not you had anything wrong. Well, that's one way to do it.

INTEGRATED PEST MANAGEMENT

To manage your garden, I recommend following the principles of IPM, which stands for Integrated Pest Management. It is a decision-making approach that looks at the problem from several integrated methods, based on the pest, its stage of development, and the site.

Foremost among these is preventive maintenance by keeping healthy plants and a healthy ecosystem. As John Davey, the father of modern arboriculture, said eight decades ago, "Good health defies disease!" It's true. Bugs and diseases pick on unhealthy plants. The sap or pitch in a healthy tree will actually blast off and drown an insect that pierces its skin. Unhealthy plants can least withstand even moderate damage.

In an earlier section I described moving some azaleas farther apart. When I did so, I added dried manure and organic matter to improve the soil. Previously they had been perpetually eaten and tortured by root weevils. Now there is only the occasional munch mark. If you follow the advice of previous sections (good soil, eliminate weeds, cut out dead wood, rake up leaves if they are diseased, not too much or too little water or fertilizer, right plants, right place), you won't have so many disease and insect problems.

If there is really a need for chemical intervention (and that's a big IF), use the least toxic and most pest-specific chemical.

When a broad-spectrum pesticide is chosen, aim it at the target pest and affected plant only. If it can harm bees, don't use it when the plant (or underlying clover) is in bloom. Don't spray everything else in the yard "just in case." Try alternative methods of control. Dormant oils can be used in the winter to smother egg masses. Oils are just that—oil—and some kinds are used to smother scale crawlers, aphid eggs, and mites, too. Timing, again, is very important. A whole line of insecticidal "soaps" is becoming more widely used—either alone or mixed with reduced concentrations of chemical pesticides. Davey Tree Expert Company is leading the way with accurate research in this program of soap-chemical pest control. The soaps are especially useful in controlling soft-bodied insects such as aphids and scale in the crawler stage.

Many diseases are aggravated by gardening practices. Watering at night places water on leaves during the cool time so leaves don't dry off. Wet leaves during warm (60° to 70°) temperatures are ideal for some fungus diseases such as powdery mildew, rose black spot, and some vegetable diseases. Early morning watering allows leaves to dry.

Proper diagnosis of the disease or insect problem will help you avoid overreacting. Find out whether you are dealing with "cancer" or just the "common cold." If you find phythopthora, a very contagious and devastating root rot, you have good cause to consider chemical treatment. If it's just a spit bug, ignore it. *Tolerance* is the watchword.

When you feel you have to, spot spray with chemicals, use the right ones, follow directions, and pay attention to timing.

COOPERATIVE EXTENSION SERVICES

The Cooperative Extension Service of your state's land grant college is a valuable resource. Many states or counties have Master Gardener programs as well. You can take a piece of affected plant and/or the bug into a plant clinic and the volunteer will help you diagnose it. Be advised that a weak plant may attract several insects or diseases and, if you are lucky, the predators of those pests. Don't assume that the first bug you see is the one responsible for the damage. The Cooperative Extension Service also has inexpensive bulletins describing common pests and their cures. Some may have taped phone messages, such as my county's "Dial-Extension." The really nice thing about the Cooper-

ative Extension Service is its staff of specialists, who are well-versed on the specific pest or soil problems and plant requirements of your own area. Their information is given on research-based facts, not gardener mythology, and the price is always right. (See Appendix.)

OTHER TIPS FOR PEST PROBLEMS

It may also be useful to know that your garden is a little more prone to pests and diseases when it's new, before the web of checks and balances has developed and your plants get older and tougher.

The problem with using garden pesticides responsibly is that you are apt to have a headache from reading all that fine print on the labels. Having to know the names and life cycles of many pests can be a daunting assignment. Keeping a healthy yard and only treating the few persistent, predictable, serious, and unavoidable problems may make it seem less overwhelming. It certainly makes better sense than trying to eliminate all pests.

In my area, the only plants for which I sometimes recommend homeowners seek chemical help (after following good cultural practice) are cherries, for brown rot; fruit trees—especially, for scab; roses, for black spot; dogwoods, for anthracnose; and blue spruce. Your area will have its own predictable problems list.

Root weevil populations in azaleas, rhododendrons, primroses, fuchsias, pieris, salal, and bergenia sometimes get out of hand and may occasionally need spraying with appropriate chemicals. Chronic chewing and shredding of leaves year after year, however, indicates a cultural problem, like poor drainage or insufficient water or susceptible species. Lists of resistant species are available through Extension Agents and nurseries. Know that you will *always* have some damage. The plants can take it—if you can.

MOLES

Mole populations occasionally expand beyond acceptable proportions. The population may "crash" naturally, or you may choose to intervene. Moles, by the way, do not eat plants. They are carnivorous. They eat worms and the like. Mice that use mole tunnels eat plants. Usually people want to get rid of moles because they are tearing up the place. (The irrational actions of some in response to molehills may be where the phrase "making mountains out of molehills" came from.)

Mole remedies number in the scores. Most problems that have 101 solutions have none that works reliably. Mole cures that don't work include pouring various nasty liquids down the hole, gassing them with exhaust from your car, windmills and whirligigs that rattle and blow in the wind (the vibration is supposed to chase them off), cat hair in the hole, various plants that they presumably hate, laxatives and, my favorite, chewing gum. The only proven cure for getting rid of moles is the scissor trap. Correct placement in a major underground arterial runway is necessary. Sometimes you need to modify the trap to catch the smaller species. Information on trapping is also available from your Cooperative Extension Service.

BEES, YELLOW JACKETS, WASPS

Bees, yellow jackets, and wasps are not created equal. Bumblebees, for example, are extremely slow moving and docile. These are the big, fat, almost furry-looking ones that are black and yellow or orange. They always make me smile—I think of them as the teddy bears of the insect world. You'll have a hard time getting a bumblebee to sting you. You'll have to step on it in your bare feet, probably, or dig around a nest in the compost pile and insult its mother. Honeybees, a little sleeker, honey to brown color, are smarter and a little touchier. Generally speaking, if you don't bother them as they go about their business collecting nectar and pollinating, they won't bother you.

Meat-eaters, like yellow jackets and bald-faced (white-faced) hornets are more likely to nail you if you get too close to their nests. The bald-faced hornets are especially hot-headed. Their white bald heads are quite distinctive. If they feel threatened, they will chase you down, drill you with their stinger, and send their pals after you, too. And they hurt! When I'm weeding and I look up to find a paper wasps' nest 2 feet from me in some shrub, my heart skips a beat. But only if a yellow jacket or hornet nest is actually too close to human habita-

tion (places like the children's play area or your front porch) do I bother dealing with it. After all, these insects are predators and serve useful functions in the garden. I just avoid working around the nests. Bald-faced hornets will not scavenge in picnic areas. However, a major problem with the common yellow jackets is that they pester at picnics, around garbage cans, and at the edge of water sources. Yellow jacket nests may need to be eliminated for this reason. I'm allergic to yellow jackets and carry pills with me for when I get stung, usually once a year, but I'm in the business, as they say. The average person won't get stung for years and doesn't need to worry unduly.

Working as a Master Gardener, I once had a woman ask for a chemical to kill aphids. I suggested she just put up with them on her maple tree. But no, she insisted. She had just had her tree radically topped so she could spray it all over to kill the aphids, because they created honeydew, and someone told her if you have honeydew, you will have yellow jackets. And her husband was allergic to their stings. People have unreasonable expectations for controlling the natural environment. You might as well stop driving because you might die in a traffic accident. The rational answer is: use good sense and be reasonably cautious as you go about your business.

For that nest just outside your door, several products will give you good control. Spray cans of hornet killer will shoot up to 20 feet, will even freeze them in mid-flight and totally wipe out the nest when you soak it. You will want to use it at first morning light or late at night when the hornets are all quietly at home, asleep, not during the day when they are buzzing around defending their territory.

SLUGS

Last on the list of common pests in this area is SLUGS, omnipresent SLUGS. I've only had to spray a few times in my yard to keep a couple of diseases in check, but I always bait for slugs. You can help keep slug populations down by destroying their hiding places and places they lay their tiny, pearl-like eggs. These places are the dark and moist nooks and crannies. Eliminate piles of leaves and debris and areas of weeds. "Organic" methods of control include hunting at night, either stabbing them with trowel or tossing them in a pail of soapy water. Other people place saucers or pans of beer (seriously!) on the ground. Do not sink the saucer to ground level or you will get the good beetle predators as well. The slugs come from miles around to climb in, get drunk, die blissfully, and dissolve. Still, this method is too gross for this gardener. I use bait. Slug bait is made of methaldehyde, usually on an apple pumice or bran base. It's very attractive to slugs and very deadly. Unfortunately, some baits may attract and poison birds and dogs, too. Therefore, you will have to hide the bait, under boards or some other way. Some people place bait in a plastic container with a lid, like a cottage cheese container. They cut a hole in the sides or lid to allow slugs entry and to keep the container off soil and away from birds, kids, etc. This also keeps the bait dry. Stores also sell small brown bait umbrellas that look sort of like mushrooms. You can push one of those over your pile of bait to hide it from the dogs, and to protect it from the rain, moist soil, and sprinklers, which will destroy its effectiveness after a few days. I sometimes use Go-West Meal™, which you sprinkle lightly around—the idea being that it's not in a big enough quantity to cause harm. It claims to have moderate effect in controlling root weevils as well.

IPM SPRAY SERVICES

The smarter companies in the pest-control business are now moving toward programs utilizing several or all the principles of Integrated Pest Management. Instead of coming home to a yard full of shrubs dripping in chemical pesticides, you come home to a pest-monitor report hung on your doorknob. It means that you are paying someone for what they know, to check your trees and shrubs regularly, assessing the pest and disease situation. They can spot early warning signs, when intervention is most successful. Most homeowners call up and ask for help when the damage has reached a peak and the pest may even be gone. If you get a really good company, they will recommend chemical controls for only the most serious problems, not for every little bug that takes a nibble. Many companies offer a full care program for your yard, including proper pruning and fertilizing. It would seem that the concept of preventive medicine through good health is an idea that is catching on—for people, for the urban environment, and for the planet as a whole.

SUMMARY

❑ Good health discourages pest and disease problems: good soil, water, pruning, garden hygiene (weeding and raking leaves).

❑ Be tolerant of a certain amount of damage because it allows enough food sources (bugs) to keep the predators alive, which will, in turn, help check the population of the pest. Just remember, some caterpillars turn into pretty butterflies or moths that become bird food.

❑ Use disease-resistant plants and correct placement. Right plant, right place.

❑ Diagnose correctly. Find out what it is, if it's really a problem, when and how to control it.

❑ Try mechanical and cultural controls.

When using chemical controls:

❑ Read the label—ALL OF IT.

❑ Time the application properly.

❑ Spot spray.

❑ Use the "most specific" and least toxic chemical.

❑ Be careful.

A Woman: A Plan: An Organization: PlantAmnesty!

This book was written as part of a larger project called PlantAmnesty. PlantAmnesty is an organization founded in the summer of 1987, "to end the senseless torture and mutilation of trees and shrubs." Mostly we concentrate on promoting better pruning —but as you can see—we address other gardening issues.

The specific task of PA is to end the prevalence of bad pruning in King County in five years, as proof that it can be done anywhere—and done fast. We have more than 500 members, to whom I send a newsletter. Our motto—*secare selecte*—is Latin for "prune selectively."

All our aspects of work are designed to answer the question, "What would it take to end bad pruning?"

The first goal of the organization is to raise awareness. Most people don't know and furthermore, don't much care, that vast numbers of living trees and shrubs are being stupidly destroyed and uglified. Therefore, we invented a campaign. We use the combination of controversy and humor to get the public's attention. We utilize the mass media— TV, newspapers, radio—to alert and educate the public to the issues of bad pruning. Hence, the annual ugly yard contest; the slide show of pruning horrors; articles about topping, poodleballing, stripping; the booth that goes to home shows and garden shows, and who knows what next. At this stage we are trying to get people to be able to identify bad pruning, and we explain the exact reasons it is considered "bad."

I am totally convinced that without the campaign no significant change in the body of public knowledge (and practice) can occur. At least not in my lifetime. Once we have the public's (and professionals') attention, we want to move immediately to, "So, you made a few mistakes. This is the better way to do it."

This is the second goal of PlantAmnesty: to give the public and professionals *all the tools* they need to prune and renovate properly. Hence this book, which is not meant to be the last word on pruning but a tool for the average yard owner, to keep him or her out of trouble. Other projects in this same vein include classes, lectures, and lessons on pruning, lots of them. I teach now, and keep track of and encourage other classes. Hopefully, free or low-cost ones will be made available by parks or by local hardware stores. We have made a video of my class and offer it. PlantAmnesty arborists already have begun to teach proper tall tree pruning to "the toppers."

Among the list of "all the tools" comes the how-to video for the homeowner called "This Old Yard," showing a real three-dimensional makeover of a yard. We are presently seeking funding and corporate sponsorship.

Another tool is the PlantAmnesty referral service of good gardeners. For people who are too busy, too tired, too old, too rich, or who tried to learn to prune but just can't get it, there must be competent gardeners.

FINDING A GOOD GARDENER

A good gardener is hard to find. Most people in the maintenance businesses are barely "literate" in their own field. Many are hardworking, well-meaning, kind, and good people who just don't know what they're doing. How is the homeowner to tell the difference? There are no state testing or licensing requirements. You could inquire whether or not they are members of professional groups like our WSNLA (Washington State Nurseryman's and Landscaper's Association), or if they've completed a horticultural degree at the local community college. These help, but I've found many "qualified" gardeners still don't know how to prune and, conversely, many people who just learned from experience and from other gardeners are quite good. Large landscape companies tend to lose control of quality and will send a different guy to your yard every month. You will have to look for a personal gardener in the classified ads of small neighborhood newspapers. Most really good personal gardeners are too busy to take on new clients, after about a year or two of owning their own businesses.

The PlantAmnesty referral service looks for people who have both education and experience. Often they are new in town or just starting their own businesses. We give them a test. Examples of pruning questions are, "Which is the worst choice to renew by cutting back hard? (A) forsythia; (B) quince; (C) star magnolia." "Which is easiest to reduce or keep under a window? (A) mock orange; (B) rhododendron; (C) choisya." My favorite is, "Under what circumstances will you top a tree?" A good personal gardener will know the botanical name of most shrubs. It's the key to accessing in-depth knowledge in the field of horticulture.

When you find and interview gardeners, just walk around and talk about your yard with them. Aside from seeing what they know about pruning and plants, you should feel comfortable with them. A good gardener shares the same outlook on your garden — really expert gardeners will learn what your individual preferences are and anticipate them, even if they are not shared preferences. But as true professionals they will temper what you want with what's good for the garden. They will be able to help you decide on design improvements and introduce you to new, rare, and wonderful plants. A professional gardener will actually enjoy the challenge of pruning a thorny shrub and relieving you of the hard physical work. Look for gardeners in the winter when they aren't rushed with work.

Some people have fears that they will be aced out of their own gardens by hiring a gardener. But many gardeners enjoy doing "background" work, which is

a restaurant term that means they will wash the pots and pans and mince the onions while you cook the stew. They will get to know you almost like a friend who's there to help.

People are reluctant to hire a gardener because they feel that keeping up on the yard is something they ought to be able to do themselves. I think this is wasted guilt for people who work for a living or have kids (also work) or are getting on in years. People don't feel obligated to bake their own bread, fix their own cars, or teach their own kids history. More and more are now opting for some help with the housework, too. Garden work can be just that— work, and skilled, hard work at that.

People also hate to spend money on the garden because it's seen as a luxury item, unlike spending money on your car, which gets you places, or for a restaurant meal, which actually provides necessary food. But keeping a beautiful, clean outdoor space should be as important as keeping your indoor "rooms" in good order.

GARDEN CONSULTATIONS

You may not be able to afford a regular gardener, but like people who remodel their own homes, you may want to bring in an "expert" to do major pruning and to consult on what needs to be done. You can save money on a major restoration project by working with an expert and doing all the hauling, wheelbarrowing, and "grunt work" yourself. Other people may only be able to invest in a one- or two-hour consultation. Draw a map of your yard and go over it with your gardener. He will identify your plants, assess the general state of the yard, and give you suggestions of where to go from there.

Good gardeners tend to be underpaid. As a class, we suffer from lack of self-esteem and feel that profit is a nasty word. We are also in direct competition with cheaper, faster, unskilled workers, many of whom cut costs by avoiding paying taxes. This keeps our rates unnaturally low. You are likely to be shocked by the hourly rate of a good gardener. It's right up there with mechanics, butchers, plumbers, and truck drivers. As self-employed workers, we must pay for our equipment, our vacations, our sick leave, our medical and dental care. We spend our weekends at the dump or buying tools and supplies. We spend our evenings doing the books, sharpening the chain saw, or talking to clients.

Weeding, pruning, and hauling as fast as you can every day is hard physical work. Being a gardener is a lot like having the flu all the time. Your body aches and your brain goes dead at the end of the day. And if you should damage your body, strain your hands or break a foot, you are out of work, with no accident insurance. So, if you hire a horticulturist be prepared to pay professional—not cheap labor—wages. You are paying as much for what they know as what they do.

THE GOAL

The last goal of PlantAmnesty is basically inspirational. We want to get people to see and appreciate the "nature" that's possible in their own backyards. We also want to engender a profound respect for nature as represented by the photosynthesizers—especially trees.

Inspirational soon turns to philosophical. PlantAmnesty is constantly being drawn into the greater "ecological" issues, such as the cutting of old growth here at home and the elimination of rain forests everywhere. I am convinced that it is the same disrespect for nature that allows a homeowner to cut an eighty-year-old oak in half to "preserve his view" of the water, as allows the logger to demand that half the old growth forest of 500- to 1,000-year-old trees, and with it the spotted owls, be eliminated to keep him employed at the same job for another five years.

I feel that at the root of this is the fairly common belief that things have value only as they are useful to mankind. Some things have this useful value only as things that we enjoy, like music or art or gardens and wilderness. People also commonly generalize things that are expedient, convenient, and useful (especially as it concerns their livelihood) into things that they think are essential for survival. Exxon's preserving of profit margin soon gets confused with preserving jobs and human life itself.

A good example of this Man versus Nature syndrome occurred fairly early in PlantAmnesty's history. I reported a story in our newsletter wherein a tree pruner on a crew was told to cut down a particu-

larly nice old elm, so that an old couple could have a view. The tree pruner refused and argued that the tree had been alive long before its "owners" and would live long after them and had, therefore, the superior right to stay. A PlantAmnesty member wrote to me to make sure that I knew that a human's life is, because God says so, more valuable than that of a tree. Somehow the tree's right to survive seemed to be in opposition to not "the view" but the lives of the people. This type of survival-generalizing is seen everywhere, like on the bumper stickers that say, "Loggers—an endangered species." Spotted owls are an endangered species if we cut down the old growth forest, and Northwest old growth forests are an endangered ecosystem. (But trees, in the tree farms we call national forests, are plentiful.) If we refuse to log the old growth forest, no loggers will die, nor will the logging industry. It will just be inconvenienced and some loggers, not all loggers, will have to be trained for a new line of work.

Ecologists and PlantActivists often defend nature by trying to upgrade it from "useful because we like it" to "useful because we need it to survive." They warn that if we don't stop cutting down the trees and polluting the environment, we will do ourselves in. They try to point out that in the disappearing plant species, we may be losing (human) life-saving compounds. They talk of the greenhouse effect and increased cancer risks. This may all be too true, yet I think it misses the mark.

What nature-lovers instinctively know and others fail to recognize is that nature (not its individual species, but entire ecosystems and bio-systems) has an intrinsic value not related to its usefulness to man. Individuals in natural systems have the right to exist in numbers large enough to preserve the health and the integrity of each system. This is why the extinction of the spotted owl is not disturbing just for the loss of that particular species, but because it indicates the elimination of an entire ecosystem; breaking habitats into ever smaller and smaller pieces until what is left is a collection of preserved wild animals but no real wilderness, fields of replanted trees, but no real forests.

What environmentalists know, just as certainly as the writer knew a human life is more valuable than a tree's life, is that it's wrong to woefully endanger nature. Wrong, not because people won't be able to "enjoy" it, but just plain selfish, stupid, and wrong.

The concept that nature has rights and that it commands our respect is immediately threatening to people who then generalize it into the humans versus nature dichotomy, assuming that our own rights to survive in good numbers have now been eliminated. It becomes an issue of dominance and survival once again. The issue is not humans over nature or nature over humans: it's humans, one species among many, *in* nature. A little self-sacrifice for the good of the whole planet and future generations is what is called for. As with pruning out branches of a tree, we need to learn to take what we need from the rest of nature, wisely taking some, leaving some, always looking carefully at the bigger picture, preserving the health and beauty of the system, and taking selectively.

No doubt it's all been said before. Perhaps someday we will act with respect. Until then ...

Secare selecte.

Please feel free to contact the author with comments, suggestions, or to learn more about PlantAmnesty:

> Cass Turnbull
> 906 N.W. 87th Street
> Seattle, WA 98117

When we plant here, let us think that we plant forever. Let it not be for present delight or present use alone. Let it be such work as our descendants will thank us for. And let us think that a time is to come when these trees will be held sacred because our hands have planted them, and men will say as they look upon the wonder and the substance of them, 'See this our fathers did for us.'

Inscription on plaque commemorating a grove of trees in Auckland, New Zealand.

Appendices

1. Cane-Growers, 173
2. Mounds, 173
3. Tree-Likes, 174
4. Best Plants for Formal Shearing, 174
5. Suckering Tree-Likes, 175
6. Tree-Likes Tough Enough to Shear, 175
7. Plants that Take Thinning or Arborizing, 176
8. Short Plants, 176
9. Easiest Plants to Keep at Mature Height of 5 Feet or Less, 177
10. Background Plants for Mass Planting, 177
11. Deciduous Plants for Group Plantings and Seasonal Interest, 178
12. Fun in the Sun Plants, 178
13. Fall Show Plants, 179
14. Plants with Interesting Berries and Things, 179
15. Plants for Winter Interest, 180
16. Plants for Skinny Places, 180
17. Author's Choice Plants, 181
18. More Choice Plants, 181
19. Tough Guys, 182
20. Small Trees/Big Shrubs, 183
21. Strange but Wonderful Plants, 183
22. Planting List for Design-Map and Hardscape, 184
23. Books, Periodicals, Catalogs, 184
24. State Cooperative Extension Services, 185

1. CANE-GROWERS

Common Name	Botanical Name
Bamboo	*Arundinaria sp., Bambusa sp.,* etc.
Beauty bush	*Kolkwitzia*
Butterfly bush	*Buddleia*
Deutzia	*Deutzia*
Forsythia	*Forsythia*
Heavenly bamboo	*Nandina*
Hydrangea	*Hydrangea*
Kerria	*Kerria japonica*
Mock orange	*Philadelphus* (can be pruned as a tree-like also)
Oregon grape (Barberry)	*Mahonia aquifolium*
Pearl bush	*Exochorda*
Red twig dogwood	*Cornus stolonifera*
Rose	*Rosa*
Weigela	*Weigela*
Wild Oregon grape	*Mahonia nervosa*

2. MOUNDS

Common Name	Botanical Name
Abelia	*Abelia*
Aucuba	*Aucuba*
Barberry	*Berberis sp.*
Box honeysuckle	*Lonicera nitida*
Spirea	*Spirea*
Burning bush	*Euonymus alata*
Cinquefoil	*Potentilla*
Escallonia	*Escallonia*
Evergreen azaleas	*Rhododendron sp.*
Evergreen euonymous	*Euonymus japonica*
Holly, small leaf varieties	*Ilex sp.*
Laurestinus	*Viburnum tinus*
Mexican orange	*Choisya*
Rock rose	*Cistus sp.*
Snowberry	*Symphoricarpos*

3. TREE-LIKES

Common Name	Botanical Name
Andromeda	*Pieris*
Camellia	*Camellia*
Cherry	*Prunus sp.*
Cotoneaster	*Cotoneaster*
Deciduous azalea	*Rhododendron*
Dogwood	*Cornus sp.*
Doublefile viburnum	*Viburnum p. tomentosum*
Elderberry	*Sambucus*
Enkianthus	*Enkianthus*
Evergreen laurel	*Prunus laurocerasus* and *P. lusitanica*
Fothergilla	*Fothergilla*
Harry Lauder's walking stick	*Corylus avellana 'Contorta'*
Highbush cranberry (Snowball bush, Guelder rose)	*Viburnum opulus*
Leatherleaf viburnum	*Viburnum rhytidophyllum*
Lilac (some prune as a cane-grower)	*Syringa*
Magnolia	*Magnolia*
Manzanita	*Arbutus manzanita*
Mountain laurel	*Kalmia*
Parrotia	*Parrotia*
Pine	*Pinus sp.*
Rhododendron	*Rhododendron*
Spindle tree	*Euonymous europaea*
Strawberry tree	*Arbutus unedo*
Winter hazel	*Corylopsis*
Winter viburnum	*Viburnum bodnantense* or *V. burkwoodii*
Witch hazel	*Hamamelis*

4. BEST PLANTS FOR FORMAL SHEARING

Common Name	Botanical Name
Boxwood	*Buxus*
Common privet	*Ligustrum vulgare*
Firethorn	*Pyracantha*
Hemlock (cannot be reduced)	*Tsuga*
Japanese holly	*Ilex crenata 'Convexa'*
Yew	*Taxus*

5. SUCKERING TREE-LIKES

Common Name	Botanical Name
Cornelian cherry	*Cornus mas*
Cotoneaster	*Cotoneaster*
Crabapple	*Malus sp.*
Doublefile viburnum	*Viburnum p.t.*
Eastern dogwood	*Cornus florida*
Fig	*Ficus*
Filbert	*Corylus*
Flowering cherry	*Prunus sp.*
Flowering plum	*Prunus sp.*
Korean dogwood	*Cornus kousa*
Magnolia	*Magnolia*
Parrotia	*Parrotia*
Viburnum	*Viburnum sp.*
Western dogwood	*Cornus nuttalli*
Winter hazel	*Corylopsis*
Witch hazel	*Hamamelis*

6. TREE-LIKES TOUGH ENOUGH TO SHEAR

Common Name	Botanical Name
English holly	*Ilex aquifolium*
English laurel	*Prunus laurocerasus*
'Otto Lukens' laurel	*Prunus laurocerasus 'Otto Lukens'*
Photinia	*Photinia*
Portugese laurel	*Prunus lusitanica*
Sweet bay	*Laurus nobilus*
Waxleaf privet	*Ligustrum japonicum*

7. PLANTS THAT TAKE THINNING OR ARBORIZING

Common Name	Botanical Name
Andromeda	*Pieris*
Atlas cedar	*Cedrus atlantica*
Camellia	*Camellia*
Deodar cedar	*Cedrus deodara*
English laurel	*Prunus laurocerasus*
Photinia	*Photinia*
Pine	*Pinus*
Portugese laurel	*Prunus lusitanica*
Rhododendron	*Rhododendron*
Strawberry bush	*Arbutus unedo*
Thread cypress	*Chamaecyparis pisifera 'Filifera'*

8. SHORT PLANTS

These plants reach an ultimate height of under 5 feet.

Common Name	Botanical Name
Bog rosemary	*Andromeda polifolia*
Brooms (some)	*Genista sp., Cytisus sp.*
Davidii viburnum	*Viburnum davidii*
Drooping leucothoe	*Leucothoe fontanseiana*
Dusty Miller	*Senecio sp.*
Dwarf bamboo	
Dwarf barberry	*Berberis sp.* and *cvs.*
Dwarf boxwood	*Buxus sp.*
Dwarf euonymus	*Euonymous fortunei* and other sp.
Evergreen azalea	*Rhododendron sp.*
Evergreen huckleberry	*Vaccinium ovatum*
February daphne	*Daphne mezereum*
Ferns	
Fishbone cotoneaster	*Cotoneaster horizontalis* and others
Funkias	*Hosta sp.* (perennials)
Heaths and heathers	*Calluna, Erica,* and *Daboecia*
Hebes (some)	*Hebe sp.*
Hellebores (includes Christmas rose, Lenten rose)	*Helleborus sp.*
Hypericum (shrub-type)	*Hypericum sp.*
Japanese holly	*Ilex crenata*
Junipers (some)	*Juniperus sp.* and *cvs.*
Lavender	*Lavendula*
Low sarcococca	*Sarcococca H. humulis*
Low stransvesia	*Stransvesia davidiana undulata*
'Otto Lukens' laurel	*Prunus larocerasus 'Otto Lukens'*
Perennial flowers	
Potentillas (some)	*Potentilla sp.*
Rock daphne	*Daphne cneorum*
Rock roses (some)	*Cistus sp.*
Rosemary	*Rosemarinus officianallis*
Roses (small)	*Polyanthas,* Miniatures, Floribundas, and some shrub types
Vanilla plant	*Raphiolepis sp.*
Wild Oregon grape	*Mahonia nervosa*

9. EASIEST PLANTS TO KEEP AT MATURE HEIGHT OF 5 FEET OR LESS

Common Name	Botanical Name
Barberry (some)	*Berberis sp. & cv.*
Box honeysuckle	*Lonicera nitida*
Boxwood	*Buxus*
Dwarf laurestinus	*Viburnum tinus cv.*
Glossy abelia	*Abelia grandiflora, cv.*
Hardy fuchsia	*Fuchsia magellanica*
Mexican orange	*Choisya*
Oregon grape	*Mahonia aquafolia*
Osmanthus	*Osmanthus delavayi*
Pernettya	*Pernettya*
Privet	*Ligustrum*
Red twig dogwood	*Cornus stolonifera*
Salal	*Gaultheria shallon*
Skimmia	*Skimmia*
Spirea (many)	*Spirea sp. & cv.*

10. BACKGROUND PLANTS FOR MASS PLANTING

Common Name	Botanical Name
Abelia	*Abelia*
Andromeda	*Pieris*
Camellia	*Camellia sp.*
Ceonothus	*Ceonothus sp.*
Cotoneaster (low)	*Cotoneaster sp.*
Cotoneaster (tall)	*Cotoneaster sp.*
Davidii viburnum	*Viburnum davidii*
Escallonia	*Escallonia*
Evergreen euonymous	*Euonymous japonica*
Heaths and heathers	*Erica* and *Calluna*
Hebe	*Hebe*
Holly	*Ilex sp.*
Laurel	*Prunus sp.*
Laurestinus (large)	*Viburnum tinus*
Mountain laurel	*Kalmia*
Needled evergreens	
Osmanthus	*Osmanthus*
Rhododendron	*Rhododendron*
Rock rose	*Potentilla*
Sarcococca	*Sarcococca sp.*
Stransvesia	*Stransvesia sp.*
Strawberry tree (dwarf)	*Arbutus unedo 'Compacta'*
Yew	*Taxus*

11. DECIDUOUS PLANTS FOR GROUP PLANTINGS AND SEASONAL INTEREST

Common Name	Botanical Name
Azalea (deciduous)	Rhododendron sp.
Beauty bush	Kolkwitzia
Beauty berry	Callicarpa sp.
Butterfly bush	Buddleia
Deutzia	Deutzia
Flowering quince	Chaenomeles
Forsythia	Forsythia
Highbush cranberry	Viburnum opulus
Hydrangea	Hydrangea sp.
Kerria	Kerria
Lilac	Syringa
Mock orange	Philadelphus
Pearl bush	Exochorda
Red twig dogwood	Cornus s.
Rose of Sharon	Hibiscus s.
Spindle tree	Euonymous europaea
Vine maple	Acer c.
Winged euonymous	Euomymous alata

12. FUN IN THE SUN PLANTS

Common Name	Botanical Name
Abelia	Abelia
Broom	Cytisus
Butterfly bush	Buddleia
Ceonothus	Ceonothus
Escallonia	Escallonia
Hypericum (shrub-type)	Hypericum 'Hidcote'
Lavender	Lavendula
Mimosa	Albizia
Montbretia (perennial flower)	Crocosmia
Phlox (perennial flower)	
Potentilla	Potentilla
Rock rose	Cistus
Rose	Rosa
Rose of Sharon	Hibiscus s.
Shasta daisy (perennial flower)	
Smoke tree	Cotinus coggygria
Sunrose	Helianthemum

For a little more shade in the summer:

Daylily (perennial flower)	
Hardy fuchsia	Fuchsia m.
Hydrangeas	Hydrangea sp.
Korean dogwood	Cornus kousa
Mountain laurel	Kalmia

13. FALL SHOW PLANTS

Common Name	Botanical Name
Abelia	*Abelia*
Aster (dwarf)	*Aster*
Blueberry	*Vaccinium c.*
Burning bush	*Euonymous alata*
Crocus (fall)	*Crocus sp.*
Crocus (false fall)	*Colchicum*
Cyclamen (hardy)	*Cyclamen*
Dogwood	*Cornus sp.*
Enkianthus	*Enkianthus*
European cranberry	*Viburnum o.*
Flame ash	*Fraxinus oxycarpa var.*
Fleabane	*Erigeron*
Fothergilla	*Fothergilla*
Ginkgo	*Ginkgo*
Hardy fuchsia	*Fuschia m.*
Heaths and heathers	*Calluna* and *Erica*
Heavenly bamboo	*Nandina sp. & var.*
Japanese anemone	*Anemone hybrida*
Kaffir lily	*Schisotylis*
Liquidamber	*Liquidamber*
Maple (many kinds)	*Acer sp.*
Oak (many kinds)	*Quercus sp.*
Oxydendron	*Oxydendron*
Parrotia	*Parrotia*
Sedum 'Autumn Glory'	*Sedum spectabile var.*
Sumac	*Rhus sp.*
Virginia creeper (vine)	*Parthenocissus cinquefolia*

14. PLANTS WITH INTERESTING BERRIES AND THINGS

Common Name	Botanical Name
Amelanchier	*Amelanchier*
Beauty berry	*Callicarpa*
Bunchberry	*Cornus canadensis*
Cotoneaster	*Cotoneaster*
Davidii viburnum	*Viburnum davidii*
Elderberry	*Sambucus sp.*
Firethorn	*Pyracantha*
Glorybower	*Clerodendron*
Hypericum (shrub)	*Hypericum inodorum*
Iris (some, seed heads)	*Iris sp.*
Korean dogwood	*Cornus kousa*
Laurestinus	*Viburnum tinus*
London plane trees (seeds)	*Platanus sp.*
Mountain ash	*Sorbus sp.*
Pernettya	*Pernettya*
Roses (some, hips)	*Rosa*
Silktassle tree	*Garryia eliptica*
Snowberry	*Symphoricarpos alba*
Spindle tree	*Euonymous europeana*
Stransvesia	*Stransvesia sp.*
Strawberry tree	*Arbutus unedo*
Willow	*Salix sp.*
Wintergreen	*Gautheria procumbens*

15. PLANTS FOR WINTER INTEREST

Common Name	Botanical Name
Branch patterns:	
Beech (big)	*Fagus*
Dogwood	*Cornus sp.*
Fishbone cotoneaster	*Cotoneaster horizontalis*
Japanese laceleaf maple	*Acer palmatum 'Dissectum'*
Japanese maple	*Acer palmatum cvs.*
Magnolia (branch and fuzzy bud)	*Magnolia sp.*
Oak (big, old)	*Quercus*
Sumac	*Rhus*
Virginia creeper	*Parthenosisus tricuspidata*
Form or texture:	
Alaska weeping cedar	*Chamaecyparis nootkatensis*
Double file viburnum	*Viburnum p.t.*
Hinoki cypress	*Chamaecyparis obtusa*
Hollywood juniper	*Juniperus chinensis 'Torulosa'*
Korean dogwood	*Cornus kousa*
Pfitzer juniper	*Juniperus c. 'Pfitzerana'*
Russian hawthorn	*Cratagus ambigua*
Thread cypress	*Chamaecyparis pisifera 'Filifera'*
Witch hazel	*Hamamelis* and relatives
Bark:	
Eucalyptus	*Eucalyptus*
Lacebark pine	*Pinus bugeana*
Madrona	*Arbutus menziesii*
Manzanita	*Arctostaphylos sp.*
'Paper bark' type trees—birch, cherry	
Red twig/Yellow twig dog-wood	*Cornus stolonifera sp. & cv.*
Scotch pine	*Pinus sylvestris*
Stewartia	*Stewartia*
Flower and scent:	
Christmas rose	*Helleborus niger*
Cornelian cherry	*Cornus mas*
February daphne	*Daphne mezereum*
Lenten rose	*Helleborus orientalis*
Osmanthus	*Osmanthus sp.*
Sarcococca	*Sarcococca*
Snow drops	*Galanthus*
Winter camellia	*Camellia sasanqua*
Winter jasmine	*Jasminum nudiflorum*
Winter viburnum	*Viburnum bodnantense*
Witch hazel and rel.	*Hamamelis*

16. PLANTS FOR SKINNY PLACES

Common Name	Botanical Name
Bamboo (can be invasive)	
Evergreen huckle-berry	*Vaccinium ovatum*
Fastigiate (tall-skinny) Yew	*Taxus b. 'Fastigiata'*
Heavenly bamboo	*Nandina*
Massed Hostas	
Massed Iris	
Massed Lilies	
Oregon grape	*Mahonia aquifolium*
'Pyramidalis'	*Thuja o. 'Pyrimidalis'*
Sarcococca, tall or low types	*Sarcococca*
Skyrocket juniper	*Juniperus 'Skyrocket'*
Vines on fences:	
Hydrangea vine	*Hydrangea a. petiolaris*
Ivy	*Hedera helix*
Plants pruned flat on the fence (espaliered)	
Cotoneaster (berries)	*Cotoneaster*
Firethorn (berries)	*Pyracantha*
Fruit Trees—apple and pear	
Quince (flower)	*Chaenomeles*
Winter camellia (flower)	*Camellia sasanqua*

17. AUTHOR'S CHOICE PLANTS

Common Name	Botanical Name
Coral bark Japanese maple	*Acer palmatum 'Sago Kaku'*
Daphne odora	*Daphne odora*
Double file viburnum	*Viburnum p.t.*
Enkianthus	*Enkianthus*
Hardy cyclamen	*Cyclamen sp.*
Hosta	*Hosta*
Japanese maples (all)	*Acer palmatum*
Kousa dogwood	*Cornus kousa*
Lady's mantle	*Alchemilla m.*
Rhododendron mucranulatum	*Rhododendron mucranulatum*
Rosa glauca	*Rosa glauca*
Royal azalea	*Rhododendron schlippenbachii*
Star magnolia	*Magnolia stellata*
Strawberry tree	*Arbutus unedo*
Tree peonies	*Paeonia sp.*
Trillium	*Trillium sp.*
Winter camellia	*Camellia sasanqua*
Witch hazel	*Hamamelis*

18. MORE CHOICE PLANTS

Common Name	Botanical Name
Alaska fern	
Ash	*Fraxinus sp.*
Astilbe	*Astilbe sp.*
Beech	*Fagus sp.*
Big Oak	*Quercus sp.*
Bleeding hearts (native and hybrid)	*Dicentra sp.*
Blueberry bush	*Vaccinium corymbosum*
Campanula (many kinds)	*Campanula*
Columbine	*Aquilegia sp.*
Cornellian cherry	*Cornus Mas*
Daylily	*Hemerocallis*
Deciduous Azaleas	
Deodar cedar	*Cedrus deodara*
February daphne	*Daphne mezureum*
Fishbone cotoneaster (on a wall)	*Cotoneaster horizontalis*
Glorybower	*Clerodendrum*
Grape vine	*Vitis*
Hardy geranium (cranesbill)	*Geranium sp.*
Heavenly bamboo	*Nandina*
Hellebore (all)	*Helleborus sp.*
Hydrangea vine	*Hydrangea petiolaris*
Iris	*Iris*
Japanese anemone	*Anemone hybrida*
Japanese red-leaf barberry	*Berberus thunbergii 'Atropurpurea'*
Katsura	*Cercidophyllum sp.*
Lacecap hydrangea	*H. macrophylla 'Blue Wave' 'Mariesii'*
Leatherleaf viburnum	*Viburnum rhytidophyllum*
Lilies (true)	*Lilium*
Madrona	*Arbutus m.*
Manzanita	*Arctostaphylos sp.*
Oakleaf hydrangea	*H. quercifolia*
Osmanthus	*Osmanthus*
PeeGee hydrangea	*H. paniculata 'Grandiflora'*
Peony (single)	*Paeonia sp.*
Port Orford cedar	*Chamaecyparis lawsoniana*
Rhododendrons (big leaf)	
Rhododendrons (species)	
Roses (shrub)	

18. MORE CHOICE PLANTS (cont.)

Common Name	Botanical Name
Sassafras	*Sassafras a.*
Scotch pine	*Pinus sylvestris*
Smoke tree	*Cotinus c.*
Sourwood	*Oxydendron a.*
Spindle tree	*Euonymous e.*
Virginia creeper	*Parthenosisus t.*
Wisteria (vine)	*Wisteria*

Good smellers:
Lavender
Lilac
Phlox
Rosemary
Roses
Sage
Thyme

Small Bulbs and Woodland Plants

Bloodroot	*Sanguinaria*
Checkered Lily	*Fritillaria lanceolata*
Coral bells	*Heuchera s.*
Crocus (species)	*Crocus*
Daffodil (dwarf)	*Narcissus sp.*
Erythronium	*Erythronium*
Iris (dwarf)	*Iris 'Harmony'*
London pride saxifrage	*Saxifraga umbrosa*
Primrose (many types)	*Primula*
Snow drops	*Galanthus*
Solomon's seal	*Polygonatum sp.*
Wind flowers	*Anemone blanda*

Groundcovers:

Bunchberry	*Cornus canadensis*
Epimedium	*Epimedium*
Sweet woodruff	*Galium*
Vancouveria	*Vancouveria*

19. TOUGH GUYS

CAUTION: Many of these plants could be considered invasive.

Common Name	Botanical Name
Bachelor's button	*Centaurea cyanus*
Bishop's weed	*Aegopodium*
Blue pimpernel	*Anagallis monelli*
Bluebell	*Scilla nonscripta* or *Endymion*
Cotoneaster	*Cotoneaster*
Davidii viburnum	*Viburnum davidii*
Epimedium	*Epimedium*
Forget-me-not	*Myosotis*
Foxglove	*Digitalis*
Heavenly bamboo	*Nandina*
Holly	*Ilex sp.*
Hosta	*Hosta*
Houtiana	*Houtiana*
Iris (wild)	*Iris*
Ivy	*Hedera sp.*
Japanese anemone	*Anemone japonica*
Japanese lantern	*Physalis*
Juniper	*Juniperus sp.*
Kenilworth ivy	*Cymbalaria*
Lady's mantle	*Alchemilla mollis*
Lamium	*Lamium*
Laurel	*Prunus sp.*
Lily of the valley	*Convallaria*
Moonlight broom	*Cistus*
Oakleaf hydrangea	*Hydrangea quercifolia*
Oxalis	*Oxalis*
Periwinkle	*Vinca*
Pyracantha	*Pyracantha*
Rugosa-type roses	*Rosa rugosa*
Salal	*Gaultheria shallon*
Snowberry	*Symphoricarpos*
Spurge	*Euphorbia e. polychroma*
St.-John's-wort (groundcover)	*Hypericum calycinum*
Sumac	*Rhus l.*
Sweet woodruff	*Galium*
Sword fern	*Polystichum*
Violet	*Viola*
Welsh poppy	*Meconopsis cambrica*
Wild bleeding heart	*Dicentra formosa*
Wild ginger	*Asarum*
Wild Oregon grape	*Mahonia nervosa*

20. SMALL TREES/BIG SHRUBS

Common Name	Botanical Name
Andromeda	*Pieris*
Bay laurel	*Laurus nobilus*
Camellia	*Camellia*
Cornelian cherry	*Cornus mas*
Crabapple (disease resistant var.)	*Malus 'Baskatong'*
'Adams'	
'Beverly'	
'Candied Apple'	
'Henry Kohkankie'	
'Professor Sprenger'	
'Sargentii'	
'Robinson'	
'White Cascade'	
Acer griseum	
Crape myrtle	*Lagerstroemia*
Eastern dogwood	*Cornus florida*
Eddies White Wonder dogwood	*Cornus 'Eddies White Wonder'*
English laurel	*Prunus la.*
Evergreen oak	*Quercus*
Fullmoon maple	*Acer japonicum*
'Aconitifolium'	
Glorybower	*Clerodendrom*
Japanese maple	*Acer palmatum*
Kousa dogwood	*Cornus kousa*
Lilac	*Syringa*
Loderi-type rhododendron	*Rhododendron sp.*
Magnolias (many)	*Magnolia sp.*
Mountain ash	*Sorbus sp.*
Paperbark maple	*Acer ginnala*
Photinia	*Photinia*
Portuguese laurel	*Prunus lu.*
Sassafras	*Sassafras*
Shadblow	*Amelanchier sp.*
Snowdrop trees	*Styrax japonica* and *obassia*
Stewartia	*Stewartia*
Strawberry tree	*Arbutus unedo*
Sumac	*Rhus*
Trident maple	*Acer buergeanum*
Vine maple	*Acer circinatum*

21. STRANGE BUT WONDERFUL PLANTS

Common Name	Botanical Name
Artichoke	*Cynara scolymus*
Bald cypress	*Taxodium*
Bear's breeches	*Acanthus sp.*
Beauty berry	*Callicarpa sp.*
Bolax	*Bolax*
Calla	*Zantedeschia*
Camperdown elm	*Ulmus glabra 'Camperdownii'*
Dawn redwood	*Metasequoia*
Fatsia	*Fatsia*
Fennel	*Ferula*
Giant onion	*Allium giganteum*
Ginkgo	*Ginkgo*
Gunnera	*Gunnera*
Harry Lauder's walking stick	*Coryllus avellena 'Contorta'*
Hollwood juniper	*J. c. 'Torulosa'*
Lamb's ears	*Stachys lantana*
Leatherleaf viburnum	*V. rhytidophyllum*
Mullein	*Verbascum*
Pampas grass	*Cortaderia selloana*
Spurge	*Euphorbia*
Sunflower	*Helianthus*
Weeping giant sequoia	*Sequoiadendron giganteum 'Pendulum'*
Weeping willow	*Salix alba tristis*
Yucca	*Yucca*

22. PLANTING LIST FOR DESIGN MAP AND HARDSCAPE

The following is the planting list for the design illustrated on page 115. The plants are listed clockwise from the upper left corner.

Backyard:
Sword fern
Western bleeding heart
Foxglove
Trillium
Solomon's seal
Hardy cyclamen
Beadruby
Escallonia
Hinoki cypress
Laceleaf maple
Arbutus unedo

Side courtyard:
Yak-type rhododendron
Black bamboo
Helleborus orientalis
Camellia sasanqua-scented white
Evergreen azaleas
Hebe 'Autumn Glory'

Front yard:
Osmanthus
Deciduous azaleas
Pieris
Mixed heaths and heathers
Low-growing needled evergreen
Kousa dogwood
Nandina
Hosta
Sarcococca
Espalier pyracantha

Back side yard:
Lacecap hydrangea

Foreground perennials and annuals:
Iris
Impatiens
Small bulbs
Astilbe

23. BOOKS, PERIODICALS, CATALOGS

Books and publications for beginners:

Sunset Magazine

Brooks, Audrey and Halstead, Andrew. *Garden Pests and Diseases*. New York: Simon and Schuster, 1980.

Phillips, Roger. *Trees of North America and Europe*. New York: Random House, 1978.

Wright, Michael. *The Complete Handbook of Garden Plants*. New York: The Rainbird Publishing Group Ltd., 1984

Books for more advanced gardeners:

Beckett, Kenneth A. *Roses*. The Garden Library. New York: Ballantine, 1984.

Brickell, Christopher. *Pruning*. New York: Simon & Schuster, 1979.

Brown, George E. *The Pruning of Trees, Shrubs and Conifers*. London: Faber & Faber, 1972.

Ferguson, Nicola. *Right Plant, Right Place*. New York: Summit Books, 1984.

Hay, Roy and Synge, Patrick M. *The Color Dictionary of Flowers and Plants for Home and Garden*. New York: Crown Publishers, Inc., 1975.

Schenk, George. *The Complete Shade Gardener*. Boston: Houghton Mifflin Company, 1984.

Periodicals:

American Horticulturist Magazine
7931 East Boulevard Drive
Alexandria, VA 22308

Avant Gardener
Box 489
New York, NY 10028

Brooklyn Botanic Garden Publications
1000 Washington Avenue
Brooklyn, NY 11225

Fine Gardening Magazine
63 South Main Street
Box 355
Newtown, CT 06470-9955

23. BOOKS, PERIODICALS, CATALOGS (cont.)

Horticulture Magazine
P.O. Box 53879
Boulder, CO 80321

Organic Gardening Magazine
Rodale Press
Emmaus, PA 18049

Pacific Horticulture Magazine
P.O. Box 22609
San Francisco, CA 94122

Catalogs:

Abundant Life Seed Foundation
P.O. Box 772
Port Townsend, WA 98368

Cloud Mountain Farm (fruit trees and edibles)
6906 Goodwin Road
Everson, WA 98247

The Herbfarm
32804 Issaqua-Fall City Road
Fall City, WA 98024

McClure & Zimmerman
108 W. Winnebago
P.O.Box 368
Friesland, WI 53935

Raintree Nursery (fruit trees and edibles)
391 Butts Road
Morton, WA 98356

Smith & Hawken
25 Corte Madera
Mill Valley, CA 94941

Springhill
110 West Elm Street
Tipp, OH 45371

Van Bourgondien
P.O.Box A
245 Farmingdale Road, Rt. 109
Babylon, NY 11702

White Flower Farm
Litchfield, CT 06759-0050

24. STATE COOPERATIVE EXTENSION SERVICES

Look in the phone book for the office of your county's Extension Service or contact the state office. Many county offices have Master Gardeners or other professionals available to answer questions.

Alabama
Auburn University
Duncan Hall
Auburn, AL 36849
(205) 826-4444

Alaska
University of Alaska
Fairbanks, AK 99775
(907) 474-7246

Arizona
University of Arizona
College of Agriculture-Forbes Bldg.
Tucson, AZ 85721
(602) 621-7205

Arkansas
University of Arkansas
1201 McAlmont
Little Rock, AR 72203
(501) 373-2500

California
300 Lakeside Drive, 6th Floor
Oakland, CA 94612
(415) 987-0060

Colorado
Colorado State University
Fort Collins, CO 80523
(303) 491-6281

Connecticut
University of Connecticut
1376 Storrs Road
W.B. Young Bldg., Box U-36
Storrs, CT 06268
(203) 486-4125

Delaware
University of Delaware
Townsend Hall
Newark, DE 19717
(302) 451-2504

District of Columbia
University of the District of Columbia
901 Newton Street, N.E.
Washington, DC 20017
(202) 576-6993

Florida
University of Florida
Institute of Food & Ag. Sciences
McCarty Hall
Gainesville, FL 32611
(904) 392-1761

Georgia
University of Georgia
College of Agriculture
Athens, GA 30602
(404) 542-3824

Hawaii
University of Hawaii at Manoa
Honolulu, HI 96822
(808) 948-8397

Idaho
University of Idaho
Ag. Science Bldg.
Moscow, ID 83843
(208) 885-6639

Illinois
University of Illinois
1301 W. Gregory
Mumford Hall
Urbana, IL 61801
(217) 333-2660

Indiana
Purdue University
West Lafayette, IN 47906
(317) 494-8488

Iowa
Iowa State University
110 Curtis Hall
Ames, IA 50011
(515) 294-4576

Kansas
Kansas State University
Umberger Hall
Manhattan, KS 66506
(913) 532-5820

Kentucky
University of Kentucky
College of Agriculture
Lexington, KY 40546
(606) 257-9000

Louisiana
Louisiana State University
Knapp Hall
University Station
Baton Rouge, LA 70803
(504) 388-6083

Maine
University of Maine
Winslow Hall
Orono, ME 04469
(207) 581-3191

Maryland
University of Maryland
College Park, MD 20742
(301) 454-3742

Massachusetts
University of Massachusetts
College of Food and Natural Resources
Amherst, MA 01003
(413) 545-4800

Michigan
Michigan State University
Agriculture Hall
East Lansing, MI 48824
(517) 355-2308

Minnesota
University of Minnesota
Coffey Hall
St. Paul, MN 55108
(612) 373-1223

Mississippi
Mississippi State University
P.O. Box 5446
Mississippi State, MS 39762
(601) 325-3036

Missouri
University of Missouri
University Hall
Columbia, MO 65211
(314) 751-3359

Montana
Montana State University
College of Agriculture
Bozeman, MT 59717
(406) 994-3681

Nebraska
University of Nebraska
Agricultural Hall
Lincoln, NE 68583
(402) 472-2966

Nevada
University of Nevada-Reno
College of Agriculture
Reno, NV 89557
(702) 784-6611

New Hampshire
University of New Hampshire
College of Life Sciences and Agriculture
Durham, NH 03824
(603) 862-1520

New Jersey
Rutgers University
Cook College
P.O. Box 231
New Brunswick, NJ 08903
(201) 932-9306

New Mexico
New Mexico State University
Box 3AE
Las Cruces, NM 88003
(505) 646-1806

New York
Cornell University
Roberts Hall
Ithaca, NY 14853
(607) 255-2117

North Carolina
North Carolina State University
Box 7602, Ricks Hall
Raleigh, NC 27695
(919) 737-2811

North Dakota
North Dakota State University
Box 5437
Fargo, ND 58105
(701) 237-8944

Ohio
Ohio State University
2120 Fyffe Road
Columbus, OH 43210
(614) 292-4067

Oklahoma
Oklahoma State University
Agricultural Hall
Stillwater, OK 74078
(415) 624-5400

Oregon
Oregon State University
Ballard Hall
Corvallis, OR 97331
(503) 754-2711

Pennsylvania
Pennsylvania State University
323 Ag. Bldg.
University Park, PA 16802
(814) 863-3438

Rhode Island
University of Rhode Island
Woodward Hall
Kingston, RI 02881
(401) 792-2815

South Carolina
Clemson University
Barre Hall
Clemson, SC 29634
(803) 656-3382

South Dakota
Box 2207
Brookings, SD 57007
(605) 688-4792

Tennessee
University of Tennessee
P.O. Box 1071
Morgan Hall
Knoxville, TN 37901
(615) 974-7114

Texas
Texas A&M University
College Station, TX 77843
(409) 845-7808

Utah
Utah State University
Logan, UT 84322
(801) 750-2200

Vermont
University of Vermont
College of Agriculture
178 S. Prospect Street
Burlington, VT 05401
(802) 656-3036

Virginia
Virginia Polytechnic Institute and State University
Burruss Hall
Blacksburg, VA 24061
(703) 961-6705

Washington
Washington State University
College of Agriculture
Pullman, WA 99164
(509) 335-2811

West Virginia
West Virginia University
Morgantown, WV 26506
(304) 293-5691

Wisconsin
University of Wisconsin
432 N. Lake Street
Madison, WI 53706
(608) 263-2775

Wyoming
University of Wyoming
Box 3354, University Station
Laramie, WY 82071
(307) 766-5124

Index

A

Abelia, 36
Adams, A.B., 161
Advice, poor, 123-4
Alternate branching pattern, 20
Amendment, 151
Amitrol-T®, 143
Apical dominance, 50-1
Arborizing shrubs, 73-4
    illustration, 74

B

Bacillus thuringiensis (Bt), 163
Balance, 105, 106
    illustrations, 105
Beds, rearranging, illustrations, 78, 81
Bees, 55, 163, 165
    killing with pesticides, 163
Bench-cutting, 50, 52
    illustrations, 52
Bloom time, 28-9
Branch collar, illustrations, 58
Branching patterns, 20, 21
    illustration, 21
Broadleaf, 114
Bt, 163
Bud, stimulating, illustration, 91

C

Cambium, 60
Camellias, layering, 74
Cane-growers, 30-4, 90
    cutting live canes, 31
    dead wood, 30-1
    illustration, 34
    plant size, 32
    pruning, 30-4
    renovating, 90
    "running," 33
        pruning, 33
Casoron®, 142, 143
Choisya, 36
Collman, Sharon, 160

Compaction, 158
Complementary plants, 81
Compost, 120, 151, 152
Conifer trees, layering, 74
Construction, 122-3
Contrast, 81, 104, 106
Cooperative Extension Services, 164
    Master Gardener programs, 164
Crowded plants, illustration, 72

D

Davey, John, 163
Davey Tree Expert Company, 164
DDT, 144
Dead wood, 25-6, 30-1, 39
    how to cut back, 25
    in tree-likes, 39
    on cane-growers, 30-1
    signs of, 25
Deciduous, 114
Design, 102-3
Diazinon, 144
Dicamba, 143
Diseases, 160-6
    host-specific, 162
Dormant oils, 164
Double digging, 129
Double leader, 62
Drop spreader, 150
Dropcrotching, 18, 50, 96

E

Edging, illustration, 127
Emerson, Ralph Waldo, 134
Environmental Protection Agency, 142, 144, 145
Escallonia, 36
Evergreens, 46, 114
    pruning, illustration, 46

F

Fall, for pruning, 28
Fan rake, 24, 26

Fan rake, cont.
    how to use, 26
    illustration, 24
Fertilizers, 149-53
    avoiding overuse of, 150
    chemical vs. organic, 150-1
    formulations, 149-50
    N-P-K, 149
    using spreaders, 150
Focal points, 104
Formal landscapes, 47
Fruit trees, 50-6
    apical dominance, 50-1
    dwarf, 56
    fruit production, 50, 53
        illustration, 53
    heading branches, illustration, 54
    heading laterals, illustration, 54
    pruning, 51-6
        for fruit production, 52-3
        illustrations, 52, 53, 54, 55
    pruning errors, 50, 51
        illustration, 51

G

Garden design, 102-4, 105, 106
    adventure and surprise, 106
    balance, 105, 106
        illustrations, 105
    contrast, 104, 106
    focal points, 104
    seasonal interest, 104
    theme, 103-4
Garden styles, 102
Gardena® system, 158
"Gardenese," see Terminology
Gardening, benefits of, 15-6
    easy to learn, 16
    physical aspects, 16
Ginkgo, 83-4
    illustration, 84
Go-West Meal™, 166
Grade change, 111
Grass, 78-9

H
Half-moon edger, illustration, 24
Hand pruners, illustration, 24
Hardpan, 120
Hardscape, 107-12
Heading, non-selective, illustration, 19
Heading, selective, 18, 19
    illustration, 19
Heading cut, 18
    illustration, 18
Health of plants, 86
Hedges, 43-6
    avoiding leggy, 43
    deciduous, 45-6
    illustration, 45
    power trimming, 46
    pruning, 43-6
        illustrations, 43, 44
    size, 45
    width, 45
Height, mature, 114
Height, ultimate, 114
Herbicides, 139-40, 142-7
    Amitrol-T®, 143
    Casoron®, 142, 143
    chart, 146-7
    dangers of, 144
    Diazinon, 144
    Dicamba, 143
    Poast®, 142
    Rodeo, 142
    Roundup®, 142-3
    Trimec®, 143
    using safely, 139-40, 144-5
        illustration, 144
Hoses, 157-8
    Gardena® system, 158
    Leaky Hose®, 158
    snap systems, 158
    soaker, 157-8
    Spray and Soak, 158
Humus, 151-2

I
"Included bark," 62
    illustration, 62
Insecticidal soaps, 164
Insects, see Pests
Installation of plants, 122-9
Integrated Pest Management, 163-4, 166
    spray services, 166
International Society of Arboriculture (ISA), 97
Irrigation, 121, 133, 154-7

Irrigation, cont.
    automatic, 154
    checking system, 155, 157
    hose splitter, illustration, 157
    installing, illustrations, 155
    semi-automatic, 154, 156
        illustration, 156
    shrubs blocking system, illustration, 156
    turf blocking sprinkler heads, illustration, 156

J
Junipers, pruning, 73
    illustrations, 73

L
Landscape, 47, 69, 101-6
    design errors, 101
    formal, 47
    low maintenance, 101
    overplanted, 101
    renovating, illustrations, 69
    theme, 103-4
    what makes it look good or bad, 101-6
Landscape materials, ordering, 128
Laterals, 53
Leaky Hose®, 158
Limb, see Tree limb

M
Maintaining yard, 133-5
Map, 107-12, 115
    how to make, 107
    illustrations, 108, 109, 115
    using, 107, 110
Master Gardener programs, 164
Mature height, 114
Micro-climates, 113-4
Moles, 164-5
Mounds, 35-6, 90
    pruning, 35-6
        illustration, 35
    renovating, 90
Mulch, 127, 136-7, 152
    using to control weeds, 136-7

N
National Arborist Association (NAA), 97
Needled, 114
NLOSS (new landscape owner's shock syndrome), 111
Nodes, 20
    cutting to, 20
        illustration, 20

Nodes, cont.
    types of, illustration, 20
Nostalgia, 87
Notebook, 118-9
N-P-K, 149

O
Opposite branching pattern, 20, 21
    illustration, 21
Osmocote®, 149
Overplanting, 118

P
Paths, 123
    illustration, 123
Pesticides, 161, 163
    cover sprays, 163
    pest/predator population cycle, charts, 161
    timing, 163
Pests, 160-6
    dormant oils, 164
    host-specific, 162
    insecticidal soaps, 164
    Integrated Pest Management, 163-4
    moles, 164-5
    predator/prey relationships, 160
    slugs, 165-6
    wasps, 165
    yellow jackets, 165
Phloem, 60
Pinching, 18
    illustration, 18
Plant size, 32
PlantAmnesty, 167-70
Planting tips, 126
Plants, 88-9, 113-20, 122-9
    arranging, 117-8
        illustrations, 118
    categories, 114, 116
    cultural requirements, 114
    how to choose and arrange, 113-20
    installation, 122-9
    overplanting, 118
    transporting, 117, 125-6
    unwanted, getting rid of, 88-9
Poast®, 142
Power trimmers, 46
Pruning, 33
Pruning, 18-20, 25-6, 27-9, 30-4, 35-6, 37-42, 43-6, 50, 51-6, 57-63, 71-2, 91, 92-3, 95
    bloom time, 28-9
    cane-growers, 30-4

Pruning, cont.
  cuts, 18-20
  cutting to node, 20
    illustration, 20
  dead wood, 25-6
  errors with fruit trees, 50
  fall, 28
  fruit trees, 50, 51-6
  heading cuts, 18
  hedges, 43-6
    illustrations, 43, 44
  lower tree limbs, 72
  mounds, 35-6
    illustration, 35
  rhododendrons, 27
  roses, 27, 32-3
    illustration, 32
  "running" cane-growers, 33
  shrubs, 71-2, 91
    illustrations, 71, 91
  spring, 27-8
  summer, 28
  thinning, 18-9
  timing, 27-9
  to reduce size, 19
  tree-likes, 37-42, 91, 92-3
    illustrations, 40, 41, 91, 92-3
  tree limb, 57-63
  trees, illustration, 95
  winter, 28

R

Renovating landscape, illustrations, 69
Renovation, radical, 90-3
Rhodes, David, 161
Rhododendrons, 76-7, 79, 80-1, 92
  regrowth, illustration, 92
  malpruned, 76-7
    illustration, 77
  moving, 79, 80-1
    illustrations, 79
Rock work, 111-2
  illustrations, 111
Rodeo, 142
Roots, illustration, 57
Roses, 32-3
  pruning, 32-3
    illustration, 32
  thinning, illustration, 33
Round point shovel, illustration, 24
Roundup®, 88, 127, 136, 139, 142-3

S

Scuffle hoe, illustration, 24
Seasonal interest, 104

Selective heading, 18, 19
  illustration, 19
Shade, 141
Sheared plants, restoring, illustrations, 75
Shearing, 18, 47-9
  drawbacks, 48-9
  formal landscapes, 47
  high-maintenance, 48
  not for controlling size, 48
  not misusing, 48
  only for tough plants, 48
  species for, 47-8
Shigo, Alex, 57, 59, 61
Shrubs, 71-2, 73-4, 75, 76, 79, 80, 91, 127-8, 156
  arborizing, 73-4
    illustration, 74
  blocking irrigation system, illustration, 156
  creating beds, 127-8
  leaning and crowded, 72
  moving, illustrations, 79
  pruning, 71-2, 91
    illustrations, 71, 91
  reducing, illustration, 76
  rehabilitating, 74, 76
  restoring sheared, illustrations, 75
  size, illustration, 80
Size of plant, 32, 70
Slopes, illustration, 128
Slugs, 165-6
Snap systems, 158
Soil, 120-1, 128-9
  having delivered, 128-9
  improving, 120-1
  ordering, 128
Sorting out, 70-7
Spray and Soak, 158
Spring, for pruning, 27-8
Spurs, 53
Square point shovel, illustration, 24
Stepping stones, illustration, 123
Story stick, 126-7
  illustrations, 126
Stripping, 73
Stub, illustration, 21
Stubbing, 18
Stump, hiding, illustration, 89
Stump grinder, 89
Styles, garden, 102
Suckers, 20, 27, 37
Summer, for pruning, 28

T

Terminal bud, 50
Terminology, 20-1, 83-7, 151-2
  "choice," 83
  "common," 84-5
  "easy," 85
  "fussy," 85
  "hard-working," 86
  "hardy," 85
  "invasive," 85
  "mature," 83
  "messy," 85
  "rare," 84-5
  "reliable," 85
  "tender," 85
  "unusual," 84
  "vigorous," 85
  "well-behaved," 85, 86
  "well-formed," 86-7
Theme, 103-4
Thinning, 18-9, 33, 95
  illustration, 18
  roses, illustration, 33
  trees, illustration, 95
Three-point ladder, illustration, 24
Timing, 27-9, 163
  pesticides, 163
Tipping back, 18
  illustration, 18
Tools, 23-4
  illustrations, 24
Topping, 18, 94
  illustrations, 18, 94
Transplanting, 79-81
  rhododendrons, 80-1
Tree biology, 59, 60
Tree-likes, 37-42, 76, 90, 91, 92-3
  illustration, 38
  malpruned, 76
  pruning, 37-42, 91, 92-3
    illustration, 40, 41, 91, 92-3
  renovating, 90, 92-3
Tree limb, 57-63, 72
  double leader, 62
  "included bark," 62
  narrow branch crotches, 62
  pruning, 57-63
    illustrations, 58, 61, 63
  pruning errors, illustration, 61
  pruning lower, 72
Tree roots, illustration, 57
Tree well, 78, 79
  illustration, 79
Trees, 60, 61, 74, 76, 94-7
  height, 96

Trees, cont.
    how they die, 61
    illustration, 60
    malpruned, 76
    pruning, 94-7
        illustration, 95
    rehabilitating, 74, 76
    thinning, illustration, 95
    windowing, illustration, 95
    wounded, illustration, 60
Trimec®, 143

U

Ultimate height, 114
Unwanted plants, getting rid of,
    88-9
    illustration, 89

V

Vines, 85-6

W

Washington State Nurseryman's
    and Landscaper's Association,
    168
Wasps, 165

Watering, 125, 154-9
    automatic irrigation, 154
    checking irrigation system, 155,
        157
    compaction, 158
    correct amount of, 158
    hand, 157
    hoses, 157-8
        soaker, 157-8
    irrigation, illustrations, 156
    plants needing less, 159
    semi-automatic irrigation, 154,
        156
        illustration, 156
    signs of stress, 158-9
Watersprouts, 20
Weeds, 70, 88-9, 134, 135, 136-41
    annual, 136
    controlling with mulch, 136-7
    errors in controlling, 141
    great, 140-1
    perennial, 138-9
    perennial woody, 139-40
    pretty, 140
    removing, illustration, 138
    seeds and flowers, 137-8
    shade and, 141

Weeds, cont.
    smart, 140
        illustration, 140
    strategy for attacking, 141
Whorled branching pattern, 20
Wildflowers, 140
Wilt-Pruf®, 117
Windowing, 74, 95
    trees, illustration, 95
Winter, for pruning, 28
Worms, 152

X

Xylem, 60

Y

Yard, 101-6, 108, 116, 133-5
    illustrations, 108, 116
    low maintenance, 101
    maintaining, 133-5
    overplanted, 101
    typical, illustration, 108
    what makes it look good or bad,
        101-6
Yellow jackets, 165